PELICAN BOO[K]

A1012

RELIGION IN SECULAR

Bryan Wilson, a Fellow of All Souls since 1963, holds, as Reader, Oxford University's senior appointment in sociology. Previously he taught sociology at the University of Leeds for several years. In 1957–8 he was Commonwealth Fund Fellow at the University of California, Berkeley, which he visited again in 1966–7 as a Fellow of the American Council of Learned Societies. Among the subjects on which he has published are education, the youth culture and the influence of mass media. His main interest has been the sociology of religion, in which field he published his first book, *Sects and Society*, in 1961. He has recently edited a volume of research studies of his own and of his associates, *Patterns of Sectarianism* (1967), and at present he is at work on a book on millennial movements. Something of a connoisseur of claret, Bryan Wilson acknowledges an 'untutored enthusiasm' for Chinese ceramics, eighteenth century music, Lieder and English watercolours. Owning no garden, he is a thwarted gardener; and, lacking time, is frustrated at being a walker 'only in principle'.

RELIGION
IN SECULAR SOCIETY

*

BRYAN R. WILSON

PENGUIN BOOKS
BALTIMORE · MARYLAND

Penguin Books Ltd, Harmondsworth, Middlesex, England
Penguin Books Inc., 7110 Ambassador Road, Baltimore, Md 21207, U.S.A.
Penguin Books Australia Ltd, Ringwood, Victoria, Australia

—

First published by C. A. Watts & Co. 1966
Published in Pelican Books 1969

—

—

Made and printed in Great Britain
by Hazell Watson & Viney Ltd,
Aylesbury, Bucks
Set in Monotype Garamond

For
Malcolm and Elizabeth Bradbury

Contents

Acknowledgements

My profound thanks are due to Mr T. M. Schuller, without whose gentle but persistent encouragement this book would probably not have been written – and certainly would not have been written so soon. His patience, sustained interest, good advice and ever-readiness to help were by no means the least of the pleasures I appreciated in the months in which I planned and wrote. To Miss Dorothy Barsby I have a previously unacknowledged debt, for her work in improving and typing the manuscript, and that I am very pleased to acknowledge. Mr John Wilson, now at Duke University, North Carolina, who read through an early draft of the manuscript, and kindly compiled the tables which appear in the appendix. I am very much indebted to Mr. T. P. Bull for all his care and attention when the proofs of this edition were being read.

Introductory

RELIGIOUS thinking, religious practices and religious institutions were once at the very centre of the life of western society, as indeed of all societies. That there were, even in the seventeenth, and certainly in the eighteenth and nineteenth, centuries many unchurched people to whom religious practices and places were alien and whose religious thinking was a mixture of odd piety, good intentions, rationalizations and superstitions, does not gainsay the dominance of religion.[1] It was entrenched, if not always strictly by law, then by some of the institutions of society, in the customs of the people and by the precept of ruling classes. That there were often countervailing forces, economic or political necessity, which frequently overrode God's will, or churchmen's apprehension of it, does not contradict the fact that religious motives, religious sanctions and religious pro-

1. The extent of man's religiosity in British and American society in the last three centuries is a matter on which opinion, and certainly emphasis, varies. For a fascinating discussion of the seventeenth century see Peter Laslett, *The World We Have Lost*, London, Methuen, 1965, pp. 71–4. Some interesting sidelights for America emerge in Emery Battis, *Saints and Sectaries*, Chapel Hill, N.C., University of North Carolina Press, 1962, who estimates that in 1637–8 some 182 of a total of 363 males in Boston were Church members and that about 1,100 of 1,600 adult males in Massachusetts were Church members, pp. 67–8 and p. 256. Elie Halévy's attribution of an important role to Non-conformity in late eighteenth-century Britain in his *History of the English People in the Nineteenth Century*, London, Benn, Vol. I, 1949, Part III, has itself raised controversy. For views which challenge the influence of religiosity see, K. S. Inglis, *Churches and the Working Classes in Victorian England*, London, Routledge, 1963; Eric Hobsbawm, *Labouring Men*, London, Weidenfeld & Nicolson, 1964, especially Chapter 3. On America see F. H. Littell, *From State Church to Pluralism*, New York, Anchor Books, 1962.

fessionals were all of them socially of very great influence indeed.

In the twentieth century that situation has manifestly changed, and the process of change continues. But change does not occur evenly, nor in necessarily similar ways in different societies. Religious *practice* may atrophy, as it has, for example, in Scandinavian countries; or it may persist in its traditional forms (and even become more extensive) whilst its social and cultural meaning changes, as in the United States. Religious *institutions* may also continue and show, as in America, remarkable resilience, but they may do so by transforming themselves from largely traditional styles to organizations which embody all the rational bureaucratic authority assumptions of other, non-religious, organizations in advanced society. Religious *thinking* is perhaps the area which evidences most conspicuous change. Men act less and less in response to religious motivation: they assess the world in empirical and rational terms, and find themselves involved in rational organizations and rationally determined roles which allow small scope for such religious predilections as they might privately entertain. Even if, as some sociologists have argued, non-logical behaviour continues in unabated measure in human society, then at least the terms of non-rationality have changed. It is no longer the dogmas of the Christian Church which dictate behaviour, but quite other irrational and arbitrary assumptions about life, society and the laws which govern the physical universe.

It is with this change in the place of religion in western society – in British and American society – that this book is largely concerned. Given that there has been change, however, it is clear that religious organizations are not merely passive and acquiescent in the process. There is a religious *response* to the changing social order and at least part of this book is concerned with the religious response to the secular society. That response has been examined in respect of the Christian tradition of two Anglo-Saxon societies. Thus if we take secularization as the experience of Christianity in these two countries, ecumenicalism, denominationalism and sectarianism are the responses which are examined in relation to this process.

The concept of secularization is not employed in any ideological sense, neither to applaud its occurrence, nor to deplore it.[1] It is taken simply as a fact that religion – seen as a way of thinking, as the performance of particular practices, and as the institutionalization and organization of these patterns of thought and action – has lost influence in both England and the United States in particular, as it has in other western societies. That this process has occurred in rather different ways, under the influence of specific historical conditions, is very much the burden of the discussion. The evidence of this process in the two societies differs, and the attempt has been made to go beyond superficial conclusions drawn from statistical evidence which assumes – as sociologists all too often do – that a unit of behaviour is, because it can be reduced to a statistic, invariably a quantity of the same weight and social significance.[2]

Although the evidence differs, the loss of religious influence is basically similar. The very recognition that a set of statistics about church attendance or ritual partici-

1. The concept of secularization is sharply criticized as a 'counter-religious' ideology by David Martin, 'Towards eliminating the concept of Secularization' in Julius Gould (Ed.) *Penguin Survey of the Social Sciences*, Harmondsworth, 1965, pp. 169–82. Many religionists, however, see it not as an ideology but as a matter of fact, e.g. the Dominican Geoffrey Preston 'The Glory has Departed', *Slant*, 2 (1) 1966, p. 11.

2. A number of examples of this rather 'mindless' use of statistics are to be found in a recent survey, *The Television Audience and*

pation can be understood only in terms of the cultural meaning of the behaviour involved, implies that if we accept that cultures differ, we should expect to find culturally different manifestations of socially similar processes. If there are broad and fundamental changes occurring which have relevance for both societies, then we should be prepared to compare a wider range of phenomena in order to come to our conclusions. We need not expect a simple-minded correspondence of specific statistics, but we should rather expect to see an explanatory structure built out of those data which seem most significant in the society concerned.[1]

The very variability of the salient evidence between societies seems indeed to illustrate the epiphenomenal character of religious institutions and religious thinking in contemporary society. From the wider social point of view it makes very little difference whether church-going is a regular habit of the majority or the determined practice of a tiny minority. That the course of modern society proceeds influenced in only the slightest of ways by such differences in expressed religious behaviour illustrates how marginal religious institutions have, in fact, become. It would require an ingenious sociological analysis to show that the development of American society was materially affected by its high rate of church-going, or that of Sweden by its very low rate.

Religion, London, Social Surveys (Gallup Poll), 1965. In asking questions about 'going to church' the surveyors obviously treat this 'piece of behaviour' as if it were a unit with common meaning to groups as different as Catholics, Anglicans and Non-conformists! Correspondingly, they were apparently surprised at the very much higher rate of support for voluntary and ancillary groups in Non-conformist Churches than in Catholic Churches, and at the different prestige of the clergy in these different organizations.

1. This approach in sociology has recently been emphasized by Donald G. MacRae.

For particular individuals, or for groups, religion may, of course, still be a powerful – perhaps the most powerful – determinant of the conduct of their lives. But that is not true of the generality of men in western society, whether church-going or not. Such behaviour and such groups are certainly worthy of sociological inquiry, and the third section of this book pays some attention to them. No less interesting are the persisting institutions of religion in societies where lay support has ebbed: in the following pages only an oblique approach to this subject is possible, in the degree to which institutional persistence and organizational loyalty enter into the discussion of ecumenism.

All of this, however, passes no judgement on the question of the theological aspects of religious thought, practice, and organization. That theological meanings are also socially evolved and perhaps socially determined is probably as near as the sociologist might wish to come to the discussion of theological issues. Churches are social institutions; men's conceptions of God are socially prescribed (and even protestations against those conceptions bear no less the mark of the social situation in which they arise). But the measure of the truth of these conceptions, or the legitimacy of these institutions in relation to some posited supermundane order, pass beyond our – and beyond sociological – concern. To discuss secularization is not to mount an attack on religious institutions, it is to acknowledge an actual social circumstance of the contemporary world. To believe, as I do, that religious ideas and religious institutions are understandable only in social terms is also to acknowledge that other men do not think so – else there would have been no religious institutions.

The sociological approach which is followed in these pages merely attempts to see religion as a social phenome-

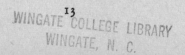

non, to interpret it and to understand it as such. It is not a highly theoretical or a highly conceptualized approach. It is concerned with actual behaviour and with actual organizations which are, in the everyday sense of the word, described as 'religious'. In a limited way the approach is – as I believe a sociological approach should attempt to be – comparative. The comparisons are between England and the United States and between these societies at different periods of the recent past.

Since the two societies with which this book is concerned are England and the United States, the religious tradition of each of which has been overwhelmingly Christian, and dominantly Protestant, it is on Christianity and more especially on its Protestant manifestations that the discussion centres. There are no more than passing comparative allusions to other religious traditions. It is perhaps no accident that the world's first secular societies as generally recognized, should be societies in the Christian Protestant tradition, but it is increasingly clear that in societies outside that tradition, of which perhaps Japan is the outstanding example outside Christendom, similar processes of secularization are in progress.

By secularization, as already explained, is meant the process whereby religious thinking, practice and institutions lose social significance. Our concern is specifically with the loss of that influence on the part of Christianity. Superficially, comparison might be made with the changes in religious thinking, practices and institutions which have occurred in the decay of other major religious traditions – the periodic decline of Buddhism in Ceylon for example, or the indigenization of Buddhism in Tibet, or of Islam at the periphery of the areas under Muslim dominance. But these are essentially dissimilar processes, in which the great tradition of a faith is gradually corroded by more pervasive, but still supernatural or magical, beliefs of a particular society. These, then, are cases where one systematic set of religious beliefs is steadily infiltrated by other usually more localized and less systematic religious ideas, and where one set of religious institutions gradually adjusts or abandons its pristine values and purposes and accepts others. Such a development merits scholarly attention in its own right, as a process of religious change: it is not, however, a process of secularization.[1]

The idea of secularization has not been popular with all sociologists of religion. There are some who would contend that what is in fact occurring in western society is not the replacement of religious ideas of life by secular ideas, but is merely the transformation, in a period of rapid social change, of the character of religion. Worship in church, the sermon, hymn-singing, the authority of a book or a bishop, are said to be out of keeping with the times, and thus man – who is taken to be religious by nature – seeks out new forms and new expressions for his religious dispositions.[2] Some who argue along these lines posit a fund of 'religiosity' in men and in society, which, like a 'wages fund' or a 'pool of ability' in the context of other arguments, is supposed to remain more or less a constant – but a hypothetical constant the means

1. On the infiltration of magical ideas into the religious practice of the major religions, see Max Weber, *The Sociology of Religion*, London, Methuen, 1965.

2. A number of theologians have recently argued along these lines. But see also, David Martin, op. cit., and Thomas Luckmann, *Das Problem der Religion in der modernen Gesellschaft*, Freiberg, Verlag Rombach, 1963; Acquaviva emphasizes the way in which a sense of holiness is communicated through ritual and symbol. Whilst he sees the decline of holiness, he sees the persistence of symbol, and does not regard the process as necessarily irreversible; S. S. Acquaviva, *Der Untergang des Heiligen in der industriellen Gesellschaft*, Essen, Ludgerus Verlag, 1964.

of measuring which have not yet been discovered. Such a concept obviously draws more strongly on theological than on sociological assumptions about mankind.

A variant of this particular idea is that man is to be regarded as essentially an irrational being, whose emotions need, and will find, expression in all and any social circumstances.[1] Worship is, as usually defined, a strictly non-rational pattern of behaviour, the ends of which are unavailable for empirical scrutiny, but which has its own intrinsic value in satisfying men's emotional demands. Given these assumptions it is then argued that if a particular pattern of emotional gratification is no longer maintained, then men must be fulfilling their desires by other means: can one define these means as less religious than those which were traditionally employed for the same ends?

The argument appears to posit a more or less universal, and unchanging, human psychology. It takes little or no account of the changing patterns of social organization, social experience and social opportunity in modifying men's emotional needs and responses. It commonly accepts the functionalist argument, that religion exists to meet certain human needs. Assuming that these needs are unchanging it is faced with the fact that none the less religion changes. Having derived the needs from religious phenomena, it now refers to the needs in order to assert that religious practices must exist to meet them. Thus if a given form of religion disappears, then some other 'religious' behaviour must be arising to take its place.

1. This idea was common to the irrationalists of the late nineteenth and early twentieth centuries, offered as a corrective to the optimistic rationalism of the eighteenth century, and of the nineteenth-century utilitarians and positivists. The most emphatic sociological exponent of this view is Vilfredo Pareto, *The Mind and Society*, London, 1935.

Thus mass-entertainment, mass-rallies, science, totalitarian political parties and ideologies, expensive consumer goods are variously credited with fulfilling some of the functions once fulfilled by religion.

It seems to me difficult to maintain that man in western society is no more rational than ever he was, within the normal usage of the word 'rational'. So much more of his ordinary everyday behaviour is controlled by cause-and-effect thinking, even if only because he knows more about the workings of the physical and social worlds. He is undoubtedly more preoccupied with immediate, empirical ends and pragmatic tests. It may be that much of this 'rationality' is derived not so directly either from an innate change of disposition or even from what he is consciously taught, as from his participation in a society which is increasingly regulated by devices and machines which operate according to the criteria of efficiency. The dominance of economic costing over spiritual aspiration in modern society, is the evidence of the growth of rationality in our social affairs, and consequently, at least in some measure, in our own habits of thought.[1]

The growth of these instrumental orientations in modern society, does not of course eliminate the emotional aspects of man's nature, nor does it solve ultimate problems of 'meaning'. Modern society does not cater, as traditional society did, for the collective gratification of the emotions, and the disappearance of religion is part of that change. But the experience of an instrumentally-oriented society may alter man's emotional responses, and even his felt sense of emotional need: it may alter the

1. An extended, but not entirely acceptable, presentation of the argument of this paragraph can be found in Thorstein Veblen's works, particularly, *The Theory of the Leisure Class*, New York, Macmillan, 1899, and *The Place of Science in Modern Civilization*, New York, The Viking Press, 1919.

age at which certain reassurances are sought, the circumstances in which they can be accepted and the degree to which they *must* be collective and institutionalized, or *may* be individual and (apparently rather than really) random. In particular, in a society where intellectual criteria dominate, it may well be that what cannot be intellectually accepted cannot be emotionally reassuring.

Modern man appears to suffer acutely from his loss of emotional reassurance. But it is also true that religion, whether in the form in which it has traditionally existed in Christian society, or in any other form which can be recognized in the common-sense usage of the term, appears no longer capable of providing this reassurance for the mass of men. To regard as 'religious' all the practices which men engage in for the satisfaction of their emotional needs appears to be no solution of the real problem which men without religion face in a world in which ultimate explanations, and ultimate satisfactions are denied them. Nor does it seem to me to be a solution to sociological questions concerning the role of religion in society.

Sociology appropriately regards religion as primarily an institutional phenomenon. This is not to dismiss the discovery of beliefs and attitudes as revealed in answers to questionnaires – they produce important results especially in the context of institutional and historical analysis[1] – but rather to recognize that religious institutions, organizations, affiliations and practices, and institutionalized belief-systems, have been of more social consequence in all societies than are the contemporary private beliefs of

1. See, for examples of particularly valuable studies of this type, Charles Y. Glock and Rodney Stark, *Religion and Society in Tension*, Chicago, Rand McNally, 1965; Charles Y. Glock, Benjamin B. Ringer and Earl Babbie, *To Comfort and to Challenge*, Berkeley and Los Angeles, University of California Press, 1967.

individuals isolated by an interview-schedule. It is with the structured position of religion within the institutional framework of society that the discussion in the following pages is primarily concerned.

Consequently considerable attention is paid – perhaps more than is usual in discussions of contemporary religion – to the professionals of religion. The clergy most fully represent religion and of this they are themselves acutely aware. Some understanding of the religious profession is essential to an understanding of religion itself, and particularly so in the secular society, where they are, more than ever before perhaps, its embodiment. In a society which is highly professionalized, and which now no longer expects to discover (amateur) saints any more than it believes in amateur clinicians, the role of the clergy becomes more distinctive within religious institutions, and becomes more specifically, and more circumscribedly, religious. They become increasingly influential concerning the future of the Churches. Just as lawyers control courts, and doctors have greatest influence in hospitals, so the clergy become, in some ways, 'the Church' (even though their tenure, like that of doctors, may be terminated by the growing power of administrators – a newer, more professional, class in all organizations). In their discussions on Church unity, this is transparently their own self-assessment.

The relations of clergy and laity are only passingly referred to in this discussion, however, and a close study of their interaction in religious institutions of various types remains to be undertaken, on a comparative basis. Such a study would need to transcend the parish level where beginnings have already been made, and would need to be located firmly in the context of major religious institutions, rather than being centred on the role of the seminary in recruiting laymen and socializing priests –

vital as such research is for a complete picture of clergy-laity relations.[1] This, and many other aspects of the sociology of religion, must wait until more empirical study has been undertaken, and until those studies have themselves been drawn together into some wider theoretical framework.

All that is offered in this essay, in the absence of the range of empirical studies and subsequent syntheses, is a tentative interpretation of some of the dominant aspects of contemporary religion, its changed role in society, its response to that change, and its degree of persistence and adaptation.

1. A large number of parish studies have been undertaken, and a number of studies of religious recruitment and training: two good examples of each subject, for America and Britain may be cited; J. H. Fichter, *Social Relations in an Urban Parish*, Chicago, University of Chicago Press, 1954; Conor Ward, *Priests and People*, Liverpool, Liverpool U.P., 1961; J. H. Fichter, *Religion as an Occupation*, Notre Dame, Ind., University of Notre Dame, 1961; A. P. M. Coxon, *A Sociological Study of the Social Recruitment, Selection and Professional Socialization of Anglican Ordinands*, unpublished Ph.D. thesis, University of Leeds, 1965.

PART I
THE PATTERN OF SECULARIZATION

I

Statistical Evidence of Secularization in England

IT is frequently argued that statistical information about religious membership and religious practice is not very relevant to a 'true' understanding of religion or its place in society. Churchmen themselves sometimes urge this view, today less so than formerly, although it has been a recurrent theme with some religionists ever since the Lord's wrath fell on David for numbering the children of Israel. Obviously the meaning of religion cannot be completely assessed by numerical means, either by head-counting or attitude surveys. On the one hand they are no adequate way of testing the strength of religious commitment, nor, on the other, can they uncover the ulterior motivations which might in certain periods persuade people that it is 'in their interests' (their mundane interests, not their post-mortem interests, that is) to go to church.

Statistics cannot reveal much of the extent of influence which organized religion might exert in the counsels of government or in the formation of public opinion. Religious responses are, in all developed societies, predominantly institutionalized responses and, even when fewer people participate in services, the institutions persist and their specialist personnel (priests and the religious hierarchy and administration) continue to command prestige and to enjoy traditional status and influence with those who have authority in other social institutions. A rather different evidence of religious influence is found in the fact that many people behave in ways which are 'religiously informed' or which carry the mark of moral training acquired through early-life exposure to religious influences. There is, then, often tacit approval of what the Churches do or preach, without personal commitment to religious belief and without attendance at church.

What can be claimed for religious statistics is necessarily limited. The ways in which men express their 'religiosity' may be changing, and church attendance and ritual may be felt by some quite religiously disposed people to be outworn patterns unadapted to the modern world. And yet, all these various considerations notwithstanding, the statistics do provide some evidence of significant religious change. They are some sort of index of secularization, taking that word at its common-sense value. The decline in organized religious participation indicated a way in which the Churches are losing direct influence over the ideas and activities of men. Since the assumed persistent religiosity of men has not been organized into self-evidently religious expression – either spontaneously or by the existing religious institutions of modern societies – we can regard the evidence of the statistics as an index of secularization in the sense of the decline of religious influence and religious organization.

The figures reveal a steady diminution in the proportion of people who go to church in European countries, and particularly so in the Protestant countries. Average Sunday attendance is as low as less than three per cent of population in Norway, and between ten to fifteen per cent in England – the English figures being swollen somewhat by the much larger proportion in the English population of Roman Catholics who are much more disposed – as yet – to let the Church influence their behaviour, at least in the matter of attendances. Although earlier statistical material is not always reliable, the figures for the latter half of the last century always revealed higher proportions of people in church, except in heavily industrialized areas. In England, in the mid-nineteenth century, the only English Census of Religion ever undertaken, revealed that the Nonconformist denominations had, collectively, almost as much strength as the Anglicans, and that something like forty per cent of the total population were church-goers.

Since the last decades of the nineteenth century the hold, first of the Anglican Church and subsequently of the Nonconformist Churches, over the English population has diminished. At the same time, partly as a consequence of persistent immigration from Ireland, and partly as a consequence of differential fertility among Catholics, active Roman Catholics have increased in numbers (which may reflect the less adequate methods of birth control permitted to Catholics, the general ignorance about birth control and the higher evaluation of fertility especially among Irish immigrants). Although the Catholic Church has undoubtedly experienced losses, particularly among second and third generation immigrants in Britain, these losses are concealed by the net gain which has accrued as a consequence of continued immigration throughout the first five decades of this century, and from the effect of the obligation exacted from non-Catholic partners in mixed marriages to bring up their children as Catholics.

The decline in church attendance is likely to affect, or to be most apparent, in the case of the Nonconformist Churches, since there it tends to be correlated with the decline in actual allegiance and self-ascription. Whereas many of those who cease attending the Anglican Church go on thinking of themselves as 'Church of England', the same is not true for Nonconformists, since Nonconformity is a much more distinctive commitment. The Church of England, like most Churches and in contradistinction to sects and denominations, rests *part* of its claim to allegiance not on voluntary disposition, but on national and ethnic differences. It has a residual claim to loyalty, as the religious expression of Englishmen – the norm to which men nominally conform. (Of course the Church of England has not, especially since the great missionary endeavours of the late eighteenth century, been particularly consistent with regard to this national and ethnic base, in becoming a proselytizing Church overseas.)

Thus, paradoxically, self-ascription to the Church of England is likely to rise as actual attendance in Anglican churches diminishes, because purely nominally self-styled Anglicans – all those without any particular religious commitment – can claim to belong, just as they belong to the country itself. (Most of these people would not hesitate to define themselves as 'Protestant', which they see in sharper contrast to 'Catholic' than is fashionably conceded by the High Churchmen among Anglicans.) That they claim to belong at all reflects a further curiosity of religious statistics. For, although church attendance declines in England, and there are fewer people 'on the books' of the Nonconformist Churches and at Easter Communion in the Church of England, there do not appear to be many more people than there were in the past who are prepared to declare themselves to be non-Christian. The vast majority profess to believe in God. Many of these assert that they 'belong' – in some residual way – to the Church of England. This is one of the discrepancies which persuades some that 'secularization' is a misnomer for what is taking place.

There is, however, a good deal of evidence other than the decline in church attendance to suggest that religious forces exercise less influence over people's lives than they did. In statistical terms this becomes apparent in the diminution of children attending Sunday school since the turn of the century. It is evident in the smaller numbers who are involved in church work of one kind and another – particularly in Sunday school teaching. Fewer people give less of their time and attention to religious thought and action. At another level, it is apparent that religious publications have steadily given place to secular publications. Despite one or two 'best sellers' (most of them works demolishing the religious conceptions of the man in the street) religious books and periodicals are today a very tiny proportion of the total volume of publications sold compared to what they were a century ago. And there is the further fact that whereas in the early nineteenth century the Church had long had dominant control of the means of communication – from the pulpit and at the church-door – by the middle of the century this dominance was broken. Today the voice of religion is small if not yet still. The services of the mass-media are open to the principal denominations but they share in these agencies along with a great many other would-be persuaders – commercial, political and recreational – and in *sharing* they severely compromise that pre-eminence of prestige which information pertaining to the supernatural enjoyed in the past. In spite of the evidence of large numbers who claim to listen to religious broadcasts, we cannot be at all sure that their level of attention is the same as that which prevails in church.

At the very highest estimate it would seem that fewer than twenty-five per cent of the adult population of England and Wales has any real claim to be in 'membership' of any religious denomination. Obviously 'membership' itself is a difficult category: Roman Catholics are disposed to claim all those who have been baptized into the Church, which means children from their earliest years. The Anglican Church tends to count those who have been confirmed, which is an only slightly more reliable indicator of people's subsequent religious disposition than is child baptism. The Nonconformist Churches make some formal admission to the Church roll their criterion, although in many individual churches they are extremely lax in maintaining the roll, and it is not uncommon, if one is permitted to go through the roll with a Nonconformist minister, that he quite readily will admit that a number of people's names are entered whom he does not know, but who cannot be struck off because of the offence which this might cause to relatives who still attend. Thus, all the Churches tend to have their own particular deficiencies in regard to the statistics which they keep. In spite of this, one thing is clear, that, with the exception of the Catholics, all of them have suffered a steady loss.

TABLE I

Church of England

Infant baptisms related to live births in England

Date	Infant baptism rates per 1,000 live births
1885	623
1895	641
1900	650
1910	689
1920	678
1930	699
1940	641
1950	672
1960	554
1962	531

'Membership' then, tends to confirm the evidence about attendance.

TABLE 2

Church of England

Confirmations per 1,000 population aged fifteen years in England

Date	Males per 1,000 living	Females per 1,000 living	Totals: rates per 1,000 living
1885	298	443	371
1895	274	404	339
1900	234	345	290
1910	298	413	356
1920	244	342	293
1930	267	360	313
1940	226	277	251
1950	232	328	279
1960	253	379	315

TABLE 3

Church of England

Confirmation per 1,000 of population aged twelve to twenty years in England

Date	Males	Females	Total
1950	27·6	34·5	31·2
1955	28·3	39·7	34·0
1960	27·6	40·9	34·2
1961	26·6	39·3	32·9
1962	24·4	36·7	30·4
1963	22·2	32·0	27·0
1964	20·7	31·3	25·9

The Church of England has, in recent years, produced its own statistics of trends within the Church.[1] In relation to baptism, which is an infant rite in the Anglican Church, the trend since the 1880s shows a slight decrease, and that a recent one. In the early 1960s some 55 per cent of the children born alive in England were baptised into the

TABLE 4

Church of England

Sunday school children per 1,000 population aged three to fourteen years in England

1885	—
1895	298
1900	296
1910	298
1920	246
1930	242
1940 (1939)	218
1953	177
1960	133

No figures are available for the period 1940–52

Church of England. A century ago the Nonconformist Churches baptised a higher proportion than they do to-day. Their decline reflects the decline in strong and specific commitment, and from this the Church of England – as residual claimant – has probably gained. Figures for confirmation show a similar downward trend since the 1880s, on whatever basis we assess them. Using as a base population those aged fifteen in a given year, about 30 per

1. *Facts and Figures About the Church of England*, London, Church Information Office, 1962 and (No. 3), 1965, on which the accompanying tables are based.

cent of this number were confirmed (it is by no means implied that all those who were confirmed were actually fifteen years old, of course). Both in the 1880s and today there is a much lower absolute figure of confirmations than of baptisms. About half of those baptized appear to

TABLE 5

Church of England

Sunday-school teachers in England

1895	196,000
1900	195,000
1910	206,000
1920	171,000
1930	163,000
1939	127,000
1953	98,000
1960	85,000

TABLE 6

Church of England

Persons on the Church Electoral Roll. Totals and Enrolment Rate per 1,000 population of appropriate age

Date	No. on roll in thousands	Enrolment rate per 1,000 population
1925	3,638	143
1930	3,693	147
1940	3,423	120
1950	2,959	96
1960	2,862	89
1964	2,692	81

be 'lost', and the proportion is growing. Baptism has retained its popularity better than has confirmation.

In Sunday-school attendance there is an even sharper decline, from 30 per cent of the appropriate age group (three to fourteen years) in Anglican Sunday schools in the 1880s, to 14 per cent of this age group in the early 1960s. Sunday-school teachers have fallen by more than 50 per cent in the same period. The marked difference between Sunday-school attendance and confirmation and, even more marked, between Sunday-school attendance and baptism, may be noted.

The Electoral Roll of the Church of England – the roll of those who have made themselves eligible for participation in those aspects of parish church affairs in which the laity have a voice – shows a steady decline, from about 15 per cent of the appropriate age group in the 1920s to just over 8 per cent in 1964. Easter Communion figures measure the really faithful in the annual Church occasion of greatest importance. In the 1890s between 8·5 and 9 per cent of the population over fifteen years of age made Easter Day Communion in the Anglican Church. In 1962 the figure was 6·3 per cent.

There are two trends which can be discerned. The first is the diminution in religious participation over the period of some sixty or seventy years in most forms of religious involvement which amount to more than one isolated ceremonial occasion. The other is the diminution in religious participation over the life-cycle of the individual. As the individual ages so he is decreasingly disposed to involve himself in religious activity. Baptism in the Church of England remains a persistent demand by a fairly large proportion of the population. We have already seen that there may have been some incidental gain to the Anglicans with the decline in commitments of Nonconformists.

TABLE 7

Church of England

Parochial Easter Day communicants per 1,000 population over fifteen years in England

Date	Rate per 1,000 population age 15 and over	Estimated number of Easter Day communicants (in thousands)
1885	84	1,384
1895	92	1,746
1900	93	1,902
1910	95	2,212
1920	88	2,194
1930	80	2,285
1940	64	2,018
1950	58	1,867
1960	65	2,159
1962	63	2,158

We must allow that there is still a high demand for this ritual, but it cannot simply be said that this represents high religious belief, especially in view of the evidence that this demand is not very extensively sustained by other religious practices. It may be rather that in a child-centred society, baptism becomes another of those things which, in a sense, is every child's right. If 'we cannot do enough for the children' as is often popularly said, then baptism is another of the welfare services to which children can be exposed certainly without harm, and possibly with benefit. Those who know industrial working-class populations well, know, too, that a child is often baptized for essentially superstitious reasons. A child who is unbaptized

TABLE 8

Church of England

Degrees of Church of England Membership, 1962 (England)

100%	41,299,000	Home population born and resident
66%	27,384,000	Persons baptized in the Church of England
24%	9,842,000	Confirmed members (44% of baptized members aged 13 and over)
7%	2,793,191	Electoral roll (13% of baptized members aged 17 and over)
6%	2,347,201	Easter communicants* (24% of confirmed members)
5%	1,892,765	Christmas communicants (19% of confirmed members)
2%	915,000	Sunday School children (18% of baptized members aged 3–14 years)

* Note this includes Easter *week* communicants.

will always be unlucky, it is said. This hardly constitutes Christian commitment to baptism – it is hardly a reason which the Church itself is likely to consider laudable, but it may be an important consideration in inducing people to have their children baptized. This then is an example rather of the persistence of magical dispositions, which in this instance support religious obligation rather than coming into conflict with it.

Confirmation may also be supported by a generalized superstition. People are still sometimes proud of having been confirmed. Its significance as a promise of religious allegiance disappears, and its role becomes that of a vague claim to status and authenticity. Usually, too, confirmation occurs at the age where adolescent religiosity and the last vestiges of firm parental authority coincide. It was

among people at the beginning of their teens that eight-
eenth- and nineteenth-century revivalists had their
greatest successes, and we may readily assume that at
this age young people are, despite stridently expressed
cynicism, still not so sure of themselves that they can
reject the claims of the sacred.

The comparison of confirmation with Sunday school,
however, illustrates how fully religious commitment goes
into decline at this period of the individual life-cycle. And
here, in the period under review, we see the significance
of a changing social pattern. The Sunday-school was in
the past both an educational and a custodial agency – an
agency of social control and of socialization. It had a protective and a formative influence. But the ethos of the
second half of the twentieth century is one in which
personal moral integrity is less emphasized than in the
half-century preceding. Relationships are more completely governed by role-expectations and there are other –
often more mechanical – ways of exacting from individuals
the behaviour which is expected of them. Religious knowledge itself, to take the other function of Sunday school,
is less highly regarded in a more pragmatic society: it
'gets you nowhere' as is often colloquially said. Even the
custodial function of the Sunday school has much less
appeal to parents. The pattern of Sunday activities has
changed from a day on which there was considerable
restriction on play in the past: it has become a day on
which parents and younger children are involved in travel
undertaken in the name of recreation. The car has, as
many clergymen have suggested, been the factor which
has altered the pattern of Sunday leisure; parents take
children out with them. The demand for more facilities on
Sunday – which increasingly means commercial facilities –
becomes a threat to Church and Sunday school. As the
fundamentalists used to say, and from their particular

perspective there is no gain-saying the validity of their comment, 'If you begin by making Sunday into Funday, you end by making it into Sinday.'

The Electoral Roll represents those 'politically conscious' of their Church obligations, although even on an electoral roll one cannot be entirely sure that all those whose names are entered are deeply religiously committed people. There may be certain local, social advantages to being entititled to vote in those limited affairs to which inclusion on the electoral roll entitles Anglican laymen. Some enjoy having a hand in running things, and others who may have let their names go forward, may in fact become apathetic and inert as they find other – more exciting – arenas, in which to exercise their franchise. Easter Communion is the peak occasion of religious devotion in the year: all the genuinely committed members of the Church might be expected to make every effort to participate in this most significant ceremony, which marks the climax of the Church year, and is the high point of drama in the Christian mythos. But the proportion of the eligible population which actually does participate is very small indeed.

We see, then, that religious participation appears to decline with age and voluntary commitment, at least in the earlier part of the individual's life-cycle. We might discover, if we had an adequate body of information that the age structure of the people in the pew revealed that in later life people are somewhat more likely to be religious than in early and middle adult life. We know, too, that spinsters are more than fully represented among the ranks of the most devout. But the figures we have examined do suggest that the church still plays its part in the lives of many more as a service facility than as an evangelistic agency, more as the provider of occasional and reassuring ritual than as the disseminator of vital knowledge or the exemplar of moral wisdom. The nexus of Church and participant has perhaps shifted. It now represents very largely what the individual wants from the Church by way of authentic prestigious and self-enhancing ceremonial, rather than what it once implied, namely the individual's obligations to the Church, the performance of his religious duties and maintenance of the Christian life. There is a continuing (if in some respects slightly declining) incidence of the demand for the *rites de passage*. From the Church's point of view these are its service functions. There is very much less demand for teaching, exhortation, prayer and facilities for worship, and even for pastoral help. The Church appears increasingly as some department of a welfare state, which might be corporately supported without personal commitment (out of 'rates' or 'taxes', although this is not, of course, the case) to be used as and when the individual requires the performance of its services.

If this is a general attitude to the Church, it is not difficult to see that this disposition will be even more to the disadvantage of Nonconformist denominations than to the Established Church. The Nonconformist Churches have depended in the past on specific and voluntary commitment. Their people were a protesting people who were conscious of their differences from the conforming and apathetic mass. But in an age in which specific religious commitment of any kind is a rare thing, there is a drift towards the standard and unexceptionable, and since the demand for the Church is focused on ritual and ceremonial, the Anglican Church, both in the intrinsic nature of its ritual practice, and because it represents the 'normal' and established thing, stands to gain.

This trend is further evidenced by the two rites of passage which mark adult life, and which we have not yet examined. Their specifically religious content is less evident than that of baptism and confirmation, which are intrinsically religious acts, with (in modern society) only very slight general social consequence. Because they are *socially* significant procedures performed for practically all members of society, the extent to which they are undertaken under religious auspices is greater than the total incidence of the purely religious rite of confirmation. I refer, of course, to marriage and burial. The accompanying table indicates the proportion of marriages performed by the different agencies approved for the purpose. It is evident that although civil marriages had a steady growth for the first nine decades after its inception, in the 1950s

TABLE 9

Marriages in England and Wales. Manner of Solemnization
(Proportions per 1,000 total marriages)

Year	Church of England and Church in Wales	Roman Catholic	Other Christian denominations	Jews	Civil
1859	812	46	75	2	65
1869	763	41	99	2	95
1879	723	41	114	2	120
1889	698	42	116	3	131
1899	678	41	125	6	150
1909	614	42	132	7	241
1919	597	52	115	5	231
1929	562	60	114	7	257
1952	496	94	99	5	306
1957	496	115	104	5	280
1962	474	123	102	5	296

Statistics not available between 1934 and 1952

the percentage of those marrying in registry offices in fact declined and now appears to have settled at about thirty per cent of all marriages. After years of decline church marriage appears now to be the steady choice of seventy per cent, but set against other religious statistics we cannot suppose that it reflects any change in sentiment concerning the religious nature of marriage as such.

The only adequate explanation appears to be that which we have intimated already in regard to other social functions of the Church – namely the sustained demand for religiously authentic rites of passage. Of all rituals in an individual's life, marriage is the occasion of greatest social celebration. The binding nature of the commitment itself, the social reorganization which it signifies, the anxiety which surrounds such a contract, the implied development of the association, and the importance of its consequences in the establishment of a home and the production and socialization of children, all predicate that the wedding day may be claimed to be the most important day in the life of the individual. In consequence there is a demand that such a day should be marked by the most dramatic, the most authentic and the most elaborate ritual possible.

In modern society the family becomes socially a more isolated unit and, as the detachment from the family of orientation enhances the significance of commitment to the family being founded, so the demand for a dramatic expression of the change of roles and the change of circumstances may be enhanced. The wedding by civil registrar lacks all these elements of drama. The tension, the idealism and the anxiety of the occasion are lost, and the civil ceremony fails entirely to enhance the meaning of what is being undertaken. Whilst for intellectuals and rationalists it may seem to be a 'sensible' way of fulfilling the legal requirements of the case, it does not satisfy the demand for some more elaborate external expression of emotion and public sentiment. In an affluent society, where lavish entertainment and spectacle are abundantly possible, it is not easy to devise ceremonial and entertainment to make the wedding stand out from other events. The one feature which distinguishes it, is the authenticity of *awe*ful ceremony. Perhaps, therefore, as long as the Church can retain its sense of majesty and transcendence, its distinctiveness from the mundane and everyday, it will find itself in high – perhaps increasing – demand for the solemnization of marriages.

The final rite of passage for which there is widespread demand is, of course, burial. Any graphic depiction of the incidence of the use of the Church for these crucial rites would reveal that even if less than two-thirds of the population of England and Wales experienced Church of England ritual for their entry into the world, a far higher proportion enjoyed its presidency at their departure. And we may safely assume that most of those who do not have the offices of a Roman Catholic, a Nonconformist or a Jewish religious functionary. Indeed, a man needs extraordinary presence of mind at death if he is to avoid religious officiation at his burial. The control of funerals is so much more professionalized than the control of baptisms, confirmation and weddings that religious officiation becomes almost a matter of routine. We can, however, except in the satisfaction of the mourners, discount this particular pattern of the individual's religious participation which may or may not be voluntarily contracted.

The case of burial left aside, it is evident that in general there is a tendency for individuals to experience a decline of religious involvement during their early lives, and that for many the Church functions as a service agency providing appropriate ceremonial for prestige and status-enhancement at crucial stages of the life-cycle. In general, there can be little doubt about the decline in church-going church-membership, sustained religious commitment, and the general standing of the Church in society. It is evident that institutionally the Church remains favourably placed, and that its agencies are well entrenched in many respects. The conclave of the Church – the Anglican Church Assembly and Convocation – remain important forums of opinion, and their debates receive publicity and attention. In their representation in the House of Lords, reduced in significance as that assembly now is, the bishops have another vehicle for the expression of Anglican opinion through which to influence the social, political and moral life of the nation. But even these facilities have more the appearance of power than the reality of it. Their influence is moral rather than political; exhortatory and not mandatory; specious in the disparity between its actual effectiveness and its appearance of solemnity and significance. There are other centres of decision-making, and other criteria of determination than those adduced from traditional, scriptural, ideological authority. As society has become diversified in its activities and interests, so individuals have gained extensive freedom in the regulation of their lives, and even though they often undertake that regulation from ill-informed and irresponsible perspectives, the Church has lost most of the authority it once may have had to control this situation.

2

Denominationalism and Secularization

THE way in which a religious ethic and religious institutions are related to the wider social structure has varied
among the different world religions. Thus in Hinduism
the religious ethic has provided a complete legitimation
of a social status system, structured in reverence to the
dominant stratum of the priestly class, and this, rather
than the inculcation of an ethical system for everyday life,
has been its predominant pattern of social control.
Christianity, initially the religion of 'outsider' groups,
has, on the other hand, always been able, ideologically
and institutionally, to accommodate new and diverse social
strata and to socialize them by an inculcated ethic for their
social roles. In feudal times, when Christianity very largely became set to the social mould, and legitimated the
pattern of the social order to the exclusion of 'outsider'
groups, and replicated that order in its own internal
offices and hierarchy, the Church may have come closer
than at any other time to fulfilling functions similar to
those of a religion like Hinduism. Christianity was, however, too centrally organized, and its own hierarchy contained too many internal status divisions, co-ordinated
with those in the wider society, for the priestly class as
such ever to have become socially dominant.

Because Christianity had an ideological history of
rebellion, it was always possible for groups which were
disinherited or disaffected to use the Christian faith as a
justification for action against the Church.[1] The kernel of
revolutionary ardour remained in the texts, and could be

1. See on this Norman Cohn, *The Pursuit of the Millennium*, London, Secker & Warburg, 1957.

invoked for transcendental legitimation for a course of action opposed to Church and State. Most of the insurrections of the Middle Ages were those of rural proletarian or newly urbanized groups, without adequate education, leadership or organization to establish any permanent counter position to that of the Church. Only when the changing economic processes of social development brought into being a new stratum, which, if without social status, was none the less literate and increasingly economically powerful, was the sectarian potential of Christianity, as an ideological accommodation for men who were outsiders, realized again. Only then was it possible to create a permanent and organized religious alternative to the universal Church, which could use Christian teachings to reinterpret its own position, and which could claim sanction and sanctity for it, and for the social stratum from which it recruited.[1]

This, then, was the transformation of Christianity at the hands of the Calvinists. The ethic of Calvinism justified and promoted the disposition to work in the calling of the townsman and trader in sixteenth-century Europe. Later, when industrial society evolved, the ethic of the Puritan was reinvoked. The same social ethic was expressed by Methodism in England, though now with an application to the masses of working men and not simply to an elect merchant class. Wesley's Arminian theology emphasized that all men had the chance to choose Christ and salvation. And this emphasis suited the new mass-society, and facilitated the socialization of a large work force, better than the aristocratic theology of Calvinism which emphasized the fewness of those who would be saved. The doctrine of assurance of salvation and Wesley's Arminian-

1. See Max Weber, *The Protestant Ethic and the Spirit of Capitalism*, London, Allen & Unwin, 1930; idem, *The Sociology of Religion*, London, Methuen, 1965.

ism were better, if blunter, psychological weapons for the working classes, than the subtle and anxiety-creating teaching of Calvin, with its final insistence on the inscrutability of the will of God in regard to salvation, and the inability of man to affect God's decisions either by heartfelt faith, or by the performance of good works.

Christianity's genius was in its adaptability to new classes throughout processes of social change. It was only as those new classes showed a firm disposition to self-discipline and organization and to establish and maintain effective social control, that permanent organizations – 'denominations' – emerged. These were the capacities displayed by the new urban merchant classes who became the votaries of Calvinism. The later alternative was for the new classes to become amenable to order imposed upon them from without and gradually disseminated to them through local leaders who were often laymen. This occurred among the new working classes and small independent men who became the supporters of early Methodism. The earlier adventist and millennialist movements which had arisen in expectation of a new dispensation with the returned Christ as its head were all too often only movements in the very literal sense of the word. Their members often had little capacity for sustained Christian commitment except as impelled immediately and unreflectingly by the intense emotions awakened in a situation of social and economic deprivation. The intensity of their feeling could sustain a march but could not bring into being a social movement which could mount a programme of sustained social action: they were incapable of compromising with the world in order to achieve their ends, which were the utter rejection of the prevailing social order.

The intensity of response of early movements reflects the deeply felt desire to alter conditions, the urgency of hope and the demand for solutions – a condition of emotional disturbance which can be expressed only in religious terms. (The urgency and intensity today manifested by Africans praying for healing for sufferers in many of the contemporary Syncretistic sects probably characterized some of the more fanatical adventist movements of the Middle Ages.) As increasingly men came to learn rational techniques and procedures, so reliance shifted from emotional attempts to control the environment, to the recognition of the value of controlled, disciplined regulation of emotional response, and the acquisition of ordered instrumental methods of controlling the intractable forces of nature and society.

Thus we see the contrast. Many of the early adventist movements, and perhaps even some which occurred up until the eighteenth century in western Europe, and even later in parts of the United States and other parts of the world, were largely ecstatic emotional outbursts reinterpreting Christianity in primitive terms and with a literal demand for the fulfilment of Biblical promises. Later sectarian movements manifested a very different disposition, interpreting Christian ideas in terms of the increasing rationality, order and organization which were necessary in their working lives. It is in this sense, and of movements like Calvinism and Methodism and their various offshoots, that one can regard denominationalism as itself an aspect of secularization.

The Puritans represented what Max Weber called a 'this-worldly asceticism', and created an ethic which was pragmatic, rational, controlled and anti-emotional. The destruction of works of art hitherto employed in religious worship was not a consequence of a mere theological conviction; it was the manifestation of a less emotional and a more disciplined and calculated religious spirit. The *Entzauberung der Welt*, of which Weber wrote, led to heightened control of imaginative excess, of romanticism and aesthetic appreciation. It was the process by which men came to terms with hard empirical facts, cut through mysteries and superstitions, mere 'feelings', whether evoked by art or fancy, and sought in hard-and-fast terms to know in a matter-of-fact way just what the truth was. In this orientation, reflecting necessarily the qualities which the man of business himself needs in the pursuit of his livelihood, there is a beginning of the secularization process.

Those societies most dominated by religious motivations are those in which diverse mysteries, powers, objects and deities are recognized. Paradoxically, considering Christianity's attempt to eliminate magic, alien beliefs and rival theories of deity, religiosity as such is stronger where such multiplicity of ideas prevails – as in Hinduism. Once order and system (theology) is introduced into man's apprehension of the divine sphere of things, and as soon as contradictions are eliminated, and the record made in some sense sensible, meaningful and in accordance with the everyday understanding of things, then the first basic assumption of the divine world becomes difficult to apprehend. Christianity militated strongly against all other religious beliefs, and in particular against magical ideas, but in doing so probably eventually – and in the very long run – made acceptance of Christian ideas more difficult. In Puritanism this process was continued and many of the persisting traditions and folk accretions to the basic essentials of the Christian faith, and the practices and usages of the Church, were now questioned. If the central ideas remained they did so in a simpler and more orderly way: if the Godhead still pertained to strong emotional forces (God as saviour, as retributor, as the judge, the arbiter, the benefactor and the depriver, even eventually as destroyer of the earth – concepts not so far removed from the attributes apportioned out to Indian deities), none the less these emotions were themselves subject to a structure of regulation and control, except perhaps in the last analysis, where the inscrutability of God continued to be asserted.

It is no accident that from among the Puritans came a significant impetus in the development of science – the manifestation of a rational spirit.[1] Again, it is no accident that it was among them and their successors that rationalism went further than mere application to theology and led increasingly to reasonable doubt about the scriptures themselves and about the accepted reinterpretation of the world. It was among the later Puritans that Unitarianism largely reasserted itself against 'irrational' doctrines such as the Trinity, and from the Puritan inheritance that early humanism found expression.

Methodism, if in some ways it emphasized some continuities with older religiosity, did so because it stemmed more directly from the Anglican Church which had largely shorn itself of its Puritan inheritance, and because Methodism became the religion of largely industrial classes, especially in its beginnings, whose condition was not such that they were prepared for a religion as rational as that even of the early Puritans. But even in the name, Methodism captures something of the new spirit in religion. It accomplished the dissemination of a work ethic to new social strata, and permitted a more emotional expression of religious commitment than had been normal among Puritans. And this emotionalism was perhaps an indispensable accompaniment of the communication of new values to the new working classes whose lives had undergone profound disorganization. But Methodism too became a disciplinary agent, producing an ethic

1. See Robert K. Merton, *Social Theory and Social Structure*, Glencoe, Ill., The Free Press, 2nd edn., 1957, pp. 574–628.

which had many resemblances to that of Puritanism. It emphasized, certainly, God's love rather than his inscrutability, but this, too, was perhaps a more appropriate and accepted emotional attribute of deity for the dependent industrial classes of Bristol and the West Riding, than the awefulness of the God who, when reason failed, could be given refuge, at least temporarily, in the inscrutability which Puritans conferred upon him.

In disseminating through religious agencies a new attitude of mind and in socializing a new stratum to its life circumstances Methodism, too, was part of the secularizing process. It defined religious commitment, eliminated superstition and disciplined and regulated men's relation to the supernatural in ways especially appropriate to the new working class. Even within one country different sections of the population will interpret the world quite differently in accordance with their relative need to exercise emotional control, and the extent to which their social control becomes important for themselves and for others. If Methodism was in some ways a 'throw-back' it was so only because it was relevant to a section of the population which was itself less emotionally mature than were the ruling classes and the established commercial classes and one which at this time was only just being brought into the class structure of modern society as its working force. Methodism was a discipline, a way of life, an ethic for people who had previously had little need of such an agency of voluntary social- and self-control – who had been controlled by community regulation, by agrarian values, by the settled patterns of landed society. Now they had to acquire an inner discipline, and in so doing rose above the brutalities of earlier patterns of social control, and eventually became themselves arbiters in large measure of the appropriate standards of decency of industrial society.

46

In developing in this way Methodists rose above the ranks of the lowest workers, and tended increasingly to represent the more respectable of the working classes. The bottom strata were again outside the effective control of society, as they had so often tended to be, and the new religious accommodation to the changing world turned out to be, for many, an agency of social mobility. In being religious, men identified with the forces of respectability, with law and order, in society, and so came to share a place which was somewhere above the bottom, and supported the prevailing ethic and the prevailing value system which was imposed on the intractables who remained at the bottom. And they, in England, as in latter-day America, were many of them migrants and immigrants.

The diversity of denominations, then, may be seen as the successive stages in the accommodation of life-practice and ethos of new social classes as they emerged in the national life. Obviously there is no complete correlation of class and religion, but the broad contours of the association can be readily recognized and will not, despite minor variations, be readily disputed. But not only have the denominations been an accommodation of classes, they have also represented, as we have here tried to indicate, a process of secularization. As Catholicism was associated with a feudal society and its values, so the various deviations of religious belief and practice, which subsequently found acceptance and became institutionalized, reflected and promoted new interpretations of society and its morality, of theology and of man's responsibilities on earth. The Reformation reduced the mystical elements in religion, and Calvinism took this process further. The development of Arianism, Socinianism and Unitarianism in the eighteenth century led to a more fully rationalized religious ethic. The Trinity, the divinity of

Christ, the miracles and the Virgin Birth all successively became open to challenge within the context of religious discussion. Tradition still had its strength, of course, but as the influence of superstition waned, so these beliefs – even where they were still strongly held – became socially less significant. They had less consequence for men in a changing social order.

We may see movements like Methodism as a reaction – a reassertion of religious values to new classes, but already embracing much of the new spirit, even if trying in some sense to perpetuate the old. Wesley's own wish for Methodists to remain Anglicans was more than he could effectively demand of a movement which was already organized along the lines of extraordinary rationality. It became the first working-class movement, the first mass movement to be structured according to rational principles, and consequently the first stable mass movement to persist over time. There were always reactions, of course; the revivalism of the late nineteenth and early twentieth centuries was exactly that. It was a demand to return to stronger and more emotional religious attitudes.

In the mass-society, with a high degree of individualism and the breakdown of community control, the revivalist movement virtually had to be Protestant in its theology, it had to espouse the individualism and the personal responsibility which were features of Protestantism. Spontaneous choice, and the will to form a voluntary community, necessarily became the criteria of religious commitment. But what such revivalism was often seeking was the stability of the religious community of that past – of the past as revivalists envisaged it. In many ways revivalism represented the attempt to re-establish agrarian values, to restore the advantages of stable community life to people who had lost all community sense. Its crudeness, naiveté, emotionalism, brotherliness, all manifested the demand for return to the security of the settled simple life, such as it was known in agricultural villages or in the communities of early industrialism after they had settled into committed Methodism. It is a recurrent demand for the fraternal society, found still among religious radicals in the mid-twentieth century.

It is not surprising that such revivals had their impact in new urban areas, full of recently transplanted rural populations. Their demand was often for the persistence of relationships and community structure which were often no longer possible in the rapidly changing conditions of industrial society. The success of revivals among rural migrants to the town, even at times among former Catholics, illustrates the strength of the emotional response and the demand for the security of life under a pervasive ethic in which stable expectations and responses have in the past provided the framework of the social order. Revivalism promises a return to the decencies of the past through a reassertion of fundamental truths. The sects which come into being through revivalism manifest the primary relationships of village society, but the effect which they have on society at large may be to disseminate standards of disinterested goodwill which never arise spontaneously without the transfer of primary affectivity to groups which in fact are themselves not primary kinship or neighbourhood communities. They create enclaves which sanctify in religious terms the structure and relationships of folk society, but because these new groupings are not groups of kinsmen, the values which they espouse may have a wider influence as they are disseminated to the society at large.

The outcropping of revivalistic reaction to the social process, and the periodic re-expression of the demand and

49

the search for social certainties which have been lost, should not, however, obscure the main line of the secularization process. The development of denominationalism is evidence of the process as fully as is the gradual demystification of society, as it is recorded in the work of such different sociologists as Auguste Comte, Thorstein Veblen and Max Weber. The denominations arising as protest movements in a particular period have gained strength for a time, and then gradually come to accept a place in the established order of society, catering for a particular section of the population whose view of the world is co-ordinated in, and expressed through, the denominational institutions themselves. The independent classes who constituted the Puritan congregations of the older English cities and the settlements of New England gradually accepted emendations of strict and early Calvinist theology, in accordance with their own interests and the view of the world which their daily activities and social situation made congenial to them. Richard Baxter in England and Governor Winthrop in Massachusetts both departed from the strict Calvinism of their inheritance. The Independents controlled in large measure their own ministry, and were able to call whom they chose, and sometimes to dislodge ministers whom they had come to dislike, and thus they had – especially in the early decades and before ministerial control of the movement increased – a special facility for adaptability of theology and ethic, which (though that Church obviously changed) was less readily possible in the Catholic Church.

Having become the appropriate religious institutions for particular strata, and subsequently gaining strength only incidentally (for instance in the eighteenth century in association with the impetus gained from Methodist revivalism), the older bodies of historical dissent in

England, the Congregationalists, Presbyterians and Baptists, continued through the nineteenth and into the twentieth century when their *specific* relevance to particular status groups diminished in importance – at least this was so in England. There is a general social phenomenon of institutional persistence, which is perhaps especially evident in the case of religious institutions, which, possibly because they are ultimate repositories of strong emotional commitment, however latent and traditional that commitment has become, manifest an especial durability.

Denominational diversity, however, has in itself promoted a process of secularization, in providing for the uncommitted a diversity of religious choice, in creating institutionalized expression of social differences and divisions, and in the very circumstance which, in extending choice, allows some to make no choice at all. The divergence of belief systems and of ethical codes in society, short of creating a persistent state of tension, is likely to reduce the effectiveness of the religious agencies of social control. Thus, if we take as a simple and perhaps trivial example a hypothetical New England community, originally Puritan we can see that once immigration brings religious diversity of belief and practice, the religious basis of social control of the community will at once be jeopardized. If we take even the relatively insignificant matter of Sunday observance, we can see that if the immigrants are Catholics, who regard Sunday as a day of recreation after their early morning religious exercise, and Jews, who might regard it as a day for business activity, then religiously sanctified practices (albeit of other religions) destroy effective social control rather than sustain it. Religious values cease now to be community values. The man who chooses to avoid religion altogether can now also escape religious regulation of his social life in a way not previously possible. In this sense he accepts, and the mixed religious circumstance facilitates, the growth of a secular ethic in which some basis of social control other than religious sanction – and thus a secular basis – has to be developed. In the particular historical circumstance, we need not be surprised that denominations which enjoyed supremacy in the New England states (and most other American states, Pennsylvania excepted) struggled to maintain it, even to the point of the persecution of religious deviants.

It must be recognized that in a different respect, denominationalism probably impeded the manifest political expression of secularism in a militant anti-religious form in Anglo-Saxon countries. In both Britain and the United States, once religious tolerance had been established, opposition to the ruling class could always be expressed as religious dissent. This led to a broad affiliation of English dissenters including the Methodists (other than the Wesleyans) with the Liberal Party in the nineteenth century at a time when the Established Church seemed to be closely identified with the Tory Party and traditional landed interests. The political and social debate was maintained within – in greater measure and for longer time than in other Christian countries – the context of religion, by the very diversity of Christian denominationalism, and the accommodation which that provided for different social strata. Eventually, and especially as the Liberal Party frequently held power, diversity of religious expression may have helped dissenters to distinguish, more clearly than could those who lived in societies where there was no religious diversity, the level of values which they shared with the ruling classes (nationality, patriotism, participation in an orderly state) and the levels at which they dissented. All of which may have contributed to the smoother evolutionary development of

Anglo-Saxon countries.[1] In societies in which economic, political and religious differences converged in one line of dominant cleavage, a more revolutionary situation existed. Thus, whereas in continental countries, and especially in Catholic countries, secularization was expressed in the development of secularist and anti-clerical movements, in the Anglo-Saxon countries it found less direct and more subtle expression.

The circumstances which induced particular strata in society to seek distinctive religious expression, at least partially in protests against those who monopolized life-changes for wealth, power and social status, tended in the course of time to disappear. The purpose of protest became increasingly less evident to subsequent generations within a particular denomination; their specific commitment became less clear. Over time protest becomes attenuated and commitment diluted in religious movements and yet institutions tend to persist. Thus denominations called into being to give expression to a certain theological position attractive to particular social strata, and recruiting largely from among them, persist when the theology has been forgotten, except by scholars, and has certainly become irrelevant to the lives of most of those who belong, and when the social circumstances of members have become quite different from those of their forebears among whom the movement began.

One of the common consequences of religious adherence in the denominational pattern is for a group to identify itself, in course of time, with the forces of moral order in the wider society, and sometimes to accept as

1. This point is not directly addressed to Halévy's contention that Methodism was largely responsible for saving Britain from a revolution of the French type, but clearly has some bearing on it. See E. Halévy, *History of the English People in the Nineteenth Century*, Vol. I, Part III, especially pp. 424–5, London, Benn, 1949.

appropriate, in all matters except those in which there are strong denominational peculiarities, the general ideal moral and social standards of the society. This is one of the ways in which, for the lowest group, sectarian and denominational religion becomes an agency of social mobility (as long as there is religious tolerance). In particular in societies in which denominational pluralism prevails, religious commitment to even manifestly outsider groups, such as the Salvation Army or Pentecostalism has often had the effect of raising the social and apparently the economic standards of those who belong. Thus it becomes the case that in the modern world there are religious denominations in Protestantism which maintain a separate existence which relates essentially to their historical position and to their organizational (rather than, for the modern world, to their social or theological or liturgical) distinctiveness.

Such denominations have in many ways lost their distinctive social meaning, but they still retain a following which is committed to a particular denomination rather than to contemporary Christianity in general, and which may derive certain special pleasures and benefits from that particular and separate commitment. The very fact that the denomination has a separate identity and that it is not part of the mass, may be a distinct attraction and comfort to some, even though they may not be well informed about the historical circumstances which brought their group into separate existence. And yet – and this becomes evident in an age in which, from sheer weakness, ecumenicalism is sponsored on every side – denominations do appear in large measure to have lost their special *raison d'être*.

Continued adherence to particular denominations is often no more than the continued adherence to particular churches, and if theological ignorance is as great as often appears, then this local allegiance is of even greater significance. This in itself has led to certain weaknesses in contemporary religion, and in particular it has become evident that it has not been easy for denominations to 'hold' their people in a society in which social and geographic mobility are so much more common than they used to be. With such mobility, locality allegiance is reduced, and if denominational allegiance is itself low there is little incentive to join up with the church of the same denomination on moving house.

The traditional Churches – Catholic and Anglican – have long organized themselves on a parish basis, on the assumption, which was no doubt realistic in a feudal society, that Church and community were mutually reinforcing and coterminal entities. But the mobility of modern man, seen both in regard to the length of time he lives in one place, and to his status in society, is such that men do not remain the same *social* entities in the same permanent localities. As they move, their social relations change, their personalities are affected, their assumptions, expectations and responses to their social world change, and they no longer have a permanent social 'self' which is locatable in a community of the faithful, whether it be of the Established Church or of a particular denomination. Although the Churches are fixed and operate on the assumption of stable local communities the assumption has become increasingly fictive.

Men perhaps no longer need the same stability of orientation to the social context or to the divine order, and in Britain the Churches find it increasingly difficult to sustain the interest and commitment of mobile people. Just as local government operates on unreal assumptions of man in relation to a small definable community with well-understood, recognized and meaningful boundaries, so does the parish. Yet men are no longer confined, permanent and settled: the social order according to which their lives are lived is of another kind, and in so many ways is incomprehensible on the basis of the assumptions of a parochial system of a static society. The Churches – especially as denominational allegiance weakens – find themselves in a continually less advantageous position for securing the commitment of their mobile clientele. Loss of members who move and fail to attach themselves to the church of their denomination in their new place of residence has long been recognized as a special source of leakage by the Churches. When friendship and shared association fail to support it, religious affiliation often proves a brittle bond.

In modern society, in which men are highly individuated by diverse patterns of social experience, in which men have considerable choice of the influences to which they expose themselves, there is no longer a widespread community of feeling to which the Churches can minister. The individuating process evident in the Reformation has continued and men have much less corporate feeling; they are less moved by local, regional or national identity than they were, and this reduces the meaning and validity of corporate worship, except in so far as worshipping, like dancing, can be economically provided only when a number of people undertake it at the same time in the same place, because they need the atmospheric context of each other to do it.

3

The Social Context of Secularization

WE have so far examined the process of secularization in the light of factors largely internal to religion itself. It would be impossible to determine the primacy of causes, but secularization is not merely a consequence of internal dialectic occurring over time within religious movements. Men's religious orientations to the world occur within a wider social context with which they interact in highly complex ways. It would be impossible to ignore the growth of new channels for man's emotional expression, new prospects for the realization of his wishes, and new agencies which function for him in ways which, in the past, have been more or less a monopoly of religious agencies. Thus, to choose almost at random, if we look at political movements, we see that the development of industrial society and the emergence of democratic patterns of political behaviour have had diverse consequences of importance for religion. The very conception that social arrangements, distributions of power, wealth, prestige, life chances and the general pattern of life circumstances, can be affected by instrumental action, and primarily by mass decision-making (or decision-making in the name of the masses) has in itself gradually altered man's recourse to demands for supernatural intervention in his affairs. The widespread religious teaching that man must show contentment with his lot, and fulfil his obligations, or, alternatively the religious hope that God will enter the human scene (again) and impose a new dispensation, are both orientations which diminish in strength as realistic political possibilities are increasingly apprehended. The change of focus from the after-life to this one has obviously been strongly associated with this development of the sense of social self-direction.

If, as is common, we recognize that we are less effectively self-directing than ideally we should like to be, increasingly we acknowledge that this is the consequence of the complexity of human purposes and emotions, and not God's disposition 'to try us in this world' or to 'give each his cross to bear'. Religious-moral interpretations of factual circumstances have disappeared and politico-moral interpretations have taken their place. Preoccupation with the morality of nation-states has largely replaced individual morality as a dominant concern of the intellectuals in modern society. Moral suppositions which are now applied to international affairs are dismissed at the individual level of behaviour.

As scientific orientations increase, and in particular those of the behavioural and organizational sciences, so we can expect conceptions of society itself to become increasingly affected by rationalistic assumptions. As social processes are increasingly subjected to rational planning and organization, so men are more and more involved in social activities in which their own emotional dispositions are less immediately relevant. Men may have become more rational, and their thinking may have become more matter-of-fact, as Veblen[1] expressed it, but perhaps even more important is their sustained involvement in rational organizations – firms, public service, educational institutions, government, the state – which impose rational behaviour upon them. The Churches with their dominant function as the institutionalization of emotional gratification, necessarily stand in sharp and increasingly disadvantageous contrast.

1. Thorstein Veblen, *The Theory of the Leisure Class*, New York, 1899; and idem, *The Place of Science in Modern Civilization*, New York, 1919.

Political movements, and the growth of organizational and manipulative techniques have not only affected our sense of social decencies and proprieties and our judgement about them, and about suitable action to be taken in regard to deviations – they have also provided new outlets for individual effort and energy. Undoubtedly religious activities – action for the Church, well-doing, voluntary organizations, participation, as well as, subsequently, the more independent activities of preaching the word – were the first outlet for the energies of new classes who were acquiring the inclination and the opportunity to interpret and shape their social world. The Nonconformist movements in Britain were not only presenting a new world-view and a new ethic, but they also provided new opportunities for the personal and active involvement of laymen in new leadership roles.

In the earlier bodies of historical dissent these roles were confined to the business and administrative aspects of the chapels, but even here the ministerial function itself was of lower status even in specifically religious matters than that of the priest or parson. In Methodism, despite its somewhat reactionary character, the process of laicization went further, and the layman acquired, despite a somewhat reluctant Wesley, the preaching role, as, in that more circumscribed context, he had previously done among Quakers. Even the celebration of the sacraments was now open to laymen. The flood-gates were open now for a wider participation of volunteering laymen in diverse religious activities. Opportunities for prestige, good-standing in the community acquired by voluntary effort, now became possible. In some ways this was the first process of mass social mobility in modern society – not necessarily involving change of occupation, income or formal position, but certainly presenting opportunities for acquiring new prestige and general respectability, which was often itself a first step to mobility of other kinds.

In Nonconformity in particular, but by imitation increasingly in the Anglican and Roman Churches as well, voluntary movements with a distribution of lay offices arose and spread. The Sunday-school movement, the Adult Schools, the Church Institutes, the Good Templars, the Bands of Hope, the Motherhoods, Brotherhoods, Bright Hours, and the Mutual Improvement societies were followed by more elaborate and more widely organized associations, the Church Lads, the Crusaders, the Boys' Brigade and so on. Initially it was the rising lower middle class who pressed forward into local leadership roles, but in course of time as voluntary associations arose with more secular aims, so the impetus of the spread of office and prestige through activities of a religious kind, or activities sponsored by the Churches, was overtaken by first political and then recreational associations in which similar prestigious roles were to be had. If they lacked the qualities and connotations of reverence, esteem and often wider community regard which attached to voluntary religious efforts, over time they often came to provide their incumbents with a wider application of power, better apparatus and equipment, until the balance has swung and religious office now appears to be less worth while as a way of disposing of one's leisure than involvement in an organization whose benefits are largely recreational and more explicitly 'here and now'. These tend to be interest associations and their spread reflects the decline of corporate and community allegiances in which religious affiliation was dominantly located.[1]

The availability of other opportunities for the exercise

1. The process is widely recognized in sociology as the shift from *Gemeinschaft* to *Gesellschaft*. See Ferdinand Tönnies, *Community and Association*, London, Routledge, 1955.

of leadership was obviously associated with the replacement of religion and church by secular activities in fulfilment of some of religion's erstwhile functions. Diversity of leisure opportunities meant that for recreational pursuits other possibilities were open, particularly in the sphere of educational and intellectual recreation which had previously been almost exclusively the province of the Churches. The growth of new techniques for the presentation of information necessarily led to the emergence of new occupations expert in production and in presentation – the development of the film industry illustrates the process most vividly.

The technical achievement in itself was sufficient to confer interest and stimulate enthusiasm. Its detachment from the agencies of social control, its competitiveness, and its profit seeking meant that from the outset it appealed to immediate appetites and emotions. There was never any inbuilt or implicit restraint about what it might offer, and it was not in the service of any particular class, national, political or governmental agency. It was ideologically uncommitted, prepared to test the market to discover what men would pay to see as entertainment, and prepared to defy social conventions and accepted morality, whenever it appeared to be in the interests of profits to do so, and until governmental interference might occur. Thus the entertainment industry – and it became an industry in the full sense only with the development of advanced technical means of presentation – was from the outset a challenge to religion, offering diversion, other reinterpretations of daily life, and competing for the time, attention and money of the public. In its actual content it may be seen as more than an alternative way of spending time, but also as an alternative set of norms and values. It replaced religion's attempt to awaken *public* sentiments by offering titillation of *private* emotions.

In this whole development, and it is necessarily a complex one, relating to the expansion of literacy and the development of a secular Press, as well as to the cinema and subsequently to the radio and television, the Church was steadily losing its near-monopoly, and at least its dominance, of the media of communication. From the times when public communication was largely from the pulpit or by notices appended to the church-door, when intellectual stimulation was almost necessarily religious exhortation, the nineteenth and twentieth centuries saw the Church's influence as a source of information rapidly eroded as the relative significance and effectiveness of its channels of communication were reduced. From being a very powerful voice in the local community, the clergyman became one of several voices with divergent religious messages, and subsequently competed further with the increasingly effective voices using the new technical means of mass-communication offering non-religious distractions.

Today, even though the Church is able to use the means of mass-communication, it does so only marginally – marginally both to its own total communication which still relies on the nexus of pulpit and pew, and on religious literature, and marginally to the total content of the mass-media as a whole. Compared to the amount of entertainment, music, news, drama, secular education and all the other types of item carried by television, radio, Press and cinema, religious information has become a very tiny part indeed. Nor are religionists as good at using the media as those who are instructing or entertaining. They have developed few, if any, new techniques for its use, and they use it by courtesy and on sufferance. They tend to be older and middle-aged men using media increasingly dominated by the young. It might not be untrue to say that they are the deference note of the mass-communicators, 'employed' to whiten the image of an industry which is frequently charged with subversive, immoral and deleterious presentations.

As long as the Church connives in using the media the media controllers can use this fact in their own defence, as evidence of their social responsibility. But given the religionist's necessary assumption that religious truth is pre-eminent and that it ought to take a dominant place in the minds of men, the relegation of religious material to a marginal place in the programmes of the mass-communications is itself a derogation of the religious message. In using the mass-media the Churches permit their own material to be reduced to the level of the medium, to be put forth without much differentiation of presentation from a wide variety of highly heterogeneous and at times incongruous material. This in itself must detract from the high claims to pre-eminence which – of necessity – religion makes for itself. There is indeed some evidence that the use of mass-media itself alters the image of the Church.[1] In the secularized society religion must accept a marginal position in the communications agencies in defiance of its own self-assessment of the relative importance of different types of information!

An important aspect of the external changes which affected the role of religion in nineteenth-century society was the growth of a pragmatic *Weltanschauung*. The expansion of science and the fact that scientific operations 'proved themselves' in the eyes of the man in the street led to a new pragmatic test for all ideological systems. Science not only explained many facets of life and the material environment in a way more satisfactory than

---

1. 'From an audio-visual point of view there is only one Church. Its head is the Pope, for whom all its members pray. Its services are held in the Anglican Parish Church ... It sings the great hymns of Charles Wesley ...' *Mainstream Religion*, Rugby, U.K., William Temple College, 1963 (mimeo.).

alternative religious interpretations, but it also provided confirmation of its explanations in practical results. The very same factors which might be said to have very significantly affected the early spread of Christianity – its efficacy as a healing agency, and as an agency which could affect material conditions – were those which furthered the development of science, at least in its public acceptability. Even if science were deficient at the level of 'meanings' men had the alternative religio-artistic approach to the world which offered emotional *rapport* and empathic involvement with nature and with other men.

All this is not to suggest that the confrontation of science and religion, which was most dramatically illustrated by Bishop Wilberforce's onslaught against evolution, was in itself essentially harmful to religion, or even that there was an incompatibility between them. Indeed, religion and science can coexist as alternative orientations to the world (often as orientations of the same person – Newton, Faraday, Lodge and Coulson would be examples from different periods). Once 'liberated' from the view of the world as depicted in a particular religion, artistic conceptions of the world may be very much more challenging to religious orientations than science is. Thus although there is no doubt that artistic orientations are in origin closely associated with, and informed by, magico-religious orientations and represent somewhat similar emotional responses, or distilled responses in which emotional sets have been transformed into something meaningful, once an artistic tradition has freed itself from the particulars of a given religion, it then becomes much more completely a rival to religion than science is ever likely to do.

The reason for this is not difficult to see: art deals, as religion deals, in emotional matters, in meaningful communications, in interpreting, evaluating, evoking responses and inviting the individual's participation in a complex set of conceptions and feelings. Science does none of these things. When its factual presentation and analysis are done there is still the opportunity for religious interpretation. The scientific procedure is itself wholly other than the religious or artistic, but it is the very fact that science is concerned with means and with 'how' questions, which leaves the field free for consideration of ends and 'why' questions.

Obviously, scientific analysis may prejudice the extent to which men are disposed to engage in these other orientations, and in the past the very character of scientific inquiry – analysis as an alternative to the intuitive and unquestioning acceptance of wholes, or doubt as a principle of operation rather than faith – led religionists to suppose that science was, in its nature, the antithesis of religion. Subsequently religious apologists have gone to great trouble to show that religious inquiry never imposed such an embargo on scientific investigation, but there is no doubt that scientific inquiry did often appear to be blasphemous to churchmen and often suffered interdiction.[1] And yet, if, in earlier periods, tension occurred because of the divergence of initial perspective, and if, in some more ultimate sense the analytical approach may rob the world and society of much of the mystical, magical and romantic elements which have been the enjoyment and the special area of concern of religionists and artists, yet in a middle area of discussion it can be held that science is merely an alternative approach to that of the arts and religion.

1. See the classic account produced in 1896 by Andrew Dickson White, *A History of the Warfare of Science with Theology*, London, Constable, 1960, 2 vols. (reissued); and also Charles Coulston Gillespie, *Genesis and Geology*, Cambridge, Mass., Harvard University Press, 1951.

This, of course, has been especially the plea of men like Coulson, and of others who stand in the tradition of the Puritans and Protestant evangelicals who were in the English-speaking world so largely responsible for the cultivation of a scientific attitude to the material world (even if they as a group stopped short of its application to mankind itself). They have suggested that in analysing and investigating, man is engaged in an act of worship, he is learning about and appreciating the wonders of God's creation. The argument is an old one, and it is manifestly not one which is so readily applied to the study of the human psyche or to human society. But as such it is an indication of the growth of a new alternative academic tradition within the intellectual (and in the context of that society, necessarily religious) stratum.

That the Puritans should have favoured science and opposed the arts – as many puritanical sectarian movements do still – is again not without significance. The arts had manifestly become the repository of the more magical and more emotional aspects of religious values and they tended, in acquiring prestige and being highly valued in religious contexts, to help to maintain older, more magical attitudes. They readily fostered the idolatry which was often not far from the surface even in an anti-idolatrous religious tradition. But, worse, as the arts as such acquired autonomy as craftsmen and artists were employed for purposes not specifically religious, so the arts came to embody values and to evoke emotional responses which were not themselves in the service of religion.

This then was a more pronounced confrontation with religious ideals than that which was provoked by science even though it was one which did not occur so dramatically. There was an imperceptible gradualism in the way in which the arts freed themselves from religious preconceptions, in literature with *moral* tales which were often intrinsically shocking, as in Defoe: in painting with the gradual romanticization of the landscape and the invocation of other gods: in poetry with the candid expression of other emotions in clearly non-allegorical contexts. But once the process began the arts still in the service of the Churches were steadily emaciated: they lost spontaneity and lost their earlier deeper sense of values and their sense of intrinsic association. Late nineteenth-century religious art, poetry and architecture make evident this emaciation. Outside the service of religion, the arts came – however uncertainly – to represent other values, whether drawn from human predicaments, political ideals, or from the theory of art for its own sake.

We have digressed to show that the confrontation of science and religion was itself misunderstood especially in the nineteenth century, and by fundamentalists until very recent times, and in some movements still. But the confrontation was one with distinct and potential dangers for the religious mission, and in their distrust of science nineteenth-century divines were perhaps more justified – even if they lacked specific awareness of the grounds for their alarm – than is, even by religionists, commonly now conceded. That the Churches today are so concerned to assert that there is no conflict between science and religion is perhaps the best indication that the struggle is over, and that religion has conceded wide territories to science. The real conflict reposed in the minds of men, in terms of their proclivity to regard science as more reliable and more valuable than religion.

Conflict came as society espoused the pragmatic values that were so much more manifest in the scientific enterprise than in religion. At the fringes there developed religious movements which sought to be no less pragmatic than the sciences, which sought to confer distinct benefits on men, and to convince them that religion – rightly understood – could also work. The whole 'New Thought' group of movements, of which Christian Science was the most effectively organized and best known, sought to assert in the last years of the nineteenth century that religion too was a set of scientific principles which would enable men to live better. These principles were applied to much the same ends as those of science at that time – the search for bodily health and material well-being. The movements had correspondingly very diminished emphasis on the traditional religious concern with life after death. It is no accident that these new religious movements arose in the U.S.A. Pragmatism was by no means confined to these marginal developments, but even in more orthodox denominations there was some growth of would-be healing cults, spiritualist 'proofs' of the after-life, and the continued emphasis (especially in America) on the value of religion as an agency of mental therapy.

The real danger of science to religion, however, was rather in the increased prestige of science and the decline in the intellectual prestige of religion. Since science had answers, and had positive tangible fruits, it came increasingly to command respect and approval. As governments became less concerned with the promotion of religion, so they became increasingly disposed to sponsor science, at first by prizes and awards, and later by ever-increasing endowments to scientific inquiry and scientific education. In earlier periods the men credited with knowledge, the 'wise' men of society, had necessarily been religionists, since the Church maintained virtually an intellectual stratum whose principal obligations had become the maintenance of cultured, civilized and educational values. But increasingly intellectual concerns passed beyond the knowledge and the ability of clergymen. Even if from among their numbers many of the early scientists had come, as science became more specialized, and as specifically scientific education developed, so the possibility for the cleric to be a scientist diminished. Science grew up outside the control of the religious intellectual strata, and a new professional grouping came gradually into being.

Reflected in this process is also the shifting reliance to science for economic advance. Whereas nineteenth-century business men in the early period of industrialization relied on religion as an agency of social control, which helped to instil a sense of discipline and order into the work force, which was still the primary factor of production, in the twentieth century, as industry became more capitalized, so machinery increasingly 'controlled' labour, and that control could now be specifically adjusted for the particular task in hand without implications for controlling men in their private lives outside the work situation. The old control, with its 'letters of testimony' ('characters' as the working class knew them) relied on a man's general dispositions to industriousness, punctuality, thrift, sobriety, willingness and reliability: the new control demanded nothing of his 'character' – the conveyor-belt could exact from him all the control that was needed. Industry has thus passed from internalized 'character' values to mechanical manipulation. Thus it has turned from religious socialization to technical devices for the means of regulating the work situation and the productive process.

Eventually, for this imperative need to control men, industry has turned to new so-called sciences, of 'management' and 'industrial relations'. In economic terms it is wasteful to demand that the whole man, in all his facets, should be self-disciplined when a more specific method of manipulation can be evolved of just that part of the man which is needed for the job. Industry has thus rejected the blanket control of religio-moral socialization of men for methods which control men very much more as if they were mechanical instruments of production. Thus, whereas once businessmen, if they engaged in philanthropy, gave to religious causes, today they increasingly pass their surpluses to the endowment of science and education – and 'education' usually means scientific education.

As science developed as a profession its professional prestige steadily rose. An increasingly pragmatic society was impressed by the results of scientific endeavour – more evident and more dramatic than anything which the cleric, or even a team of clerics could produce. Ancient wisdom was more slowly gained, and less dramatically transmitted and operationalized, than the new learning. As prestige rose in science, a more important consequence followed: science increasingly attracted the better minds, provoked more public concern, gained increased access to the media of communication, and won higher rewards in terms of salaries. Whereas the minister of religion had been a specialist at earlier stages of social development, with the advance of scientific disciplines, and with application of science to many occupations, the clergyman was left as a distinctly more amateur practitioner. His special expertise – his knowledge of theology and liturgy and his licence to perform sacramental acts – were increasingly less relevant to a pragmatic society. Indeed the prestige of scientific procedures was such that it came in some measure to affect theology itself. The canons of objectivity, neutrality, empiricism were evidently strongly present in the movement towards the Higher Criticism, which placed religious authority under scrutiny – often in ways not altogether conducive to the maintenance of the actual authority of the priest in the pulpit.

The steady development of science meant the gradual emergence of separated disciplines which had earlier been

embraced within – embedded within – a general theological interpretation of the world and society. The older
sciences had freed themselves over centuries as Comte had
illustrated in his sociological treatise of the Three Stages,
and by the nineteenth century the Church had little claim
to provide the basis of cosmology.[1] As geology and
biology developed so the authenticity of the Christian
interpretation of the world became patently less tenable,
and steadily, often with bad grace and sometimes with
scant respect for objective procedures for the discovery of
the truth, the churches retreated from their earlier assertions concerning geological and biological facts. Psychology and sociology in which specific propositions capable
of testing are more difficult to formulate, have not experienced the same dramatic confrontation with Church teaching, but their attempt to create dispassionate, non-evaluative
approaches to man and society are undoubtedly as much, if
not more, totally at variance with the religious orientation
per se, as any of the earlier sciences.

Churchmen have, of course, sought to make use of
these disciplines, to harness them to their purposes.
Science is always easily restricted to the realm of means,
and is neutral concerning ends. The very development of
the Higher Criticism was a considerable concession to the
scientific spirit by theologians. To recognize that sacred
books must, despite their sacredness, have been written
by men, and must contain human apprehensions of the
deity, was in itself a remarkable admission of the spirit
of empiricism and reason to the theological sphere. It is
true that when the results of such inquiry proved grossly

1. Auguste Comte, *Cours de Philosophie Positive*, English translation by Harriet Martineau as *The Positive Philosophy of Auguste
Comte*, London, Chapman, 1853. For a short exposition of Comte's
ideas see *Fundamental Principles of the Positive Philosophy* (translated
by P. Descours and H. Gordon Jones) London, Watts, 1905.

inconvenient, and fell under pontifical disfavour in the Roman Church in the first two decades of this century, then the interest of the clergy shifted from historical to mystical interpretations of the beginnings of Christianity. Steadily, however, a scientific orientation has persisted, not only in textual matters, but in stylistics, archaeology and in the interpretation of the Dead Sea scrolls. The attempt to offer counter-scientific interpretations of the physical world, which religionists sought to do so urgently in the nineteenth century, have been largely abandoned. More radically, clerics have increasingly recognized religion as itself a subject of psychological and sociological interest.

Thus the sociology of religion, or religious sociology as it is more often called in that context, has been developed by clergymen as an aid to pastoral theology and missiology, particularly in France.[1] Other clerics have taken the insights of psycho-analysis, particularly in the Jungian tradition, and have invoked them in their preaching – sometimes with dramatic success in audience appeal. Clinical theology has emerged as a study of the therapeutic aspects of faith and congregational participation. There has, of course, also been widespread suspicion of disciplines of this kind within the Churches, and what have been taken to be the moral consequences and moral implications of these subjects have frequently been attacked as anti-Christian and ungodly. The point, however, is that not only has knowledge of the material world, and the ability to pronounce upon it, passed from the clergy, but so, too, has systematic knowledge concerning the minds of men and the organization of society. It is not uncommon today to see clerics as students in universities, particularly in the social sciences, where –

1. See F. Boulard, *An Introduction to Religious Sociology*, London, Darton, Longmans, Todd, 1960.

little more than half a century ago – those who would have been teaching what there was to know on these subjects would themselves have been clerics, and this was not much less true in America than in Britain. Even in their pastoral functions, the clergy may be said to have lost influence, and to have been transformed, by the growth of specialists in social work, into amiable amateurs.

We have already associated the growth of science with the development of rational pragmatic attitudes in society, and we must not omit mention of the specifically named creed of rationalism itself. In its militant form, rationalism was opposed to religion, and sought to show that religious beliefs were irrational, superstitious and unjustifiable. A view of man in which the discovery and application of rational principles would lead to a more fully ordered and sane universe, was promulgated, and with it the assumption that man could acquire, as part of the evolution of the species, a completely rational approach to the world and his fellow man. To this rationalistic impetus sociology, too, owes a good deal for its early development.

Rationalism was in many ways a shallow creed, but its promulgation in a diverse range of works and from a large number of thinkers – its affiliation to English Utilitarianism, Comteanism, Marxism, Pragmatism, and its widespread acceptance in socialist movements – illustrates the pervasiveness of the new credo. When the anti-rationalist thinkers emerged, aware that men were not capable of rationality in the naive way which had been supposed, and recognizing the persistent demands of men for emotional satisfactions, for conservatism and the retention of the habitual, and as the mechanisms of these irrational dispositions were laid bare, and man's emotional despair was revealed, so it might have been expected that such a contradiction of the anti-religious rationalists would in some measure restore religion.[1]

The anti-rationalists were, however, themselves employing scientific and rational techniques in their analysis and exposition. Although their theories frequently made evident the needs which, for example, religion served – in the case of Freud, Pareto, Durkheim – none the less they were not themselves advocates of religion, and were by no means themselves completely devoid of some of the rationalistic spirit of those whose naive rationalism they condemned. Rather they laid bare the religious motivations of men, and in some sense made them less creditable than they had appeared under the more open opposition of the rationalists. Whereas the rationalists were opposed to it, the anti-rationalists explained it. Whilst they and their successors acknowledged that religion might be beneficial for society they also made apparent its intellectual untenability. Thus the currents of thought which followed the hostility of nineteenth-century rationalism were, if less disposed to evoke hostility towards religion, more potent in reducing its credibility.

1. For a discussion of the importance of Nietzsche, Freud, Sorel and Pareto as the dominant anti-rationalists, see Stuart Hughes, *Consciousness and Society*, New York, Vintage Books, 1961.

4
Religion and Other Social Institutions

IT would be very easy to exaggerate the significance of purely ideological developments in the process of secularization. Although religion itself is largely concerned with the maintenance of an ideology, it is inevitably very much more than this, and its continuance is associated as much with its institutional persistence as with the plausibility and resiliency of its ideology.

The very fact that the Churches exist as structures, with a thoroughly independent and systematically organized professional service to operate them, their concerns and their auxiliary activities, is the best insurance of their continuance. Even if they lose social importance (whether by actual loss of numbers attending them, as in England, and indeed throughout Europe, or merely by loss of influence over even increasing numbers who affiliate with them, as in the United States) they are unlikely to disappear. Their ministry, even if somewhat depleted in its ratio to the general population, persists as an institutionalized order.

Professional autonomy and the accepted place of religious functionaries in the social structure is the crucial factor in the continuance of religious organizations. The ministry may change its functions in some measure, and may become less committed to specific religious formulations – a process which has been most evident perhaps in the Church of England, and in less measure evident in the Nonconformist Churches and the Calvinist and Lutheran Churches in Europe – but it continues as an independent profession often enjoying independence not merely as a professional body setting its own standards and controlling its own conditions of work, but also in the individual professional's own freedom to accept, reject, emphasize or ignore particular doctrines, practices and ethical prescriptions, and to establish whichever of the many styles of relationship to his clientele most suits him.

Nor is this degree of flexibility of role and function the only facet of religious institutionalism which has a preservative effect. The past significance of religion, its institutionalized channels of communication, the status of its leaders, the very sacredness, solemnity and seriousness of the pronouncements of religious functionaries, also ensure that religious influence persists in society. It often persists by continuing to operate in, or in close association with, central governmental agencies and with the chief political offices (the bishops in the House of Lords, for example, or the national importance of the General Assembly of the Church of Scotland, or the influence of Christian political parties in various European countries). The assemblies and councils of the Churches have been used to exerting strong influences on the political, social, moral, and, in the more remote past, the economic, institutions and activities of men. They have been significant powers in these matters, originally as arbiters of conduct, and subsequently as leaders of public opinion, and more recently as organized interest-groups and pressure-groups.

Even today, when this influence is by no means as central as it once was, the resolutions of Church leaders, of the hierarchy or the clergy are given very considerable attention by the Press, and it is perhaps rather through agencies of mass-communication that religious opinion is clearly formed than by the truths learned in church itself and applied by church members in their daily lives. It is in the organized religious conferences that the most acute and clearly crystallized responses to the events taking place in the wider society are articulated and it is here that religious leaders commonly pronounce on social and moral – and sometimes on economic and political – issues. In the Catholic Church, with its stronger hold on its following (a hold directly associated with the elevated and authoritative conception of the priesthood, and especially of the higher echelons of the clerical profession) pronouncements on birth control, on aspects of medical practice, on divorce, and on education, still have important political and sometimes economic significance.

The Protestant Churches have not had this type of control of the laity: indeed, there is a sense in which such authority would inveigh against the rights of conscience and individual responsibility which have always been stronger elements of Protestant (including Anglican) faith. But the pronouncements of Protestant leaders still gain prominence, even if, because of the much greater amenability to external influences, and the wider and more liberal discourse to which Protestant clerics have generally been exposed, the Press and the public recognize that there is here much more concession of divergence of view, opportunity for change of opinion (as in the case of the attitude of the Anglican Church on marriage and birth control during the first half of the twentieth century). There is far less disposition to claim that the opinions of the clergy are expressions of the will of God towards men and their concerns.

Despite the continuance of religious organizations, however, what is more apparent than the continued influence of the Churches through their institutional apparatus is the fact that the social institutions (using the word now in its more specifically and usual sociological sense) have, in industrial societies, tended to grow apart from each other. The economic sphere of production has become separated from consumption; the family and its concerns have separated from the productive sphere; education has acquired autonomy. All of these developments, together with the earlier distinction of the political and judicial areas of social life, and the more recent separation of recreational facilities from the community and the family, have tended to leave religious agencies very much less associated with the other social institutions than once was the case. There has been a compartmentalizing of life; religion which once had a general presidency over the concerns of men, and endowed their activities with a sense of sacredness, has increasingly lost this pre-eminence and influence.

Life activities have been secularized, and the sense of mystery, the religious meaning of objects and acts, has steadily waned. This de-mystification of the world has meant both that everyday thinking has become more instrumental and matter of fact, that emotional involvement with nature, with the community and with other men has been reduced, and that the external world has been 'drained of meaning'. The process has been twofold, in the loss of the 'religious sense' of activity, the disappearance of the religious interpretation of the purpose of life, and the actual loss of influence of the institutions which embodied these sentiments. It is not merely that the Churches have lost members, but that men have largely ceased to think of – or respond to – the world with a sense of mystery and awe.

In practice this process has meant the steady loss of influence by the Churches over the various agencies of social life. The process can be readily illustrated and documented. Whereas traditionally religious institutions dominated education, for example, from the days when the Churches had a virtual monopoly of learning, so steadily education has passed from religious control. In Europe the universities, and even at a later date the schools, were controlled by priests. In England as recently as 1900 there were more Church schools than state schools, and the state system itself had originally been begun merely to fill in the gaps in the educational system left by the inadequate coverage which the Churches provided. In America, the case was necessarily different because of the purely secular assumptions of the constitution, and the emphasis (and from 1833 the reality in all states) of separation of Church and state, even though freedom of religion was promoted, and God was invoked, in the constitution. Steadily in Europe – occasionally dramatically – the Churches ceased to control education, and priests ceased to be regarded as the teachers. As knowledge itself became increasingly secular so priests became less appropriate as teachers, and as the content of education shifted from a religious-moral concern (developed at least partially in the interests of the maintenance of social control) to an increasingly instrumental-technical concern (developed in the interests of increased economic productivity), so education emerged into an institutional order in its own right.

Not only did secular schools replace Church schools, but within the secular schools, the significance of religious education diminished. Although it appears that in England at least there is still widespread public support for some religious instruction in schools (if questionnaire inquiries may be relied upon) there is a competitive situation between expanding disciplines for time in the over-crowded curriculum. There is increasing pressure for a wide range of new instruction (languages, mathematics, the sciences, physical education, road-safety and car-driving to mention but a few). Against all this, religious knowledge quickly loses its priority and becomes very much a residual claimant for curriculum time. It has low status as a subject, and is often regarded as make-weight to complete formally the demand for examination passes in a certain number of subjects. Institutions of higher learning do not usually regard proficiency in this subject as a 'good predictor' of abilities in more developed and rigorous fields of intellectual inquiry. Finally, it is an open secret that in many schools the period allotted to religious instruction is often used for talks on current affairs.

The recession of religious influence in education is paralleled in other areas of social life; in many of them the separation of religion from other social concerns occurred earlier, and is, today, even more complete than in the case of education. In politics, we see that despite the persistence in some countries of religious parties, these parties behave very much more in response to particular economic situations than at the prompting of specifically religious interests. It would be hard to say in exactly what policies the Christian Democrats in Germany (C.D.U.) were specifically Christian. Equally, the parties which make no claim to being specifically Christian, and which in the past were often hostile to the political activities of the Churches, are now so indifferent to religious issues *per se* that for marginal electoral advantage they will sometimes promote legislation favoured by the Churches. Thus in Nieder-Sachsen, a dominantly Protestant *Land*, the Socialist party (S.P.D.) entered, in 1965, into a concordat, despite its own secularist traditions, with the Vatican about religious instruction in schools, despite strong local resistance and its own traditional opposition to the religious affiliation of the opposing Christian Democrats.

A case of this kind illustrates the relative marginality of religious issues to the political parties in the secular society: religion is no longer a matter on which the parties feel sufficiently concerned to quarrel. The days when the Church of England could be described as 'the Conservative Party at prayer' have certainly passed, and there is today no more than the faintest association, and this mainly in the Celtic fringe, between Nonconformity and the Liberal Party. Even the Labour Party – a party inheriting something of the old Nonconformist conscience as well as a certain secularist tradition – legislated in 1966 for more favourable financial support for religious schools, which in practice means for Roman Catholic and Anglican schools. On such issues as recently as 1906, real radicals had gone to prison on refusal to pay rates which might be used to support Church schools. If further evidence were needed, the marked loss of religious fervour in Northern Ireland in the decades since the end of the Second World War, and its diminished consequence in political terms, illustrates the declining relevance of religion for politics.

Obviously there are some correlations of particular religious persuasions with particular parties. Studies on Britain suggest that Roman Catholics are more likely to vote for the Labour Party than are Anglicans and Free Churchmen.[1] None the less the identification of Catholics with the left-wing and Protestants (especially evangelicals) with the right-wing, for example in a city like Liverpool, have clearly declined in recent years. In the United States, too, class position appears to determine voting behaviour more markedly in the case of Protestants than of Catholics, who tend in all social classes to be more disposed to support Democratic candidates.[2]

Lipset has suggested on the analysis of opinion poll data that 'the general political set of a Protestant denomination is determined largely by the average socio-economic status of its adherents. When segregated by denomination and occupational status, it is clear that every Protestant group is more disposed to back the Republi-

1. See Robert Alford, *Party and Society*, Chicago, Rand McNally, 1963, pp. 134 ff.
2. ibid., pp. 241–7.

cans than Catholics or Jews are.'[1] He finds that Protestant religious beliefs serve to reduce the relation between class and party among church attenders: 'Low-status fundamentalist churchgoers vote less Democratic than their class position calls for, while high-status Protestants who attend religiously liberal churches are less Republican than one might anticipate, given their social position.'[2] He considers that in America religion affects political choice in two independent ways, as a source of beliefs and as a determinant of status.

. . . the two variables operate at cross-purposes among Protestants. Active membership in a liberal high-status church pulls one towards political liberalism; nominal adherence primarily serves as a source of status and hence strengthens the political conservatism associated with high position. And the opposite pattern operates among the inactive and active adherents of the more fundamentalist low-status groupings.[3]

There appears then, in the United States, to be some association with active liberal Protestantism and more liberal political sentiments than might, on the evidence of social status, have been expected among those of high social status; and more association with conservative political responses among low-status active Protestants in fundamentalist Churches, than their status would have led one to suppose. Even if there is some religious influence on voting behaviour, however, this is far from indicating that political parties are today much concerned about religious issues in principle. The evidence from Europe suggests that even parties with no religious tradition make gestures to religionists when it suits them. The

1. S. M. Lipset, 'Religion and Politics in the American Past and Present', in R. Lee and M. E. Marty, *Religion and Social Conflict*, New York, Oxford University Press, 1964, p. 98.

2. ibid., p. 101.   3. ibid., p. 102.

general dissociation of religious and political concerns, except perhaps at the political extremes, is illustrated in the way in which a Catholic and a Disciple could run comfortably as Democratic American presidential and vice-presidential candidates in 1960, without their religious persuasions being thought to be more than marginal disadvantages in their political campaign.

In countries in which Catholicism eliminated religious minorities or prevented their growth, religion may still be a factor in politics. In these cases – Italy and France in particular – Catholicism as the established Church was for long closely associated with political power, and political opposition necessarily also become anti-clericalism. Without Nonconformity to 'contain' this animosity within an at least broadly Christian framework, such as existed for instance in England, the political struggle (often in part though never wholly a reflection of an economic struggle) often become also a religious struggle. The intolerance of the Catholic Church created anti-clericalism, whereas the tolerance (albeit a slow and reluctant tolerance) of Anglicanism prevented or impeded the expression of anti-establishment politics as anti-clerical agnosticism, since alternative religious expressions existed.[1]

The same process of institutional segregation may be seen in relation to law. In England the ecclesiastical courts gradually lost their jurisdiction over the moral aspects of social control, and adultery and divorce ceased to be subjects for them at all. Blasphemy and sacrilege, whilst still technically punishable offences, came to be left unpunished, and, where punished, more as invasions of

1. Some interesting material on religious and political allegiance in France is presented in Charles Y. Glock and Rodney Stark, *Religion and Society in Tension*, Chicago, Rand McNally, 1965, pp. 201–12.

property rights than as immoral acts in themselves. But not only have specifically religious agencies – in this case the ecclesiastical courts – lost their jurisdiction in the general growth of the distinction between religiously-defined 'sin' and judicially-defined 'crime', but the secular courts themselves have become increasingly indifferent to the moral aspects of social control. As society has grown more technical in its operation so law has increasingly embraced technical concerns, regulation of mechanical operation. The growth of legislation concerning the motor car and the enormous growth of litigation concerning it, are an illustration of a trend which can be discerned in other departments of public affairs – town planning, and public health, for instance. Simultaneously, those who apply and those who make the law have come increasingly to accept the law's indifference to purely moral matters although in divorce law there is still a tendency to punish immorality, but rather for its antisocial consequences than intrinsically for its own sake.

At levels of social control other than the formal operation of law, there has been an increasing recognition that morals are private matters. People are less prepared to be their brother's keepers, and the force of community opinion about what is 'done' and 'not done' and what is decent, diminishes as local community life itself diminishes. Those attitudes of moral regulation of one's fellow men, and of each by all, were of course, in western nations, entrenched in strong religious attitudes, and underpinned by Christian values. In the twentieth century we have seen a general relaxation of moral and religious demands made on the individual by the community. It is no part of the purpose here to evaluate this process, to applaud it or to deplore it. That increasing moral freedom is enjoyed by man individually, but is costly to society as a whole, is a truism which can be readily accepted: that there is a limit beyond which private interest and indulgence must be restrained in the interests of the community, is equally self-evident. What is apparent is that the age of economic *laissez faire* has introduced an age of moral *laissez faire*, and, in western Europe at least, just at the time that economic *laissez faire* is itself under heavy attack and has, in some departments, given way to regional or national planning.

Previously society was, if not exactly morally planned, at least morally regulated (a Thomistic or a Puritan system of moral theology may be seen as a type of 'plan') and that regulation extended to economic concerns. As those concerns have escaped from religious regulation, and come to be regarded as largely matter-of-fact, morally-neutral areas of behaviour, so the process has continued in other areas of life, until the texture of social relationships itself has, for many, perhaps even the majority, passed from direct religious control. Social relations are no longer informed, except indirectly, traditionally and at second hand through persisting institutional frameworks, by religious ideas and ideals. Standards of decency, in so far as they are a matter of actual consensus in any society (and that in itself is at least questionable) are informed by generalized secular standards, ultimately supported by a framework of legal regulation.

That men still seek the approval and goodwill of their associates, and seek to be thought well of, is self-evident. But the terms in which one expects approval, and the acts for which it is elicited, have changed. Most important of all the strong subsidiary motivation of 'serving God', 'doing what is right in the sight of God', and so perhaps of winning God's approval, or at least conforming to ideals which, however inscrutable He might be, God demanded and which he might not entirely ignore at the day of judgement – all this has gone. Many aspects of behaviour which were once moral matters supported by religious attitudes are now morally neutral. Thus, for instance the matter of dress was in various societies and at various periods regulated by religious conceptions. The early Methodists went so far as to specify number of petticoats and their height from the ground, and the Scriptures themselves make prescriptions about a woman's head and a woman's arms. Today, with certain reserves about public decency (and these are subject to open disputation), dress has become a morally neutral matter.

What is even more significant in this matter of social control is the changing response of the Churches themselves to changing social practice. At one time moral values were held to be derived, if not actually prescribed, by Him, from the word and will of God. In such a circumstance prescribed morality was unchanging and authoritative. But the Churches have increasingly faced the circumstance in which the authoritative will of God has made less and less impact on men in a society where social and legal control have become increasingly separate from religious control, and where men cease in large measure voluntarily to put themselves under the guidance of ecclesiastics. In this circumstance the Churches have faced a dilemma – whether to uphold their traditional moral prescriptions or whether to seek new interpretations of God's word and God's will in the light of changing social conditions, and changing social practice.

From being the arbiters of moral behaviour, the Churches have steadily become more like reflectors of the practice of the times, gradually and hesitatingly endorsing change. In the emphasis on 'getting up to date' the Churches tacitly recognize their own increasingly marginal capacity to influence society. The shifts of Church response on the issue of birth control illustrate the way in which moral theologians have attempted to come to terms with the changing moral practice of societies which they increasingly realize they know very little about. The Lambeth Conference of Bishops declared in 1908: 'The Conference regards with alarm the growing practice of the artificial restriction of the family, and earnestly calls upon all Christian people to discountenance the use of all artificial means of restriction as demoralizing to character and hostile to national welfare.'

In a memorandum the Committee of Anglican Bishops (with the approval of most of the Diocesan Bishops of the Church of England) declared to the Commission on the declining Birth Rate, instituted with official recognition by the National Council for Public Morals in 1916, their limited approval, in extenuating circumstances, of use of the 'safe period' method of birth control. Thus where a wife suffered ill-health 'it seems a legitimate application of self-restraint that in certain cases intercourse should be restricted by consent to certain times at which it is less likely to lead to conception' and this they were prepared to regard as self-denial and not as self-indulgence; they did not believe that this practice was 'condemned' (presumably in Scripture or by Church tradition?). But they gave an 'unhesitating judgement' that the use of artificial appliance and drugs 'is at once dangerous, demoralizing and sinful ... it is condemned as unnatural by healthy instinct in men and women. A society in which it is practised will lose all delicacy of feeling, and the refinement ... which comes of keeping the natural instincts of modesty and reserve untarnished.'

By 1958, theologians had begun to accept the lead of social scientists. They refer to 'the quantity and complexity of sociological information', and add 'in matters which are treated by the social sciences, the kind of preparation that used to be thought adequate to justify theological pronouncements is no longer adequate.'[1] The Scriptures, revelation, papal and episcopal pronouncements had ceased to be accepted, even by clerics, as adequately prepared guidance for society. Having, in 1930, recognized contraception in very special cases, they proceeded to examine the situation again in the 'very different . . . circumstances of today'. With appropriate theological weight, they came to new conclusions:

The theological revaluation of coitus as a symbol of and means to the union of man and wife in one flesh was then [1930] only in its early stages. Today few would command prolonged abstinence from intercourse as 'the primary and obvious' method of preventing conception; for if coitus is the characteristic act of marriage which differentiates it from other relationships and the seal of marriage union, then prolonged abstinence is contrary to the nature of marriage and requires either special vocation or strong circumstancial justification. . . . today it is recognized that nature itself provides for purely 'relational' intercourse; it is generally allowed that such intercourse is permissible during natural infertility; and the question at issue is whether such infertility may be reproduced artificially, and, if it may, in what circumstances.[2]

The theologians then confessed themselves defeated by the task of arranging in order of importance the various ends of coitus, but they found it an act of unique quality, involving the whole person as a psychosomatic unity, expressive of the whole life and attitude to God. They rejected the idea that the only good act of coitus in marriage was one which had generation as its end, since this could be true of an act which none the less exploited one spouse by the other. Thus they conceded that coitus

1. *The Family in Contemporary Society*. Report of a Group convened at the request of the Archbishop of Canterbury, London, S.P.C.K., 1958, p. 120.
2. ibid., p. 136.

could be relational, and that all acts of coitus should be relational, and some both relational and generative. They acknowledged that the use of scientific techniques to attain certain ends did not render such practices 'unnatural' or 'artificial', and they declared: 'Because of its deep involvement with man's personality and its instrumentality in the expression of relational values coitus transcends the simple functionalism of natural copulation.'[1]

Our concern, it must be emphasized, is not with the rightness or wrongness of the theologians' judgement in a matter of this kind, but only with the evidence of the steady adjustment of religion to the life-styles of secular society. Thus what the Church condemns as sinful at one time, it acknowledges as perfectly appropriate at another – in the course of just half a century in fact. The increased acceptance of divorce in the Free Churches might provide illustration of a similar kind. Leaving small sects aside, the Roman Catholic Church has proved most conservative of all Christian bodies in the west in its moral attitudes, but here too there have been changes in the emphasis, if not in the content, of Church teaching.[2]

In other moral matters Church regulation steadily changes. Thus in the Catholic Church the old laws of usury were tacitly abandoned. Annulment of marriages –

1. ibid., p. 145.
2. The Church, of course, maintains that its teaching has not changed, though its acceptance of the 'safe period' method of birth control amounts to a change in practice, if not in theology. In 1930, Pope Pius XI claimed to pronounce definitively on birth control from a Christian truth 'handed down uninterruptedly from the beginning'. The pronouncement was followed by twelve condemnations of contraception issued by the Sacred Penitentiary between 1816 and 1916; John Peel, 'Birth Control and Catholic Doctrine', *London Quarterly and Holborn Review*, October, 1965, pp. 315–27.

in some Catholic countries rising to quite high rates – has been a loop-hole round the rulings on divorce. The safe-period method of birth control has been a casuistic compromise between what the Church feels it must go on asserting and what it knows from various studies of the practice of Catholic laymen is a widespread practice. In Puerto Rico, widespread contraceptive practices have had to be accepted in spite of the dominance of the Roman Catholic Church on the island.[1]

Thus it becomes apparent that religion loses its effect as an agency of social control except as a public court of appeal, as a traditional force and in such effect as sermons and religious literature may have on those who voluntarily expose themselves to these influences. The traditional elements persist in many forms, but they are not always influential. Often they have become social fossils, persisting in part through institutional inertia, in part because they have acquired other functions, and in part to satisfy those to whom obedience is more than mere lip-service.

The oath in the court of law is one such case. That many men – and particularly most of those who are convicted – feel constrained by the solemn oath on the Bible actually to tell the truth, few can now believe. In simple societies and perhaps in the feudal stage of social development such an oath had effect; in some societies indeed there would be no possibility of lying in such matters. But today, it can impose intrinsic constraint on very few. That it functions to impress the solemnity of the occasion, or to give a formal and familiar start to a proceeding (which may reassure, ritualize and introduce an element of shared

1. See J. Mayone Stycos, *Family and Fertility in Puerto Rico*, New York, Columbia University Press, 1955; and J. Mayone Stycos, Kurt Black and Reuben Hill, 'Contraception and Catholicism in Puerto Rico,' *Millbank Memorial Fund Quarterly*, 34, 1956, pp. 150–59.

expectation in a situation about which anxiety-creating uncertainties persist) is undisputed. But these are subsidiary functions, different from those which an oath manifestly purports to sustain. Today those who refuse the oath, and choose to affirm – sometimes causing a slight flurry among the court officials to whom the form of affirmation is not always familiar – in some way invoke more awe, and make perhaps, a more earnest impression of intention to tell the truth.

The change has been very much a twentieth-century affair: Bradlaugh today would not create a *cause célèbre* by the honesty of refusing an oath in which he did not believe. Many who do not actively worship accept a religious oath because it is of no consequence to them, and because they are in some very residual sense unprepared to face the open intellectual and emotional issues involved in coming to terms with religious commitment (or its rejection) at all. What is true of oaths, is no less true of other institutionalized and patterned responses in which religious values are asserted or invoked. The grace which begins meals in many institutions may be thought today to function more either as a common courtesy or as a starting-pistol than as a genuine expression of dependence on, and gratitude to, God.

But even in entrenched contexts, religious values do not always persist. The military which, in a variety of ways, has shown itself a profession and an institution generally favourable to conventional and established religion, has abandoned its compulsory church parades in England. Schools often allow, informally at least, their periods for religious instruction to pass into general discussions of 'civics' or social affairs. Colleges are built without chapels. Civic marriages have ceased to be a procedure causing people to suspect that all cannot be well with the affairs of the betrothed couple.

In England they have now established themselves as about a third of all marriages performed. Church marriages persist not so much as an expression of the religious commitment of those concerned, as from general preference for an occasion which admits of display, ceremonial and solemnity – all of which are lacking in the matter-of-fact affair which is conducted by a civil registrar. In an affluent society, bells, choirs, vestments and photographs in the (preferably period) church door are some of the status-enhancing items which money *can* buy. But the Church may function in additional ways, which in themselves have little to do with the specifically religious interpretation of the marriage ceremony: it confers dignity and decorum as little else can. In a society in which commercial bunting is a commonplace; in which men are used to gimmickry and used to seeing through it, traditional ceremonial transcends the pervasive cynicism. As a largely traditional agency the Church has a certain style of integrity, a certain authenticity which may yet be an important element in its appeal.

Finally, in relation to the Church's loss of influence, its tendency to lose some of its pastoral functions must be recognized. As an agency conferring solace in institutionalized forms for the persisting afflictions of society, and the ultimate philosophical and emotional traumata which embrace men in their lives – associated most dramatically with illness, misfortune and death – the Church has long had perhaps its most immediate and intimate access to the generality of men. It has furnished explanations, and emotional reassurances. But, as modern society has grown more complex, and as scientific explanations have superseded essentially religious interpretations of life – replacing the suggestion of 'meaning' with the closer analysis of empirically verified fact – so the pastoral function of the Church has been affected. From being a socially recognized inevitability, death has become an embarrassing private trauma in which almost any outside solace, except from intimates, has become an intrusion. The disappearance of religiously-supported public grief (in mourning rites) has meant that 'public' interpretations of the situation, and public solace, have become less and less acceptable. Modern man avoids the unpleasantness and the unhygienic nature of death, and thus demands no meaning of a kind which religion has traditionally supplied.[1]

If man in modern society demands rather less by way of consolation than he has traditionally demanded, yet it is also evident that men today are under greater continuing strain in their daily lives, and have evolved means of handling this situation other than through religious agencies. The welfare services which once were prompted by Christian motives and a sense of charity, have been almost completely secularized. What was once done from Christian duty is now an accepted state provision as part of the extension of general political, civic and social rights which have been universalized in many countries, and noticeably in Britain, in the past century.[2] But not all men's problems in industrial society resolve themselves into mere legal and economic provision, and it is clear that the state and its apparatus are not equal to the task of providing the reassurance and the security which, as long as society had strong elements of community, were spontaneously afforded to individuals. Reassurance was largely expressed as the sacred value of life itself. But

1. See for a popular discussion, Jessica Mitford, *The American Way of Death*, London, Hutchinson, 1963; and, for England, Geoffrey Gorer, *Death, Grief and Mourning*, London, The Cresset Press, 1965.

2. See T. H. Marshall, *Citizenship and Social Class*, Cambridge, 1950 (reprinted in idem, *Sociology at the Cross Roads*, London, Heinemann, 1963).

even in this function the Church has lost its hold as the basis of social organization has shifted.

If the problems of identity and anxiety have become worse, they have also become susceptible to new methods of treatment. If man is more alienated in the industrial society, the decline of religion and the loss of widely accepted meanings and emotional orientations has been part of the process. The Churches are no longer in a position to undertake their preventative therapy, and special agencies of mental hygiene arise.[1] The mental health agencies cannot provide *general* social reassurance; they operate as essentially private rehabilitation services for individuals with specific and acute problems. The cost of the affluent industrial society is a high incidence of mental ill-health, widely diffused strain, addiction to drugs, high rates of suicide, crime and delinquency, the disorientation of youth in a social context increasingly bewildering and in which older moral and religious shibboleths no longer seem valid.

Religious orientations are part of what have been surrendered in the development of this type of society, and since common consensual solutions appear impossible, it is evident that individual priests and ministers of religion contend with a pastoral problem which in the social struc-

---

1. Paul Halmos, *The Faith of the Counsellors*, London, Constable, 1965, records that in the period 1901–51 clerical professionals in England and Wales fell from 56,210 to 51,198 whereas medical and para-medical personnel rose from 95,777 to 278,236. Taking into account population increase in the same period, this meant that there was one clerical professional for every 579 people in 1901, and one for every 843 in 1951 (an increase of 43 per cent of population per religious professional), against one medical and para-medical professional for every 340 in 1901 and one for every 157 people in 1951 (a decrease of 54 per cent in the number of people per professional). A considerable part of this increase in medical professionals was in the field of mental health.

tural character of its origins exceeds their competence, and in its magnitude exceeds their resources. The means of coping with the problem, such as they are, are by private therapy and elaborate applications of techniques which increasingly leave less and less to the will of the individual (drug therapy, electrotherapy, leucotomy, etc.). Certainly there is little prospect of relying on such 'preservative values' as might still persist within the social order. Even where personal counselling is the remedy, it is the specialist techniques of psychiatry, and not religious pastoral care, which society calls for. Mental health and moral behaviour become 'research problems' and scientific inquiry moves to ever more elaborate analysis, and to manipulative remedial action, in sharp contrast to the synthetic and socially-wholistic approach of the Churches. In spite of developments such as psycho-therapeutic theology, and work with 'experimental congregations', the operation passes out of the control of the Churches.

5
Secularization and the Clerical Profession

THE loss of association with other major social institutions has not been accomplished without some effects on the religious profession itself. We have already seen that the clergy tend to have lost social standing. Scientists have increasingly replaced them as the intellectual stratum of society, and literature and the arts have passed almost completely out of the religious sphere. The scepticism of modern society has affected the clerical profession profoundly. The attempt to find other levels at which religious propositions are true – that is to say, levels other than the common-sense and literal level – has led to widely diverse clerical interpretations of religion in its contemporary meaning. Clerics have now come to disbelieve in the ultimacy of any answers which they can supply about social questions, as they did earlier about physical questions. As the range of empirical information has increased, acquisition of the knowledge of it and the skills to analyse it and interpret it pass beyond the range of clerical education. The awareness of the relativity of modern knowledge has made the cleric more guarded and less confident in the intellectual content of religion. The man-in-the-street, even if less concerned by this relativity in a society in which he is bombarded unceasingly with information and exposed mercilessly to persuaders, has developed a protective cynicism about what is being 'put over'.

One consequence of the expansion of modern knowledge has been its increased influence on theological studies. Without usually becoming expert in such disciplines, theologians have recognized how vulnerable is their discipline to influences from outside – of which archaeology, comparative religion, anthropology, psychology and sociology are perhaps the most relevant. Many of the early exponents of these disciplines were, necessarily in societies in which intellectual roles were predominantly in clerical possession, clergymen. These subjects have increasingly passed out of the hands of clergymen together with older disciplines the personnel of which was once also ordained. The influence of these intellectual developments has been, however, to make the laymen's grasp of religious ideas more tenuous. It has been more difficult for the Churches to reconcile their traditional claims to wisdom and the increasing acceptance by the clergy of modern branches of knowledge which cast considerable doubt on what the Churches have for centuries been teaching. The man-in-the-street has not the permanent commitment to inquiry of the intellectual. He is not interested in the subtle shifts of academic debate, although clergymen of this cast of mind, and educationalists generally, often assume him to be. Thus what for the clerical inquirer is an interesting academic problem, and part of a long-sustained and continuing debate, may be merely a source of new confusion for the layman. The professional can afford to play an intellectual game. It is not difficult to present such discourse as thoroughly appropriate to his job, and, since heresy trials no longer occur, that his job is very secure. But laymen very often want only assurance and certainty – of a kind which clerics feel increasingly less able to provide.

That some clergy themselves become sceptical, and cease to believe in many of the things which laymen believe in as essentials of the faith, or believe in them in an entirely different way, can only be a source of confusion and despair to those who want to believe in certain, and usually simple, truths. A Bishop Barnes of Birmingham in the 1930s and 40s, a Bishop Pike of California, and a Bishop Robinson of Woolwich, in the 1960s, are only sources of bewilderment to ordinary believers, some of whom are impious enough to wonder why, if men think as they do, they continue to take their stipends from Churches which commit them, in honesty, to rather different beliefs. The alienation of the clergy is one of the remarkable phenomena of the Church of modern times. But even in this alienation from less intellectual laymen, the clergy have little chance of rapprochement with the secular intelligentsia, since they are committed to at least a framework of debate which is normally quite unacceptable to most other intellectuals in the secular society.

The speculative intellectuals among the clergy resemble in their professional position (and I make no judgement of the warranty of their specific ideas) the charcoal-burners or alchemists in an age when the processes in which they were engaged had been rendered obsolete, technically or intellectually. The clergy become a curiously placed intelligentsia, many of them uncertain of their own faith, uncertain of the 'position' of their church on many matters, and unsure whether they agree with that position. The more advanced among them sometimes suggest that simpler men believe the right things for the wrong reasons. They themselves are institutionally entrenched but intellectually foot-loose. They have no real continuity with the actual beliefs of the past, but only with the forms, the rituals, the involvement in a persisting organization. At the same time they have no part in the faster-moving intellectual debate within their own society. Neither the scientists nor the literary intellectuals seek theological opinions, and least of all the social scientists.

Obviously there are many issues of a less specifically intellectual kind on which Church opinion is called for, and, even if not called for, is none the less freely given. In the moral field, which was once the area in which the Church's judgements held complete sway, Churchmen have become, as we have seen in the matter of birth control, much more aware of their own difficulties in making pronouncements on moral issues, without the benefit of 'scientific' information. There is, then, no longer much confidence in God's word or in God's guidance about the issues arising in contemporary society. Thus before an Archbishop feels equipped to comment on the moral implications of television, he calls for an inquiry into its effects. What is surrendered by the Church, then, is the claim of religion to guide the course of social policy, the decisions of statesmen, the operation of social instituttions, *and*, latterly, even the everyday behaviour of the man-in-the-street.

The loss of general standing of the clergy in relation to other professions, and the diminution of their social influence, has been accompanied in England by their increasing average age as the accompanying table[1] illustrates for Church of England clergymen in England.

TABLE 10

Percentages of Anglican clergymen by age at various dates in the twentieth century

	Years of age at appropriate dates						
Date	22–34	35–44	45–54	55–64	65–74	75+	Total No.
1901	20·23	24·91	20·90	16·43	11·66	5·87	23,670
1911	16·39	22·03	24·63	18·61	11·97	6·37	23,193
1921	10·70	19·47	23·95	24·01	14·27	7·60	22,579
1951	9·71	23·37	17·27	19·26	18·66	11·73	18,196
1961	15·28	14·71	25·19	17·90	14·95	11·97	18,749

1. *Facts and Figures About the Church of England*, No. 3, London, Church Information Office, 1965, p. 21.

Thus, whereas in 1901 over 45 per cent of Anglican clergymen were under forty-five years of age, and only 17 per cent were more than sixty-five years of age, in 1961 just over 30 per cent were under forty-five years of age, and almost 27 per cent were over sixty-five years of age. No other profession would show an age distribution of this kind, and no other profession would have so high a proportion of members over the normal retiring age. An ageing profession may, it can be expected, be less efficient than one with a more normal age distribution, and this may hold for some branches of the work of the clergy, notwithstanding the fact that the clerical role has many non-instrumental aspects. Age may not much affect a priest's competence in the performance of ritual (and the Church has been growing steadily more ritualistic), but it might very much affect pastoral visiting, contact with the population and the ability to counsel them about 'modern' problems.

One other feature of the statistics concerning the Anglican clergy is worth noting. That during the sixty years in which the number of clergy fell from 23,670 to less than 19,000, the population of the two provinces (Canterbury and York) to which the figures relate was growing steadily, from 30·6 millions in 1901, to 43·6 millions in 1961. Thus in a period in which the Anglican clergy in England have declined by more than 20 per cent, the population has increased by more than 40 per cent. Although in the same period there has been a remarkable increase in the numbers of Catholic priests in England, which very much more than 'makes good' the losses in clerical professionals in the Church of England, there has still been an overall decline in the number of religious professionals. For England and Wales the number of religious professionals (including clergy of all religious bodies, monks, nuns, itinerant preachers, scripture readers, etc.) fell from over 56,000 in 1901 to a little over 51,000 in 1951.

The fall in relative, and absolute, numbers of clerical professionals in England clearly reflects a number of facts about contemporary religion, and the due weight of the various matters involved has yet to be assessed. It would appear that the religious profession has grown less attractive. Certainly there are fewer people coming forward for the Anglican ministry. In 1959 there were 757 candidates, which fell to 646 in 1961. Even a campaign under the slogan *Pray for Your Clergy – Pray for more Clergy* in 1962–3 took the figure up only to 737 in 1963, and it fell again to 656 in 1964.[1] Among the intake into the Anglican ministry, the age of entry itself has also risen; about 14 per cent of candidates recommended for Holy Orders in 1959 were thirty years of age or over, whereas in 1964 it was more than 20 per cent; and whereas 3 per cent of those recommended in 1959 were forty years or more, this figure was 12 per cent in 1964.[2] The 'late entrants' constitute a similar proportion among both English and Canadian Anglican ordinands.[3] Clearly a profession which draws an increasing proportion of older entrants will *continue* to have an abnormal age-structure.

The diminished appeal of the clerical profession has had a further effect, at least in England, of attracting to it a decreasing proportion of men who are university graduates. In the four years from 1960 to 1964 the proportion of non-graduates among Anglican candidates rose from

1. *Men for the Ministry*, London, Church Information Office, 1965.
2. *Facts and Figures*, op. cit., p. 43.
3. A discussion of problems involved is contained in A. P. M Coxon, *A Sociological Study of the Social Recruitment, Selection and Professional Socialization of Anglican Ordinands*, unpublished Ph.D. Thesis, University of Leeds, 1965.

just over 50 per cent to just over 60 per cent of the intake.[1] Thus a declining educational level tends to characterize the Anglican ministry, at a time when almost all, if not all, other professions are characterized by increasing educational standards and more exacting professional qualifications. The Catholic Church, which more completely controls its own methods of professional education has not, of course, been exposed to changes of this particular kind. It may, however, especially in more affluent societies where there are, and have been over the past two decades, abundant work opportunities, have failed to draw forward candidates of the same quality as in the past. This, however, rests on the assumption that fewer candidates have been drawn forward. This appears to be true of the various religious orders. Since there are still many relatively non-affluent areas in which the Catholic Church is the dominant Church, this problem may not yet have become acute.

If recruitment to the religious profession becomes more difficult in an affluent society, the difficulty of retaining the recruited exacerbates the professional situation. We have very little detailed information about those who abandon their spiritual vocation. There is certainly considerable defection from the ranks of those who enter training for the priesthood; in America it has been estimated that 'less than one-sixth of those entering the freshman year of [diocesan minor] seminaries eventually enter the priesthood.'[2] In England a prominent Baptist, estimating that in a ten-year period the Baptist Church had lost 305 trained and ordained men from pastoral ministry, contended that 'the central problem of our ministry lies,

1. *Men for the Ministry*, op. cit.
2. J. H. Fichter, *Religion as an Occupation*, Notre Dame, Ind., University of Notre Dame, 1961, p. 187.

plainly, not in recruitment, but in the retention of our ministers'.[1]

An important feature of the Protestant ministry in England has been the relative decline in the clerical stipend. In an inflationary society other incomes have tended to increase more rapidly than those of the *rentier* class (and the parson with his freehold had some association with that class), and more rapidly than the stipends of the clergy. By the standards of other professions the ministry of the Established Church in England is badly paid. It bears little comparison with the medical and legal professions, as once it did, and stands now in rather closer relation to the schoolteachers. In America, where there is no establishment and where clerical stipends depend rather more closely on congregational generosity, the minister's salary has been more responsive to changing monetary values. The relative poverty of English Nonconformity (among Baptists, for example, the minimum stipend has in recent years been lower than the national average wage) is not reflected in the salaries of the American clergy in the same denominations among whom success as a clergyman may even be measured in monetary terms.[2] For Catholics, of course, with expectations of poverty, and with an obligation to celibacy which eliminates the expense of dependents, the stipendiary situation is, in both societies, radically different. The principal work on *Religion as an Occupation*, which is strictly Catholic in interpretation, has no direct mention of the payment structure of the Church: money reward is dismissed as irrelevant.[3]

1. R. E. O. White in *Baptist Times*, cited in E. J. Carlton, *The Probationer Minister – A Study among English Baptists*, unpublished M.A. Thesis, University of London, 1964, p. 30.

2. Philip J. Allen, 'Childhood Backgrounds to Success in a Profession', *American Sociological Review*, XX, 2, 1955.

3. J. H. Fichter, op. cit.

Salary may be an uncertain test of the social evaluation of the ministry, although in England it must be acknowledged that the salary of the clergy has fallen relative to that of the professions with which they like to be compared, and that society at large makes no effort and voices no concern about clerical stipends. With ministerial salaries often lower than those of some of the better paid among industrial occupations, there is a tendency, despite frequent complaint of the deterioration of the quality of the clergy, for the past association of the clerical class with the gentry to be gently re-emphasized. Yet if the clergy are increasingly drawn in as late entrants to the profession, and are increasingly educated as priests after no higher education other than that of the theological college, in terms of modern objective criteria of social status their position increasingly approximates that of schoolteachers, whose ranks also include a high percentage of non-graduates, and whose professional qualifications, in training colleges are conferred without very much rigour of selection.

The elaborate ranking scales which have sometimes been employed to assess status by asking people to place different occupational groups in order, may (perhaps particularly in the case of the religious profession) rather over-state society's actual evaluations. There are the spiritual affinities of the occupation which induce respondents to give relatively high rating to clerics, since people with any religious dispositions at all cannot but pay some attention to the traditional claim of all religious professionals to have the highest calling of all. In all traditional cultures religious functionaries tend to claim high status, and usually gain it, if only because of their access to higher and potentially dangerous sources of power. Fichter says that Catholic priests share the generally high status of clergymen in America: 'the social position of clergymen is colored by two thousand years of church history'.[1] Of ninety occupations which the respondents of the American National Opinions Research Center were asked to place in order of rank, clergymen came twelfth: physicians and academics were accorded higher status, but lawyers and architects were given lower status.[2]

The comparable English evidence, based on a more limited sample of respondents, placed clergymen fourth among thirty occupations, following surgeons, general practitioners, and solicitors, and immediately above university lecturers, grammar-school masters and dentists.[3] On the basis of this evidence it appears that most of those entering the priesthood of the Church of England are individuals who are rising in the social scale. Nearly ninety per cent of the ordinands in Coxon's extensive survey were the sons of men in occupations with lower social status than clergymen. Becoming a priest, then, if not exactly the 'way to the top' (and within the clerical profession in the Anglican Church, prospects for promotion are very limited)[4] is none the less a way of enhancing one's status. Most ordinands, according to Coxon, identify with the middle class.[5]

It appears then, that on objective evidence English

1. ibid., p. 124.

2. Albert J. Reiss, *Occupations and Social Status*, Glencoe, Ill., The Free Press. 1961, p. 54.

3. Noel D. Richards, *An Empirical Study of the Prestige of Selected Occupations*, unpublished M.A. Thesis, University of Nottingham, 1962, cited in A. P. M. Coxon, op. cit., p. 254.

4. According to the analysis of Leslie Paul, *The Deployment and Payment of the Clergy*, London, Church Information Office, 1964, pp. 99 ff., only 8 per cent of clergy have posts above that of ordinary incumbents (1 per cent as Archbishops, Bishops, Deans and Provosts; 2 per cent as Archdeacons and Residentiary Canons, and 5 per cent as Rural Deans).

5. A. P. M. Coxon, op. cit., p. 236.

society accords its clergy relatively few of the material advantages normally associated with high social status, although subjectively it awards priests, a reasonably high place in the social scale. The discrepancy reflects, perhaps, a pious sentiment and the traditional ascription of high status to religious professionals. High status must not be confused with high reward or with social influence. Social systems can, like that of Tonga, carefully dissociate real power from the elevated status of sacredness. The priest's work is not accorded much importance; society in general does not account its welfare to the efficacy of those who spend their lives praying for it, nor does it confer very high rewards on those who seek to bring men under the influence of God.

The decline in religious observance occurring in Western Europe, may yet leave the clergy as an entrenched profession with diminishing functions. It is true that the demands for the 'service functions' of the clergy – baptisms, marriages and burials – show little sign of diminishing, and that some clerics report themselves as being overworked, and yet that work is for a declining number of religiously-committed people.[1] The priest's role in the secular society of England has steadily lost its social definition (it retains, of course, its theological definition). The search for social justification may in part be responsible for various trends evident among some of the clergy. Responses to the situation differ: some obviously see social work and welfare as their appropriate role, from work with youth groups to organizations like the Samaritans. Others see themselves as responsible for social protest against the political structure of society, and enlist themselves into movements like C.N.D. and Anti-Apartheid, substituting for traditional hymnology the music of protest. This appears to be one of the easiest

1. See Leslie Paul, op. cit., pp. 71 ff.

ways for religious vocation to rediscover social relevance, though often with slightly *passé* reverence to nineteenth-century revolutionaries: even Roman Catholics display this tendency.[1] Similar manifestations are perhaps even more evident in the United States, where Marxist terminology (there is an especial fondness for the concept of 'false consciousness') is to be found strewn throughout much recent, theologically-inspired social commentary.[2] Among parish priests and congregational ministers it is the younger elements who are most conspicuous in the Civil Rights movement and other activities of social protest, but the parish ministry – with dependence for the livelihoods on their lay following – are less likely to espouse radical causes than ministers serving in such roles as campus ministers or university teachers.[3]

Other ministers emphasize pastoral work in their communities and attempt to salve the abrasions which man living in highly institutionalized society is likely to suffer. While the more politically conscious clergy tend to mani-

1. Fully manifested in the semi-Marxist Catholic periodical *Slant*: '. . . we hope to see emerging the full implications of Christian radicalism: to show that the Church's commitment to the creation of a fraternal society, its function as the sacrament of human community, the relations between its liturgy and a common culture, imply a revolutionary socialism.' Vol. 2, No. 1, February–March, 1966.

2. For examples of this style of contemporary theological writing, see Harvey Cox, *The Secular City*, New York, Macmillan, 1965; Gibson Winter, 'Theological Schools: Partners in the Conversation' in Keith R. Bridston and Dwight W. Culver, *The Making of Ministers*, Minneapolis, Augsburg Publishing Co., 1964.

3. Evidence is provided in Ernest Q. Campbell and Thomas F. Pettigrew, *Christians in Crisis*, Washington D.C., Public Affairs Press, 1959; and in Phillip E. Hammond and Robert E. Mitchell, 'Segmentation of Radicalism – The Case of the Protestant Campus Minister', *American Journal of Sociology*, LXXI (2), September, 1965, pp. 133–43.

fest contempt for these 'comfort functions' of the church, the American laity demand precisely this of their clergy.[1] Still others turn to ritual, as the irreducible religious function, capable of extension and elaboration, and the real professional expertise of the priest. The burgeoning of theological and quasi-theological academic and quasi-academic disciplines is another way in which churchmen keep their institutions alive. If they cannot fill the churches they might, in the sociology of religion seek out the reasons why people fail to attend or discuss the relation of worship and architecture, comparative liturgies or group therapy. All of these are the new responses, the defence mechanisms, mounted for professional survival. Not least important, there is the ecumenical movement.

1. See Charles Y. Glock, Benjamin B. Ringer and Earl Babbie, op. cit.

PART II
SECULARIZATION IN AMERICA

6

Religion in America: A Contrasting Pattern

THE evidence of a process of secularization in Europe is clearly established. In the United States we are presented with figures of a very different kind. Instead of a decline in Church memberships, there has been a steady increase over the past sixty years; instead of diminishing attendance at Church services we find rates of attendance which are far higher than those prevailing in most European countries, particularly in industrial European countries, and this in spite of the predominance of Protestants in the United States. Protestant countries in Europe have shown higher dispositions to secularization than Catholic countries.

The statistics available indicate that religious memberships have increased rapidly in America – more rapidly than population growth during the course of the twentieth century. Thus in 1926 only 27 per cent of the population was in membership in Protestant Churches, and 16 per cent in Roman Catholic Churches. By 1958, 35 per cent were claimed as members in Protestant denominations and 22·8 per cent were claimed as Catholics. (Of all those who were in membership with a church, 56 per cent were Protestants and 36 per cent Catholics in 1958). Whereas in 1880 only 20 per cent of the population had Church membership, in 1962 the figure was 63 per cent of the nation. Attendance at churches has remained fairly steady during the decade from the early 1950s to the early 1960s (with some slight but unsustained increases in the later fifties): about 45 per cent of Americans attend church each week.[1]

It must be pointed out that the reliability of American statistics on Church membership has been challenged, particularly on grounds of duplication occasioned by the high residential mobility of Americans. The attendance figures are drawn from Gallup Poll data, however, and if, as seems likely, they are themselves fairly reliable, the ratio of attendance to memberships seems thoroughly plausible. It is clear that Church membership has become more easily and lightly contracted, but this anticipates the argument to be followed here concerning the course of secularization. On the other hand, it has also been argued that the figures relating to the past underestimate the religiosity of Americans in earlier periods. Thus foreign observers are cited who were struck by the great religiosity of Americans (they were also struck by the superficiality of religion in America!), and estimates from 1832 of 90 per cent of the population in church membership.[2] On the other hand, another authority puts church membership figures at 5 per cent in 1776, 6·9 per cent in 1800, 15·5 per cent in 1850, 35·7 per cent in 1900 and 50 per cent plus in 1926, and writes 'the new nation [of the United States] was a heathen nation . . . for the major part of the nineteenth century, Protestant and Catholic missionary societies in Europe were sending to it mis-

1. Figures are drawn from Benson Y. Landis (Ed.) *Yearbook of American Churches* (annually), New York, National Council of Churches of Christ (various dates).

2. This argument is developed by S. M. Lipset, 'Religion in America; What Religious Revival?' *Columbia University Forum*, II, 2, 1959; a further discussion will be found in Charles Y. Glock and Rodney Stark, *Religion and Society in Tension*, Chicago, Rand McNally, 1965, Ch. IV.

sionaries, tracts, and money to save the New World from relapse into utter irreligion.'[1]

For our purpose, we shall take the figures we have originally cited, acknowledging that there may be inexactitudes now, and almost certainly were in the past (whether travellers' tales and impressions, or Church statistics). With over eighty large religious movements with impressive organizations and large incomes (these account for all but a few per cent of Church members in America) and perhaps two hundred small ones, no one can doubt that religion is institutionally and organizationally well entrenched in America. In attendances it has a record which is increasingly impressive in comparison with European statistics. Religious practice, even in Catholic countries in Europe, tends to fall below the American level: thus the percentage of those adult Catholics obliged to attend Mass in various French and Belgian cities in the late 1950s was discovered to be only between 11 and 25 per cent (11 per cent in Marseilles and Toulouse and 24 per cent in St. Etienne, among others). In Vienna it has been shown to be less than 20 per cent; in German large towns between 24–40 per cent of Catholics attend Mass (only Osnabrück and Münster had figures of over 50 per cent). Although practice in Italy and Spain appears, on the survey undertaken, to be higher than that of the United States, in Lisbon one inquiry revealed practice of less than 18 per cent.[2] Protestant countries tend to have a worse showing. The percentage of population in church (of all denominations including Catholics) on an ordinary Sunday has been

1. F. H. Littell, *From State Church to Pluralism*, New York, Anchor Books, 1962, pp. 23 and 29.

2. These figures are assembled in Sabino S. Acquaviva, *Der Untergang des Heiligen in der industriellen Gesellschaft*, Essen, Ludgerus Verlag, 1964, pp. 53 ff.

variously estimated at between 10 per cent and 15 per cent in England and Wales, and these figures are bolstered up by the much higher proportion of Catholics than of Anglicans and Free Churchmen who attend church. In Stockholm church attendance has been less than 3 per cent for the last five years.[1]

Superficially, then, and in contrast to the evidence from Europe, and particularly from Protestant Europe, the United States manifests a high degree of religious activity. And yet, on this evidence, no one is prepared to suggest that America is other than a secularized country. By all sorts of other indicators it might be argued that the United States was a country in which instrumental values, rational procedures and technical methods have gone furthest, and the country in which the sense of the sacred, the sense of the sanctity of life, and deep religiosity are most conspicuously absent. The travellers of the past who commented on the apparent extensiveness of Church membership, rarely omitted to say that they found religion in America to be very superficial. Sociologists generally hold that the dominant values of American society are not religious: '. . . American culture is marked by a central stress upon personal achievement, especially secular occupational achievement. The "success story" and the respect accorded to the self-made man are distinctly American . . .'[2]

The paradox of high church attendance in a markedly secular society has been resolved by a now famous thesis.

1. Berndt Gustafsson, *The Influence of Television on Church Life in Stockholm* (Abstract of Research Report No. 24, Stockholm Institute of Sociology of Religion), November, 1965.

2. Robin M. Williams, Jr., *American Society. A Sociological Interpretation*, New York, Knopf, 1961, p. 417. See also Robert K. Merton, *Social Theory and Social Structure*, Glencoe, Ill., The Free Press, revised edn., 1957. Ch. IV.

Will Herberg, an American theologian, has suggested that being a Protestant, a Catholic or a Jew are three acceptable ways of expressing American identity, that being religious has become in fact an evidence of adherence to national values.[1] This is to say that in the recent historical development of America instead of religion being the source of such values as patriotism and the sense of national allegiance, as was the case in Europe, the acquisition of American nationality (which was, for most, a conscious and decisive act when, as immigrants, they chose to go to the United States) has come in time to need a further affirmation, and that affirmation has been found in religious affiliation.

The evidence of being a complete American has been provided by commitment to a religious belief and to a religious organization. Herberg attempts, at the outset of his argument, to resolve another American paradox – that of highly diverse denominations present in the nation from the time of its origins. Taking Durkheim's theory of the functions of religion – that religion supplies a common value system to society – he is faced with a difficulty in the existence of some two hundred and fifty religious denominations and sects.[2] What Herberg asserts is that most of these (eliminating only the consciously divergent sects) do in fact uphold a common value system, and that of these many denominations there are in fact only three principle positions – those of Protestants, Catholics and Jews, the major differences recognized, for instance, by the American military authorities in

1. Will Herberg, *Protestant, Catholic, Jew*, New York, Doubleday, 1955.
2. This theory is expounded in a study of religion among Australian aboriginal tribes; E. Durkheim, *Elementary Forms of the Religious Life*, Glencoe, Ill., The Free Press, 1954 (translated J. W. Swain).

accrediting chaplains to the armed forces. Thus, implicit in this argument is the idea that the denominations are separate organizations with certain doctrinal, historical and organizational differences, but that these differences in no significant way affect the underlying values of religion as such.

Further, Herberg argues that the values of religion are not in the normal sense autonomous, but are in fact themselves derived from national values: going to church is one of the values of American life; having a faith is expected of all upright citizens. Thus the argument holds that whereas in the small primitive society which Durkheim took as his model for the analysis of the functions of religion, religion is the repository of values, and sustains by common practices and solemn occasions the unity of the society, in America religion is simply a value of the society itself. What one sees here then is the germ of an idea – unexplored by Herberg – that with the emergence of effective state organization, the basis of social unity shifts from community values to the maintenance of an institutional framework, but that this skeleton of social order is more acceptable to men clothed in the mantle of decency which religion provides. Religion then, does not dictate social values, but rather reflects those values, and consequently all denominations – small sects apart – fulfil this function.

Herberg also advances other arguments which seek to explain the high incidence of Church membership and attendance in America. In a country in which the tenor of life is highly impersonal; in which individuals are often exposed to manipulation; in which the economic organizations of society have reached giant proportions and threaten the very identity of the individual, so there is likely to be a persistent demand for something which provides a less associational and more communal orientation.

Since, in many areas, Americans are often on the move – with travel to and from work, for pleasure, and, in the longer time-span and for the sake of their careers, frequently moving house – community values are difficult to establish. There are few spontaneous agencies to support community life, and in this circumstance the Church takes on functions and provides facilities which even if they do not actually rest in a community structure, give the impression of doing so.

The Church, then, represents the values of the agrarian ⟩ or communal pre-industrial society: its forms are moulded from that stage of social development, and it participates in the warmth, stability and fundamental mutual involvements of a type of community life. That this community is, in the nature of American society, not so much a fossil as a reproduction piece, is less damaging in the eyes of those who have little experience of community life than in the eyes of visiting Europeans. The synthetic nature of the community-orientation of many American Churches is evident to those from more traditional cultures; the personalized gestures of the impersonal society acquire an almost macabre quality for those who have experienced the natural spontaneous operation of rural community life, in which the Church may fit as a part. And yet it seems evident, whether the Church does fulfil genuine functions of this kind or not, men obviously get some, perhaps purely sentimental, satisfactions from pretending that it does.

This circumstance is obviously related to the trauma of the immigrant, who, though experiencing better economic conditions, may miss the community values of the (usually) peasant society from which he came to America. That many of the early Churches were the repository of immigrant values is evident. In the Church, as nowhere else in the new society, immigrants could continue their language, their customs, their folkways.[1] Even if these customs were not specifically identified with the Church in the countries from which the immigrants had come, the immigrants' churches were the only place where they could persist. In economic activity, in education, in general social contact, American ways had to be learned, even including the consumption patterns of family life. But in the Church – so insulated was religion from these dominant aspects of social activity – all the old values could find expression. Although, with the Americanization of the second generation, the influence of the Church waned, and its distinctive religious and peasant values lost their vigour, the Churches held on, as institutions tend to do, and became for the third generation important agencies for the reassurance of identity in terms of origins. As, in the mass society and the mobile society, the problem of identity become more acute, so the search for the meaning of the present in the past is likely to be intensified. Thus the Churches of the grandparents – rather like the American preoccupation with genealogies – became important because they provided evidence of the link with the past, and provided some sense of continuity and identity.

To Herberg the Churches in America fulfil their function of supporting the nation, however, only by losing their distinctiveness of tradition. Thus he notes that the teaching of the Churches tends to grow more vacuous. Were they to persist in their distinctive theological orientations they would become new agencies of divisiveness in American life, and, in a nation of many different sorts of immigrant, divisiveness would be intolerable. As

1. Two different studies which discuss this issue are: N. Tavuchis, *Pastors and Immigrants*, The Hague, Nijhoff, 1963; and E. Franklin Frazier, *The Negro Church in America*, Liverpool University Press, 1964.

the second generation settled into American-ness so they tended to ignore the Churches which reminded them of their diversified past. Only as the Churches became similar to each other in function, and indistinct in ideology, could they significantly satisfy the various needs of the third and subsequent generations for community life and reassurance about the past, and – simultaneously – their commitment to American nationality. 'The American way of life' thus embraced 'going to church' as one of its facets, without much concern about which church anyone went to. Religion became privatized, and different prefer-/ences became as significant as different brands of cigarette or different family names – at least in the case of the major denominations. In some ways, the functions of the churches as community centres are facilitated, by different brand images for rather similar products. Thus when President Eisenhower could assert that a man should have a faith, no matter which it was; and when President Johnson (a Disciple) and his wife (an Episcopalian) could assert that their daughter's conversion to Roman Catholicism did not disturb them, since religion was a private matter, they made evident the American faith that one religion is as good as another. But this, be it noted, is an *American* value. It is not a Christian value, and has no respectability of pedigree in Christianity.

Belonging to a faith in America thus becomes unconnected with distinctive belief to an extent quite unparalleled in Europe. Precisely because Church adherence still has a content of distinctive teaching, and precisely because commitment to one organization means more than merely 'preferred religion' (as American official forms refer to religious allegiance) and implies the belief that one denominational creed is true in at least some respects in which others are false or less than wholly true, so religious commitment means rather more in Europe. The point being made here, then, is that it is a gross fallacy, too often made in statistics, to assume that one membership in one denomination and in one country can be regarded as an equal unit of comparison with others. Statistics of this kind tell us nothing without the historical and sociological cultural context in which the statistics exist.

The contrast with which we are presented then is that of a process of secularization in two different societies – America and Europe – which has taken radically divergent forms. That it has been, in each case, a process of secularization, can hardly be in doubt. Clearly the sociologist of religion must seek to explain divergences of this kind, particularly so in light of the general sociological tendency to seek similarity of patterns and processes in the structure and change of human societies at similar levels of economic and social complexity. Explanation for divergence must be sought in historically specific circumstances in the two cultural areas. We shall take the case of England to compare with that of America, since the situations of European countries are themselves too diverse to admit of easy comparison. We are faced then with a traditional society in which religious adherence and church attendance have sharply declined during the past eighty years, and a new society in which a sharp increase of membership and attendance has taken place over exactly the same period. It is true, of course, that this decline in England has not been uniform in all branches of Christianity. As Anglican attendances have decreased, and those of the Free Churches have followed, so the Catholics have gained in strength, and sustained a high level of attendance among their self-confessed adherents. But this circumstance is itself largely a consequence of the fact that many Catholics in England are immigrants or the children of immigrants – a circumstance similar to that in which religious resilience has occurred (on a wider scale) in America. There is, however, reason to suppose that Catholicism too suffers some – if slower – loss of adherents over time. There is a tendency for lapsed Catholics to cease even to call themselves Catholics, perhaps because to do so is to invite the attentions of the Catholic clergy, who, armed with greater authority and a more absolute conviction of truth, make much of a Catholic's duty to attend Mass – a sanction which Protestants can scarcely invoke. Self-styled Anglicans do not receive attention of this kind. But even allowing for the Catholics in England, the broad patterns of the two countries are still radically divergent, and in the United States the Protestant denominations appear to have gained as many new adherents as the Catholic Church – despite high immigration of Catholic Puerto Ricans – and appear to enjoy the same high attendance rates at services.

The central difference as a point of departure is of course in the fact that Britain, as a traditional society, was 'naturally' a religious society. Its Established Church, though one which had experienced change, and at times dramatic change, represented a religious association of the powers and the people which could reasonably be regarded as 'from time immemorial'. Implicit religious commitment was thus posited in the existence of the society; at any particular time, religion could be assumed to be part of the order of things. A religious view of the world was officially held, and the institutions of religion were established and continuing. Men inherited a religious *Weltanschauung* which changed only slightly and only gradually over time, at least until the mid-twentieth century. Furthermore, religion was entrenched and privileged, and although increasingly admitting of challenge, it was deeply involved in all areas of national life.

Only as recently as the eighteenth century an ecclesiastic sat in the highest offices of secular government; only in the nineteenth did education *begin* to surrender to secular influences; only then, too, did subscription to the formularies of the Anglican Church cease to be necessary for admission to a degree in Oxford and Cambridge; only then did Church demands on the nation's economic product cease; only then did the Church lose control of juridical procedures affecting persons other than ecclesiastics. Today, still, the episcopacy has its reserved seats in the legislature; the monarch presides over the Church as its temporal head; the Church supports some of its own schools, and there is religious instruction in state schools; and the Church still maintains its own courts for the regulation of its own discipline. These then are continuities from an ancient religious identity of the nation.

The American case is almost directly the contrary. Despite the piety of the early settlers, and their early experiments in near theocratic government in New England, the state, once independently established, chose to be a secular state. Although God was invoked in the federal constitution, none the less religion was to be free and divergent religious creeds were to be tolerated – hence the secular state. In eliminating by 1833 (in Massachusetts) the last remnants of an established church, America also eliminated anything which could be called Nonconformity. The state proceeded as a secular institution, and just as judicial and legislative and executive functions were separated from each other, so religion was separated from all – a voluntary affair in which, almost as an extension of strong Protestant sentiments, each man was to wrestle with his conscience. Religion was apart; commitment to it, and to a particular branch of it, was a matter of voluntary choice.

The American nation assumed a formal secularity from the outset, and this despite the genuine religiosity of many of those who formed its early citizenry, and in particular, its governing strata. The very diversity of religious commitment imposed the assumption of secularity, since only in this way were different religious persuasions accorded equality. Thus, in the United States, opposition to the state or governmental agencies has no implications for religion – neither in the promotion of secularism, as on the continent of Europe, nor in the promotion of Nonconformity, as in England – itself a less direct process of secularization. If, as sociologists often suggest, secularization is a feature of industrializing societies, then in America, because of these specific historical circumstances, it had to take a different form from that which occurred both in continental Europe and in England.

If religion in America was to be closely involved in the sense of national identity which the country obviously found so imperative in the years of immigration, it could become effectively involved only as religious differences were themselves eroded, so that all faiths might serve the same end, and become more similar to each other in doing so. Religious commitment and Church allegiance *have become* elements in the American value system, accepted parts of 'the American way of life', so we can see that the cost of this increased association has indeed been the diminution of religious divergence. Those values which were claimed as intrinsically important in a specific denominational commitment, are the very items which have been surrendered in the growth of indiscriminate approval of religion of all and every sort. As religious denominations have been reabsorbed into the mainstream of national life, so they have lost their distinctive qualities. Religion has placed its common values at the service of the political and social institutions of the nation, and has become one of the various approved values of American culture.

This development seems itself almost implicit in the religious pluralism of American society, but as surely as Luther conceded the supremacy of state authority above priestly authority, so the American Churches have, in effect, if less explicitly, subordinated their distinctive religious values to the values of American society. Thus, though religious practice has increased, the vacuousness of popular religious ideas has also increased: the content and meaning of religious commitment has been acculturated.

In England, the very existence of an Established Church predetermined a quite other course of development. The religious institution was an institution of the state, and this implied that as religious belief became threatened in the various ways which we have examined, so the state itself became more secular. Since English society, like all traditional societies bounded within an effective political structure, posited an assumption of social consensus, the spontaneous social forces which challenged this consensus tended to find expression at an ideological level which diverged from the 'official theory' of state power, social stratification, etc. – that is to say, protest meant religious Nonconformity. To challenge the state religion was a way, and in many respects the most fundamental and yet least dangerous way, of challenging the state, and its economic social and political establishment. Religious toleration came sooner and extended further throughout the social structure than political toleration. T. H. Marshall's famous depiction of the winning of three orders of social rights – civic, political and the rights of social welfare, overlooks the significance of the gradual but earlier acceptance of the rights of religious conscience. Since men had religious rights before they had political rights, religion was, in England, as it has since been in many less developed societies at certain stages of their history, the agency for general discontent and disaffection.

Nonconformity in England was the expression of much more than mere ideological disagreement about transcendental verities. It was the social expression of divergent values, divergent life-styles and hence of social strata whose claims to status rested on quite different grounds from the criteria of distinction in the existing status hierarchy. The very existence of an Established Church made it more appropriate to regard religious dissent as at least in part a manifestation of political dissent. Thus in England Nonconformity was a challenge to the idea of social consensus implicit in the existence of an Established Church which assumed itself to be the religious expression of the nation.

In America Nonconformity is clearly an inappropriate concept. There was no expectation in the early days of the colonies of more than local, state or regional consensus, and no established religious institution to express the ideology of consensus. And yet, in the forging of a new nation, and in the need to induce immigrant groups to accept the American way of life, there was pressure in America for the creation of institutions which would weld disparate elements into one community. It was, of course, impossible that migration to the new world would lead men directly to accept a new religion – America had no such official religion to offer. The search for freedom from European persecution had been too important an idea with the early settlers to allow such a religious establishment to develop in the whole federation, though it did occur in particular states. New circumstances do, however, demand new explanations and justifications, and although the forms and nomenclature of older religion was transplanted, it was only to be expected that in time religious ideology would adjust to meet the social and material conditions of American life. New 'American' religions did, of course, emerge as marginal phenomena, of which Mormonism and Christian Science were the most prominent – the former playing a part in inducing European immigration to the promised land.[1]

The vast majority of immigrants, if they were religious at all, brought their traditional religious conceptions with them, and were often followed by religious professionals from their homeland. Clearly such divergent religious affiliations could have persisted as divisive elements which no new nation could afford: the unconscious and subtle pressure of circumstances was to bring about a certain 'homogenization' of religious values. The second generation tended to desert the Churches, to assert American nationality. The third found themselves Americanized and acculturated, but in need of confirmation of identity and nationality, and so returned to them. By this time the Churches were assuming a rather different role in American society. In a society in which there was, apart from the long-settled areas, much less stability of community life than Europeans had been used to, the role of the Churches was increasingly that of providing an agency for community orientations and loyalties.

So the Church – in England a fixed, stable centre of and organized expression of the 'natural' community, in which there was a spontaneous and continuing association of the generations – in America forged for itself the role of providing a community dimension to a way of life all too likely to be dominated by the associational interest-

1. On European migration of Mormon converts see William Mulder, *Homeward to Zion*, Minneapolis, Minnesota University Press, 1957; and P. A. M. Taylor, *Expectations Westward*, Edinburgh, Oliver & Boyd, 1965. For a sociological account of Mormonism see, Thomas O'Dea, *The Mormons*, Chicago, University of Chicago Press, 1957.

group assumptions of an increasingly rational and routinized social organization. The Church, then, became an agency of synthetic community life. The diversity of Churches offered people a choice ('religion of your choice' is an American phrase which amuses Europeans), but, as with so many other choices of the mass-society, the choice was increasingly less real, as the values of the Churches increasingly approximated each other, and as they all came to reflect increasingly the American way of life. That there were many Churches, which appeared different from the outside, was an accident of the diverse sources of population recruitment in America. None of them could be discriminated against in the interests of keeping tensions down in a society with so many potential sources of division – ethnic, regional, linguistic; all of them were to be identified with the American way of life as an expression of dominant consensus.

In effect, the Churches adapted themselves to this role more readily than their emphatic assertions of distinctiveness of theological commitments, and the primacy of ideological positions, would have led one to suppose. From the very earliest days it was evident that the immigrants had to come to terms with the permanence of their new circumstances, and the role of the Churches in maintaining continuity with home became muted in all the crucial areas of life – continuity was only in the sentimental recollection of things now past. Thus the pastors of the Norwegian Lutheran Churches, called out from Norway, and expecting to return there, found themselves with basically different assumptions about America and the problems of assimilation from the immigrants who had chosen the new country and who expected to stay there.[1] The social orientations of the Churches necessarily had to change: the relatively painless way in which it

1. See N. Tavuchis, op. cit.

occurred illustrates the malleability of religious dispositions.

Despite the convergence of ideological position among
the American denominations, and the diminishing significance of doctrine in religious life, the tendency towards
amalgamation has not proceeded quite as far among
American denominations as might, from these indications,
have been expected. The churches had enjoyed a context
of friendly rivalry, open competition and formal equality.
They have, in consequence, grown increasingly alike in
their organizational structure, and in their evangelization,
fund-raising, overseas missioning, publicity, social welfare and many other activities (and American churches
have extensive social programmes). The similarity of
style, and the loss of ideological distinctiveness has not,
however, given a very strong impetus to church union –
perhaps because the 'brand images' are still significant,
even though the labels bear little relation to actual differences of denominational belief and practice. Some tendency to polarization between fundamentalist and liberal
wings has occurred, but in general this has (the Southern
Baptists and the Missouri Synod Lutherans apart, among
the major denominations) occurred within denominations – which nonetheless still hold together, so unim-
portant is doctrinal difference – rather than between
them.[1]

1. See the discussion of the 'New Denominationalism' in C. Y.
Glock and R. Stark, *Religion and Society in Tension*, Chicago; Rand
McNally, 1965.

7
Religion and Status: America and England

THE assimilation of immigrants and the creation of communities were the first social processes to affect the accommodation of European religion to the American context. But in the emergence of a new society, and one with unparalleled opportunities for expansion, other social imperatives follow. Religious movements had to adapt first to the immediate local requirements of their clientele. That clientele had eventually to adapt to the wider social pressures of the new American society. It was evident that religious divisions would either approximate to other more imperative social divisions, or that the Churches would increasingly approximate each other in their general orientation to the wider society. In succession, both processes occurred. The Churches adjusted to the cognizance that their members were becoming Americans in a permanent sense, with a mixture of sentiment for the peasant European past, and realism concerning the increasingly urban and suburban American present and future.

As groups of immigrants settled and strove for economic advancement in American society so the Churches reflected their aspirations for social and economic status. The groups outside the Churches found new, often indigenous religious expressions appropriate to their social situation, and the imported Churches took on characteristics of the level of social status which their clientele attained.

The correlation of religious and social status, which became a marked feature of American religious life, was not, as it had been in England, a religious division of those identified with, and those excluded from, participation in the mainstream of national life in the established and dissenting Churches. There was, precisely because of the wider political tolerance, the reality of economic opportunity, the buoyancy of the American economy and the expansion of the physical and subsequently the technical, frontier, no necessary religious bifurcation. All religious groups could claim a prospect of a share in the American future. But here lies another distinction between the denominations in America and those in England. Both had some relation to social status, but the rapidity and normalcy of social mobility in America gave their denominations an association with particular groups whose status was, especially throughout the nineteenth century, increasing. The appearance in England – although there was some tendency for Nonconformists to rise in the social scale – was of much greater fixity. Such social mobility as occurred was much less recognized, certainly it did not acquire an overt ideology, and members of particular denominations were not constantly faced with adjustment to an improved status position.

It was no accident that, in the later nineteenth-century, post-millennial adventism, and the optimistic mood of movements like Universalism, New Thought and Christian Science, should develop in the longer settled urban areas of the American continent, just as revivalistic and holiness sects had emerged from rather earlier periods – and continued to emerge – in the rural areas and in the newly settled and fast growing towns. Both represented a religious adjustment to a situation of rapid social change. The more established Churches could alter their perspective from the traditional despair for the world and the hope of heaven, to a steady belief that men would bring in their own millennium only after which would all that they had achieved receive the divine imprimatur.

The newer cults were an echo of the same faith in progress among less accommodated populations. The revivalism and the holiness movements were adjustments, in this context of groups not as yet advantaged by the course of the nation's development, and often temporarily dislocated within it.

If the new sects which emerged among the new urban immigrants and the least advantaged members of the society were often remote in emotional tone and liturgical style from the older established bodies in which the wealthy and influential were religiously accommodated, even so there was in this contrast no suggestion that the new sects were politically or socially a threat to the well-to-do. Rather, indeed, the opposite: the opportunity for emotional expression in the religious context might be seen as a deflection of concern from social inequalities. The emphasis on fraternity made possible a certain religious tolerance of extreme outsider groups, including even their economic support by men who were themselves of different religious persuasions.[1] The assumption of the equality of men led to an assumption of the equality in some sense of the differing religious opinions of men. There was less opportunity for the expression of distinctive superiority of particular faiths *per se*, except as reflections of divergent social statuses. The expansionism, freedom and tolerance of the United States in religious matters had profound consequences for the development of religious movements, and were in themselves fundamentally different from conditions in England.

Because America was a society in which status ascription – the fixity of social positions – was never a social

1. For a discussion of this see the classic work of American sociology of religion, Liston Pope, *Millhands and Preachers*, New Haven, Conn., Yale University Press, 1942.

assumption as it was in England; because, indeed, social mobility rather than occupational succession was the likelihood for the majority in an expanding society from the very beginning, the believers in a particular movement never needed to define their relation to those in a dominant Church in specific status terms. They, too, had the prospect of 'moving up' in their society, and consequently the status connotations of religious affiliation were of much less permanence in the United States than in England. In consequence, even sects which recruited from outsiders and underprivileged groups showed a capacity to change which was never approximated by sectarian movements in Britain. The social mobility of individuals was reflected in the possibility of the social mobility of the movements to which they belonged. The demand for congruence of status – social, religious, cultural, occupational, educational – was most easily expressed, and most quickly effected, in relation to religious affiliation.

The immigrants to America had to adjust to radically different assumptions about social mobility from those which prevailed in Europe: these ideas, often in an exaggerated form, were one of the pull-factors of migration, of course. European societies assumed basic stability and the fixity of status, to a degree which permitted one sociologist writing in the 1890s to describe even 'great exhibitions' as a circumstance which upset men's ideas of the norms of social life, and the appropriate bounds of aspiration.[1] (Today the equivalent consequences on more massive scale follow from tourism.) In such a society as

1. The implications of these differences in attitudes towards social mobility can be drawn from a careful reading of Emile Durkheim, *Suicide*, London, Routledge, 1952 (a translation of *Le Suicide*, (1st edn. 1897) by George Simpson) and Robert K. Merton, *Social Theory and Social Structure*, op. cit., Chs. IV and V.

Europe was, part of the function of religion was to vindicate the ascribed and fixed status of society. In the words of the nineteenth-century hymn:

> The rich man in his castle, the poor man at his gate,
> God made them high and lowly and ordered their estate.

In America, entirely different ideas about mobility necessarily prevailed. It was a society of opportunity, for men to become 'self-made', for getting on, and even for assuming the life-styles and claiming the status limited, in Europe, to an hereditary elect. Religion necessarily had to adjust to this circumstance, to make itself at least compatible with direct and naked goals of competition, self-seeking and social mobility. Thus religion in America necessarily abandoned some of the functions it had fulfilled in Europe. Even in the mid-nineteenth century, it was already emphasizing love, joy and personal security, rather than the social control functions of hellfire. Universalism and Christian Science were emphatically American products. Religion in Europe has much more slowly adjusted to the idea of high rates of social mobility, and perhaps for this reason has prospered less well in the more affluent society.

Two distinct processes can be observed in American religious development. One was the gradual acquisition of enhanced status by whole movements, and the other was the tendency for individuals who rose in status more rapidly than the generality of their fellows within a religious movement, to shift allegiance to a denomination which more adequately expressed the congruity of religious and social status. Thus the developments of the Disciples, an extreme Baptist denomination in the mid-West, and originally recruited from relatively poor and partly rural groups, illustrate a process of steady enhancement of social status. From simple and undecorated meeting rooms to Gothic-style churches with stained glass windows; from hymns unaccompanied by musical instruments, to the building of large organs; from contempt for education and scholarship, to the eventual endowment of colleges supporting even secular educational aims: this was the process occurring in that denomination as its membership found themselves in greater association with the outside society, sharing increasingly their values and undifferentiated in terms of economic success and economic goals.[1] The history of other groups reflects a similar process – Methodists earlier, and the Church of the Nazarene later.[2] In the latter case the Church of the Nazarene had originally arisen from among groups of Methodists and others who were concerned to find expression for the teaching of holiness which had become rather out of favour with many Methodists, as savouring a type of enthusiasm which they had largely abandoned. The early Nazarenes were undoubtedly people of lower social status and of little education. They recruited many of the lower classes. As their members rose in social status – pushed up from below in some respects by the new tides of immigration – and as the discipline and orderliness of religious commitment led to habits of frugality and responsibility which increased opportunities for economic gain and social respectability, so the Nazarenes ceased to be so dominantly identified with the very lowest sections of society. They gradually came to manifest the concern for status, prestigious buildings and display which characterized other denominations.

The alternative process, of individual mobility and changing religious affiliation is less adequately docu-

1. See Oliver R. Whiteley, *The Trumpet Call of Reformation*, St Louis, Mo., Bethany Press, 1959.

2. On the Methodists see E. D. C. Brewer, 'Church and Sect in Methodism', *Social Forces*, 30, 1952, pp. 400–408.

mented, but the Churches themselves often reported the tendency – and this was something which occurred in some measure in England as well as in the United States. Certainly, it is evident that an individual rising in the world cannot afford to continue in association with religious groups that practise rituals which are strongly associated with lower classes. The man who has been brought up as a Holy Roller is likely, as he advances in the world, to find it less and less attractive for a businessman with a public reputation to roll in the aisles with the least sophisticated members of the locality. So we find, more strongly marked in America than in England, although the point has some application in both societies, a tendency for status discrepancies within a Church to disappear and for a congregation to be drawn dominantly from people who find themselves not simply religiously congenial in terms of belief and ritual practice, but who also find themselves socially and economically compatible.[1] Where the denomination fails to manifest this degree of social and economic conformity, none the less the local church often does so. It is of course a commonplace that Churches have in the past often divided into separate divisions of the same broad religious persuasion largely on economic grounds, and although the relationship does not hold completely, it is often sufficiently approximated to be arresting.

The tendency for denominations to move upwards in social standing does, however, illustrate the extent to which religious movements in America have shared in a system of ultimate values about their society. There is not the same strength of social antagonism expressed between

1. See W. R. Goldschmidt, 'Class Denominationalism in Rural California Churches,' *American Journal of Sociology*, 49, 1944, pp. 348–55; and Lloyd Warner, *Democracy in Jonesville*, New York, Harper, 1949, pp. 153 ff.

them as was marked by the divisions of Anglicans and Dissenters in Britain, nor the same political and social divisions of affiliation which prevailed when the Church of England could be described as the Conservative Party at prayer, or the United and Primitive Methodists be accused (by Wesleyans) of too close an association with the Liberal Party. Social mobility did occur in religious denominations in England, of course, but in a society in which status has been at least partially ascriptive and perhaps is still, the opportunity for mobility has been less obvious – perhaps even less real, in terms of the acquisition of social honour. (This may be suggested despite the conclusions of Lipset and Bendix – whose findings relate only to occupational mobility and this on a crude measure of manual and non-manual professions.)[1]

There appears to be little doubt that those who became Methodists or Salvationists did in fact rise in social status, became respectable by adopting religious beliefs which if themselves heterodox at least led to attitudes which were socially laudable. They provided themselves, in being members of such bodies, with virtual certification of reliability, honesty, self-esteem and self-discipline. They embodied, indeed, the virtues of Victorian society. But the limitations of this social mobility must also be stressed. This was laying a claim to a position in society, it was far from being an assimilation to the standards of social conformity assumed by the ruling classes and the Anglican Church. The Nonconformists of the nineteenth century were always aware that they stood outside and apart from that national institution and its social and political correlates. Such upward mobility of denominations as there was, was very much slower than that which occurred among the denominations of the United States.

1. S. M. Lipset and R. Bendix, *Social Mobility in Industrial Society*, London, Heinemann, 1959.

The assumptions of the social context were different, and the expansionism and optimism of American society were inevitably lacking; the creed of progress had not as yet found its social dimensions in Britain. More important, of course, the very attitude of the Nonconformists was that they did not want to move upwards into a position of parity with, much less association with the Anglican Church, which – particularly in its Anglo-Catholic forms – was to them clearly a betrayal of the principles of Christ.

Where individual mobility occurred, it tended to occur steadily and inter-generationally. Nonconformists who prospered in business sometimes sent their grandchildren to boarding schools, and so, perhaps unwittingly, often exposed them to circumstances in which occasional and nominal conformity were much more laudable than committed Nonconformity, which clearly singled a boy out as an oddity, and as coming from the 'wrong' sort of background. There was not in England that American ease of movement – often reflecting the ease of geographical mobility – which allowed a man to move up religiously as he moved up socially.

Perhaps the crucial factor in contrast to the upward mobility of American denominations and their increased assimilation to a high status norm of Gothic architecture, decorous services, elaborate liturgies and sacramentalism was the very fact of the Established Church. English Nonconformists knew, from the very institutional position of Anglicanism, what they were against. They had a measuring rod against which to set themselves. They knew what they were not, and they knew the signs of movement towards 'churchiness' and how to resist them. Although, in the very broad sweep of two or three centuries there has been an undoubted tendency for English Nonconformity to get 'higher' and to espouse

customs which were once known only to the Anglicans –
and sometimes only to the Church of Rome – none the
less the process was, in comparison with the American
experience, a very slow process indeed.

It is thus evident that denominationalism represented,
and in some measure still represents, albeit in an attenuated form, something very different in the English context from what it means in the United States. The Americans 'inherited' their original denominations. Those
which evolved there, grew largely in response to the
prevailing social conditions – the rawness of the middle-
west, or the depression of the urban slums, the disloca-
tion of immigrants (both in America, and from rural to
urban America) or the need for justification and Ameri-
canism in the drawing rooms of Boston. They did not
stem so emphatically from a circumstance of social protest, from conditions in which men felt themselves
excluded from, or too restrictedly admitted to, the
presence of God. The absence of an established church,
the assumption of the equality of men, and hence the
equality of their religious faith, made reasonable the
expectation of each sect that it should be regarded as
being as fully prestigious and worthy as the next. It
meant, then, an implicit willingness to compete, not
simply in terms of the religious ideologies which were
disseminated, but also in terms of the purely social,
architectural and economic style which each sect adopted,
and thus denominations vied with each other in their
buildings, social standing, patriotism and social acceptability. There was, then, a willingness to be assimilated to
the wider society and its values.

However much competition there may have been between denominations in America, their competition was
in similar terms, without any one Church being able to
claim superiority or advantages in the social and political

sphere, and without the relentless antagonism which was implicit in the dichotomization of society into conforming and nonconforming groups. There was, in the American situation, no clear religious group, with its distinctive values, which other movements knew that they were, from their basic charter, against. Hence, it was always possible in the American context that religious movements would increasingly approximate to each other in practice, ideology and organization. And the more fully the movements were exposed to the wider pressures of American society, and the more sensitive they were to these pressures, so increasingly they would tend to respond in similar ways, lacking that vigour of social protest which characterized English Nonconformity.

Given the need in America for the country to assimilate immigrants and to Americanize their home-life and their religious values – those two areas of their experience which were most likely to be least directly affected by life in the new country – it was clear that American denominations were quickly to be exposed to social pressures, and were to reflect the demand that immigrants should become Americans. English denominations were obviously under no such pressure from the wider society – religious divisiveness, indeed religious hostilities constituted no such ultimate threat to social order, and were, on all counts, to be preferred to more explicitly political divisions. In the United States, because there was competition, there was, then, also a certain agreed framework within which competition could take place, and this too promoted that similarity of ultimate orientation, and the accommodation to American values of which Herberg has written so persuasively. As individuals expected to 'get on' so each religious movement absorbed the expectations of growth, progress, enhanced social status and a better place in the sun. These aspirations were, of course, alien in particular to the more sectarian groups in the first place, in America as in England; and in England, much as denominations might have wanted growth, they wanted it not by approximating to the Church of England, and imitating those practices and attributes which made that Church socially pre-eminent, but rather by the dissemination of their own distinctively divergent ideals and values.

It becomes evident that whereas the secularization process in England was reflected in the diminution of religious attendance, by the emptying churches in the late nineteenth and especially throughout the twentieth century, in the United States secularization occurred in quite different ways. The growth statistics of the American Churches conceal the growing vacuity of American religious belief and practice. Obviously membership comes to mean something quite different in a society in which distinctive religious commitment has in almost all major denominations come to be so purely nominal. Whereas in England secularization has been seen in the abandonment of the Churches – as in other European countries – in America it has been seen in the absorption of the Churches by the society, and their loss of distinctive religious content. Whereas in England religion continues as a compartmentalized marginal item in the society, in America it remains institutionally much more central, but ideationally much more bankrupt. In many ways religion is still, for historical reasons, well represented in Britain, and has more apparent association with government and central authority and with education. In practice, apart from this sphere of institutional influence, however, it is evident that religious practice – worship – is much less prevalent in Britain than in America. The very voluntary element of religion appears to have made Americans more compulsive about Church affiliation, but it is evident that, in a society which is relatively little informed by distinctive religious values, a society which has been described, religious statistics notwithstanding, as the most secular society in the world, Church allegiance is a matter of social respectability.

Church affiliation has different cultural meaning in the United States and in England. We must distrust statistical presentations which suggest that there is direct comparability on the assumption that similar behaviour carries similarity of meaning in different cultural contexts. Clearly it does not. What the difference of statistics does demand, however, is some interpretation of the functions, not of religion, but of institutional affiliation in the two societies. If the religious content of Church practice has declined, then we may assume that the increased attendance in America and its decrease in Britain, reflects differences in the functions of institutional attachment in the two societies. Herberg has, though he is concerned only with the American case, suggested the appropriate explanation here. In America, the Churches act as agencies for the expression of community feeling. Such communities are not natural communities, of those who live in face-to-face contact for generations, rarely moving, and rarely receiving strangers. Such was the condition of traditional societies, and from such a context the European sense of community persisted into modern times. But in America, particularly as immigrants were dispersed, so such stable community life as existed in the early settlements went into eclipse.

The resettlement of the country meant that a steady process of movement became inevitable, and the benefits of stable community life were lost (that such stable communities might also have disadvantages, on a modern assessment, must be clear, but does not affect the present argument). The Church, which had for the immigrants become, as we have seen, the repository of sentiments and practices from the past, was obviously the focus of community life as displaced people knew it, and so the Church became the one agency which appeared to sustain the various functions which communities had once performed. In a context of social and geographical mobility, however, the Church could obviously not forge a community life of the kind which had persisted in traditional societies – that was necessarily abandoned in the development of a modern industrial society. It could, however, maintain the sentiments of community, and so the Churches became the agencies of synthetic community life, drawing people together as 'neighbours' even though many of the natural features of neighbourhoods, as they had existed in Europe, were no longer evident.

This development gave American Churches that distinctly 'welcoming' characteristic on which Europeans so often (and by no means always favourably) comment. People who did not know each other, whose lives, though temporarily lived in physical propinquity, impinged relatively little on each other, except in secondary relationships, could go through the fiction of being a community. It was, after all, a pattern of response to which they were accustomed, and about which they had heard a great deal from their parents and grand-parents, and from literature, even though it now had a very different relevance for their own lives. The search to retain community; the felt need for sociability and association with those around; the persisting desire to 'belong'; the need for a context in which to claim status and display status; the persistence of an affective need to be 'someone' in terms of the actual direct responses of others, and not simply in terms of abstract consideration of receipt of wages; acknowledgement of identity with the 'nation' or 'the state' – all of these elements were probably involved in the steady growth of the American Churches. The stability of the organized institutional framework could create the illusion of a stable community life, even if the gestures of friendliness and involvement necessarily had to be prostituted by their extension to relatively anonymous people.

In England, where the community has certainly also been in process of attentuation, it can be readily observed that the process has – even after the Second World War – gone less far, and been less obvious. The increasingly fictional quality of assumptions of settled community life, of parishes and local government units in which people have a genuine stake, is a feature of modern life in Britain, but the very steady evolution of the process has had different consequences. There are still in many places, and particularly outside the large metropolitan centres, many neighbourhoods with a continuity of communal life, and there is a continuity of community expression and community institutions, even though they suffer steady attrition. There has never been the need to think consciously of 'creating' community agencies, except in the marginal circumstances of new towns and large new housing estates, and there the experience has been far from an unmixed success.

In the decline of community institutions, the Church itself has suffered. It has not been able to assert itself as the agency of community identity, and the need for that reassertion has been very little expressed in Britain. Those who have felt such a need have been content with the traditional, continuing if declining, agencies. In a country with an uncertain but diminishing place in world affairs, there may also be a loss of nerve, an uncertainty about whether the values and institutions of the past are still worthy of credence. Thus, loyalty, even to immediate personal and local objects, has been thrown into doubt because loyalty seems to be associated with the patriotic and imperial mission of the past, which now has had to be disavowed. Decency is questioned because it, too, belongs to the period of confidence. Religious beliefs become untenable because they took on so much from the matrix of the vigorous, secure, morally righteous society which flourished until a quarter of a century ago. The loss of political and economic dominance has been met with the almost joyful abandonment of large parts of the nation's cultural inheritance which were somehow associated with it.

The rejection of the past has meant not only the open rejection of religion, but also of the institutions and circumstances which supported it. The local community, the home, the school are no longer focal points of allegiance in British society, and the discontinuities of a keenly cultivated mobility make religious traditions difficult to sustain. Thus young people are early bent on 'getting away from home', from small towns and villages, to college, to work, 'and to lead a better life'. It becomes apparent, then, that the social meaning of the Church is different in the two cultural contexts and in England is not yet a repository of sentiment concerning the community life of the past – partly because there are still sufficient remnants of community life to make this development unlikely, partly because the past appears suddenly bankrupt, partly because there has been no conscious hankering after a return to community, and that in turn because there has been no such radical break in people's experience as occurred in the uprooting and migration of peoples in the United States.

The Churches in the United States are an expression of status differentiation in some measure, whereas they have had much less importance as a status-confirming agency in Britain. The denominations in Britain expressed rather the basic divisions of social, political and economic orientation, and these divisions in turn had reference to a class stratification of society which needed no further confirmation in religious terms – it was already evident enough. Only in the uncertainty of an increasingly homogenized society, with few elements of ascriptive status (abolished as all the remnants of the pre-immigrant past had to be eliminated) was it necessary for achievement and the struggle for status to find adequate social expression. Thus one circumstance which helped to maintain the denominations in being and to impose additional functions to those of community-identification, namely status-reassurance, existed in America but not in Britain.

But in both countries the significance of denominational differences has diminished, albeit for somewhat different reasons. In America the denominations were, as we have seen, committed to a system of status-distribution and engaged, necessarily on increasingly equal assumptions, in the status-race of the ordinary American citizen and church-goer. Those assumptions were drawn from the experience of an expanding society, a strong optimism, experience of social growth and increasing affluence. It is a commonplace that in richer nations the differences between rich and poor are less profound than in poorer countries. In America this circumstance is intensified if one excludes the Negro community (legitimate in this argument, since they have separate religious denominations of their own). Consequently among Protestant white Americans, the early differences of socio-economic status between denominations has tended to diminish.[1] Even outsider Churches have, in considerable measure, been able to assume the approved role of offering to their adherents status enhancement.

1. See Robert Lee, *The Social Sources of Church Unity*, New York, Abingdon Press, 1960.

As the specific teachings of the different denominations have been less emphasized (and Herberg has commented extensively on this) so they have persisted as different but increasingly similar organizations. As the pressure of competition in the field of missioning abroad, evangelization at home, maintaining good community services, fund-raising, welfare work, educational development and the like has developed, so Churches which at one time had little central organization have developed it, and they have done so, necessarily, on increasingly similar lines. The organizational imperatives of large-scale operation in modern society have forced the Churches into the adoption of similar methods and consequently similar structures for all these auxiliary operations. Thus even in groups like the various Baptist denominations which subscribe strongly to a theology and an ecclesiology which assert that God's will is revealed directly to individuals and to individual congregations of the saints but not to the denomination, the Church Assembly, the conference or the department within a rational bureaucratic machine, these developments have occurred. The Baptists, theology notwithstanding, have been obliged to develop denominational conferences and to accept the establishment of rational bureaucratic planning with departmental divisions of responsibility for denominational work at a national and international level. Their ecclesiology and their theology sit uneasily under the shadow of the bureaucratic machine which has grown up in spite of these ideological commitments.[1] American denominations, then, have largely come to terms with the wider society in their organization, their value-orientations and their acceptance of the prevailing cultural response.

In Britain the drawing together of the denominations

1. See Paul M. Harrison, *Power and Authority in the Free Church Tradition*, Princeton, Princeton University Press, 1959.

has in large measure proceeded for reasons somewhat different from those which have been influential in America. The pressure of rational bureaucratic organization has played some part even in the less rationally organized and more traditional society which Britain represents. The Nonconformist movements expressed, in the past, the general social and political nonconformity of their members – their dissociation, at the transcendental level, from a religiously constituted society, reflected their sense of dissociation from secular society as well. But inevitably, social divisions change; the class-orientation of the different denominations has weakened. We have already noted that acceptance of religion tended to enable a man to become socially mobile, and we can also note that the disabilities under which the Nonconformist Churches laboured gradually eased, and their dissociation from the wider society lessened. They themselves gradually gave up their distinctive life-styles, their moral peculiarities, and their sense of being distinct outsiders from both Church and state.

As the state became increasingly secularized, so the automatic dissociation from both could be modified. When Nonconformists were increasingly voters they had the prospect of influencing social and political affairs in increasing measure, and this immediately compromised and eventually diminished their social nonconformity. Inevitably, as its social and political base was eroded, religious Nonconformity lost something of its force. Historical differences prevented, within a society which retained strong traditionalism even in nonconformity, a too rapid transformation of Nonconformist attitudes. The separate organizational structure, the reinforcement of allegiances through long segregation, almost into separate community structures, resisted the effect of the disappearance of the social and economic conditions which had made Nonconformists express themselves as a distinct people with a different approach to the transcendental. The old cleavages in society no longer required religious expression, and that diversity of religious expression had now to justify itself in its own terms. And yet, in a context of secularization, it was evident that religious ideology and long persisting communal and organizational separateness were insufficient to preserve Nonconformity in its earlier form. Such new divisions which existed in society no longer required religious expression, having more direct outlet in social or political movements, and these were not drawn from sections of the society in any way co-incident with denominational divisions.

If social processes have reduced religious differences between major denominations to merely verbal responses, liturgical patterns and organizational arrangements, has religion then no significant social influence in contemporary society? In the late 1950s an American sociologist attempted to assess the extent to which the Protestant ethic – the commitment to work, free inquiry, and individual initiative among other values – was still influential in the United States. Max Weber himself would not, perhaps, have expected Puritan values to have persisted as a distinctly religious differential in a context so remote in time and place, and in a society so manifestly un-Puritan. From a survey of citizens of Detroit, a city of mixed religious composition, Gerhard Lenski concluded that there was still a significant religious factor at work in affecting the dispositions of Protestants and Catholics. He found that Jews and Protestants had a positive attitude towards work, and Catholics a negative attitude; that Jews and Protestants regarded it as important that a child should learn to think for itself; Catholics that it should learn to obey. He found that Catholics attached more importance to kin-groups, and he believed that Catholic family life might interfere with the development of motivation towards achievement and mobility.[1]

Lenski's findings, however, have been directly challenged in a study of religious adherence and career aspirations by Fr Andrew Greeley, whose principal stricture on Lenski's work is that it did not take into proper account the differences in ethnic background and degree of assimilation to American society of the Catholics in Detroit. Greeley found little evidence of differences between Catholics and Protestants, that Catholics increasingly accepted general American standards and values, and that once the Catholic has been assimilated the distinctiveness which Lenski noted, entirely disappears. It is only the time-lags in the outworking of this assimilation which create discrepancies between the Catholic and Protestant contributions to the scientific profession for example (in which, hitherto, Protestants have been more than proportionately represented). Greeley found that among his sample of graduates drawn from all over the United States, Catholics in fact made a much more than average choice of business as a career; that Catholics were much more interested in making money than were Protestants; that they were fully as achievement-oriented. Nor did all-Catholic schooling affect Catholic respondents in these various ways.[2] It seemed that American Catholic graduates behaved as fully in accordance with the values of the old Protestant ethic as did American Protestant graduates, and in some respects even more fully.

If Lenski's work was perhaps affected by his failure to isolate ethnic background as an important determinant of attitudes which he took to be specifically Catholic,

1. Gerhard Lenski, *The Religious Factor*, New York, Doubleday, 1961.

2. Andrew Greeley, *Religion and Career*, New York, Sheed & Ward, 1963.

Greeley's work may have been influenced by the particular age-group and educational-group which he took as his sample for investigation. Young people, and especially those just emerging from universities, are more likely to be achievement-oriented, anxious to get on in the world, than a more representative age-group. They carry with them the values of the institutions – the schools and universities – in which they have spent most of their lives. Both sets of findings have all the limitations of questionnaire procedures, but the conclusion which might be tentatively reached is that whatever the Protestant ethic may have contributed to the general values of western – and particularly American – society of the present day, it appears now to have become effectively disconnected with its point of origin. Catholics appear to be as manifestly imbued with Puritan values in relation to work and achievement as are Protestants in the modern world. Whatever religious diversity prevails in contemporary America, at least as between the two major variants of religion, appears to contribute less and less to social diversity.

It is too simple a thesis to suggest that religious diversity originates in social diversity, and that religious unity will occur as social diversity diminishes. The relation of religion and society is by no means so constant for a thesis of this kind to reveal the really significant changes that have been occurring. Although contemporary society, and this is especially true of American society which was so much more divided in the past, has lost some of its diversity, its regionalism, patterns of stratification and, in some cases, ethnic divisions, none the less the moral unities of European societies of the past have been destroyed rather than restored. The sense of moral rectitude which once extended to almost all social and personal activities even in peasant societies (to dress, forms of speech, eating, courtship, attitudes to strangers, neighbours, kinsmen, etc.) although they were often highly localized moralities were a manifestation of local social unity. Many of these moral orientations were entrenched within a religious view of the world, and both the influence of religious morality and of the religious beliefs which supported them have been largely swept away.

Church unity may be a response to social change, but perhaps not so much to the diminution of social diversity, as to the changed role of religion in society. Mass-media, mass production, rational bureaucratic organization, extensive social and geographic mobility, have been important determinants of the diminution of social diversity. But all of these forces do not 'produce' religious unity. Once religious interpretations of the world have ceased, for the vast majority, to be important (whether organizational affiliation and participation increases, as in America, or not, as in Britain) the barriers to religious unity are lowered, but it is unity at a different level. Even then, it requires perhaps the determined efforts of a profession facing adversity to bring it about, and to promulgate the ideology which will dissolve the hard core of organizational persistence.

8

The Clergy and Ecumenicalism

'THE problem of ecumenism is the order of the day,'[1] writes a Catholic theologian. An outside observer might have thought that the problem of secularization could much more suitably have been chosen as the special problem of contemporary Christianity. But the Churches have, in response to the situation in which they find society in the twentieth century, become very much more concerned with themselves – and by the Churches what effectively is meant, is the religious profession. In the last two decades ecumenicalism has become the dominant clerical cause. In an age when Christianity has been demythologized, when traditional ideas about God have been radically challenged by bishops of the Church, ecumenism becomes a new faith – something to believe in. There has been something like a mass conversion of the clergy. It is not a spirit which has suddenly overtaken the Churches, it is a campaign which has been actively, almost aggressively, canvassed.

Ecumenicalism has been supported by a variety of arguments, some of them mutually exclusive. A popular argument has been that the divided condition of the Churches has been not only a sin in the sight of God, but a cause of the decline of religion: it has enabled the man in the street to say to the Churches, 'How can I choose among you?' and, consequently, to abandon religion. In

1. George H. Tavard, *The Century of Ecumenism. The Search for Unity*, Notre Dame, Ind., Fides, 1960, p. ix.

the American case, an argument of this kind has less force, since choice and competition have for a long time been highly prized values of American society. But the disappearance of ethnic, class, and regional differences, and the endorsement of American values by all the major denominations, has erased their individual distinctiveness.

Whereas the low religious practice in England appears to imply considerable commitment on the part of the small minority of regular worshippers, in the United States it appears that much higher church involvement is associated with relatively low commitment to religious values. Whereas in Britain doctrinal positions of denominations still bear something of the distinctiveness of the past, but denominational organization has grown weak, in the United States denominational doctrinal distinction has little consequence, but organizations, enjoying wide lay support, are relatively strong. In America, ecumenism has been limited; in England its canvass has been extensive. It seems that organizational strength is a more effective impediment to unity than persisting doctrinal and liturgical distinctiveness.

In general, we are seeking confirmation of the hypothesis that organizations amalgamate when they are weak rather than when they are strong, since alliance means compromise and amendment of commitment. Of all social organizations, religious movements have most difficulty in altering their commitment, since their purpose is supposed to be 'given' from a higher source. The truths of religion are generally supposed to be apprehensions of the divine, and particular movements have come into being to give expression to truths which they found unrepresented in existing religious practice. The ecumenical tendency illustrates then the extreme weakness of religious commitment and belief, since, much more markedly than for organizations which have purely instrumental ends, amalgamation implies surrender of principles, or their attenuation.

What then appears to be the case, is that, whereas most denominations began as protest movements, over time there is a distinct attentuation of protest. Even in a traditional society, where young people are socialized to the norms of the denominational way of life, it is difficult to communicate fully the meaning of belonging to an 'outside' group, with standards and values of its own. Two distinct circumstances make this evident. In the first place, the original recruits to Nonconformist religion are likely to be those who understand the point and purpose of contention against the prevailing establishment. They are, in some sense, disposed to mild rebellion. (They are not, of course, as extreme in their revolutionist ardour as the converts to adventist sects, which, in their initial vigour, are frequently quasi-revolutionary movements, revelling in the expectation of an early overturn of the social order.) But even if not so extreme, Nonconformist *converts* were men who had at least opted out of the deference system and status ascription of the wider society in its traditional form. Their children, however, are brought up within the Nonconformist system, which, all too often, has evolved a new status order of its own. The very inheritance of religious attitudes implies a certain acceptance of authority, a certain acquiescence. The ideology of the movement may itself be still fervently anti-establishment, but since the movement is likely to evolve an establishment of its own, and since its second and subsequent generation of converts are themselves not those who have had to forge (and sometimes to fight for) their beliefs and their organization, we can expect – and indeed we see – that denominations tend to lose something of their pristine vigour; their expression of protest becomes attenuated, even by circumstance of these purely internal considerations.

The second factor is, of course, the changing external context. As the process of secularization has continued, so the differences between denominations have lost their social significance. Fewer issues are decided in terms of religious differences; fewer aspects of social experience are affected by them. The very stuff of religious regulation and the moral order of the denominations – which was always an important feature of their religious protest – have become increasingly irrelevant as the pattern of social life has changed. With the increasing emergence of the mass society, so the social experience of people has become more and more similar, and its reinterpretation by distinctive religious philosophies has become less and less tenable. The denominations cease to reflect distinct types of social experience – cease to have 'meaning' in any other terms except the religious terms in which they present themselves, and religion has itself become a departmentalized and separated aspect of the individual's life and social experience.

It is thus clear that although ecumenicalism has captured the imagination of the leaders of the Churches, this process has in part been a growing recognition of the essential weakness of religious life in the increasingly secularized society. The spirit has descended on the waters and brought peace between churchmen of different persuasions only as those churchmen have recognized their essential marginality in modern society. The choice, in a country like England, appeared to be between becoming odd-men-out for those few who remained religiously committed, or the continuance of religious activity with ever less influence and loss of inner integrity, as in the American case.

In both Britain and America, however, the *appearance*

of success has considerable attraction, and many church-men are – understandably in regard to their history – anxious not to lose their identification with national insti-tutions. They are keen to remain part of the normal ex-pression of social life, even if this is at the cost of more distinctive religious values. Ecumenicalism is a policy which is entirely convergent with this choice, since it also means the surrender of distinctive beliefs and practices, and the attenuation of positive and distinctive denomina-tional commitment.

There are clear reasons for the choice. No profession cares to see its activities under-valued, nor to see its functions becoming superfluous. Even loss of substantive influence (and in England that influence is still institu-tionally entrenched and protected in certain respects) is to be preferred to the disappearance of large numbers of appointments, the abandonment of institutional and organizational arrangements, and the loss of relative status, and perhaps, relative income. Disestablishment in Britain, or perhaps even the affirmation of a more earnest religious commitment, might lead to the loss of chaplain-cies in various institutions where they still persist from an age when most public and many private organizations recognized the indispensability of the services of religion. If the Churches were to refuse to compromise with the irreligious dispositions of the increasingly secular social order, such consequences would follow. Religion would risk being totally disregarded, except for those with a private predilection for it. Having been much more clearly committed to contra-distinctive religious values the Nonconformist denominations in Britain have less effective choice than American denominations. In a society with no fixed orthodoxy, and used to change, the Churches adjusted without the acute consciousness of the surrender of historic positions which has faced denominations in England. Religious commitment was one of the points at which tradition was enshrined in a traditional society. Only ecumenism, and it now has a long history in the experience of English denominations at home or overseas, could justify the compromise with the secular society, under the guise of compromise with fellow Christians. Ecumenicalism permitted an adjustment to the secular society that has been generally attractive at least to the clergy of the Churches and denominations in England. The laity, who have less vested interest in this level of operation of their religious denomination, have shown themselves less enthusiastic about it.

The final study of ecumenicalism and the professional religious mind has still to be undertaken, but it seems evident that those whose profession involves them in some sort of appraisal of the specific commitment of their denomination, some recognition of changing historical circumstance, should become especially sensitive to the problems of division. Quite apart from the possible loss of professional roles by the decline of the Churches, there is the experience of lesser status. For those without the intensity of that protest-orientation which transvaluates human statuses in heavenly terms, the sense of being an inferior professional because one's profession is religion must be harrowing. For those professionals in denominations which began in protest the gestures of ecumenicalism from larger Churches are obviously attractive because they reduce the immediate sense of inferiority, and offer ultimate prospect of equality with professionals in more 'orthodox' Churches. There are abundant evidences of the way in which the ministers of dissenting or free denominations experience some sense of flattery to be approached on practically equal terms by the clerics of more 'orthodox' denominations.

Quite apart from the status and economic considerations which are important for a profession facing decline, there is the extent to which the ministries of different movements have been involved in a shared experience of professional specialization. In some ways ministers have got further away from their own laity by the very development of specialization in the wider society. Although religion has not evolved the technical expertise which has occurred among many professional groups, and although the secular trend of Protestantism was distinctly towards laicization of the Church, none the less the inevitable tendencies by which a profession seeks to enhance its status, cultivate its own universe of discourse, and claim its own field of special competence has affected religious functionaries hardly less than others.

The existence of an intellectual tradition in Christianity was such that Nonconformists could not for ever ignore the need to participate in the religious intellectual debate: nor could they ignore their own need to justify, as intellectually as possible, their own development. Intellectual concern was in itself a way in which the ministry of even a dissenting denomination could claim some parity of status with 'orthodox' churchmen, as well as being a way of enhancing the respectability of the denomination as such. The development of ministerial education in the denominations – often attended by disputes between those who held to a much more experiential approach to religion, and those who urged a much greater reliance on intellectual and institutional traditions – was not an easy development and it does not concern us here. But the participation in an intellectual debate on theological issues, and sometimes on other issues, was such as to draw Free Churchmen into close association with those similarly exercised in the older established Churches. This development inevitably meant that at least the *élite* of the ministry addressed themselves as much to the 'informed minds' of their professional counterparts in other branches of the Church, as to the 'honest hearts' of their own laity.

There is one other important aspect of the ecumenical drift, which reflects the interests of religious functionaries rather than of laymen, and this is the wish of the minister to maximize professional specialization. The history of dissent is largely the history, as Max Weber long ago noted, of an *Entzauberung*, a process of demystification, in which the functions of the religious specialist were increasingly shorn of mystical or magical attributes. The denial of the doctrine of transubstantiation by Protestantism, the rejection of the idea that priests could forgive sins, the rejection of the immediate efficacy of churchly rituals, and of the confession were all aspects of emerging Protestantism, and particularly so as expressed in the Presbyterian and Independent movements, which reduced the mystical elements of the priest's role. The very concept of priest was changed once the priesthood of all believers was asserted, and the religious functionary now became a pastor, a preacher or a minister, his functions became directed to the community and ceased to be those of an intercessor between community and God. In Quakerism the process was even more radical and the element of inspirationalism – although circumscribed in time as older 'weighty' Quakers increasingly dominated proceedings in the nineteenth century – gave a genuine lay character to the movement.

Subsequently in Methodism, lay preaching was institutionalized, and a wider range of Church offices was disseminated throughout the lay membership of the chapels. The sectarianism of the nineteenth century took this process even further, and many such movements – the Plymouth Brethren being one of the earliest and most influential – held a professional ministry to be a corruption of Christian organization. Thus, the process of advancing Protestantism was in the direction of the diminution of the distinctive status of the priesthood as a professional body, and of increased insistence that all religious functions could be performed by any committed and sincere believer. This development occurred with the growing individuation of men in modern society, and came to its fulness in a period in which individualism, freedom of contract, the political doctrines of liberalism and liberty of the individual, and the economic doctrines of *laissez faire* were all of them in the ascendant. The professional priesthood stood for a basic and almost ascriptive inequality among men. (This was especially so in religious systems where religious functions were inherited, which was never true of Christianity of course, although there was a tendency for higher religious positions to become the possession of the lesser sons of the aristocracy and gentry – those who held ascriptive status in the secular society.) In the process of history in which ascriptive status declined in importance so the prerogatives of the clergy as a class set apart also declined in appeal, and new movements arose, even in non-revolutionary societies, among those who rejected clerical claims to officiate for them.

There is then a process of decline of the clerical role in western history. Large sections of the population came to deny the supernatural basis of religious specialization and laymen appropriated at least some of the functions formerly the monopoly of the clergy, and denied the value of others. None the less, in all western countries, even when it lost dominance, the old system persisted, either at the margins of the social order or in attenuated form. But a counter-process has also occurred. There is, as we have noticed, an attenuation of protest in dissenting movements. And there are also tendencies for new power structures and status systems to arise even in movements with strong egalitarian ideologies. Thus even among dissenters there has been a reassertion of ministerial authority and an enlargement of the differences between priests and people. In most of these movements the ideological and intellectual justification for a reassertion of mystical priestly power could not be directly provided, of course, but steadily there has been a return to practices and traditions which are more those of the Churches from which these movements broke away, than of Protestant dissenters.

The ministerial class within these movements has appeared to hanker after specialist functions, and not to have been content simply with a gradually more elevated intellectual status. The ministries of the Free Churches came increasingly to emphasize their educational qualifications. Parity of esteem with other denominations has certainly been one factor inducing Free Church ministries to elevate their own role in relation to their lay members. As theological knowledge has ceased to be regarded as socially very important or interesting knowledge, and as advanced theologians have made their reputations more by the abandonment of traditional views than by their reassertion, thus accepting assumptions of the 'progress' of intellectual disciplines which prevail in secular subjects, so the ministry have come to seek other validations for their role. One of the most attractive to them has been the irreducible performance of essentially religious functions. As theology appears to have become bankrupt, so liturgy has burgeoned. The Churches have steadily returned to a stronger liturgical expression, the elaboration of the artistry of worship, even though they have simultaneously grown less certain about the nature, the history and the morality of the deity who is worshipped. This has been essentially a movement among the priesthood rather than among the laity, and it has been a development which has manifested itself in a wide range of denominations, many with traditions of a very contrary kind. The dissenting ministry have found for themselves status-enhancing functions by restoring forms and expressions of worship which are very much more ritualistic and very much 'higher' in their assumptions than those of their forebears or their lay followers.

The new movement to churchiness is clearly the expression of a number of forces. It expresses the attenuation of protest and the loss of historical identity among the laity of the denominations, who often persist in commitment for community and family rather than for well articulated ideological and intellectual reasons. It is a movement which coincides well with ecumenicalism – as the overtures are made by larger Churches to smaller denominations, so the semblance of forms of worship closer to those of the higher Churches facilitates conversations towards union. The sense of professional identity which Nonconformist ministers come to enjoy by fuller liturgical practice enhances their status by acquisition of greater parity with colleagues in Anglican and Catholic Churches. It restores personal self-confidence in a world in which religion is under attack and in which the minister must have become increasingly anxious about the way in which he is evaluated in society at large. It is a compensation for the relative loss of income (in comparison with other professions).

Thus what are for the ministry largely professional reasons overcome the resistance of the laity – a resistance which, it must be conceded, is often more associated with essentially communal feelings about churches and chapels and even denominations, rather than something which is grounded in a strong sense of historical distinctiveness. The liturgical movement is clearly part of the process in which the Churches are driven steadily back to the role of gratifying the demand for emotional expression, to the function of catering institutionally to emotional needs. Whether modern man has emotional demands which can be adequately expressed in religious terms, whether his emotions do not now manifest themselves in quite other – though not necessarily more satisfactory – social forms, and whether Church liturgies can now be more than a mere 'going through the motions' remain open questions.

What does appear is that the dissenting movements of Protestantism, which were lay movements, or movements which gave greater place to laymen than the traditional Churches had ever conceded, pass, over the course of time, under the control of full-time religious specialists. Thus, it is not only that second and subsequent generations of dissenters lose something of the fire of protest. It is not only that the children of rebelling parents become somehow 'conformist' within the terms of the movement in acquiring as 'received truths' ideas which their fathers had to struggle to assert. It is not only a loss of the historic circumstance in which protest had meaning, and was a sufficient concern for the direction of one's life and its purpose. It is very much more that, over time, movements which rebel against religious specialization, against clerical privilege and control, gradually come again under the control of a clerical class.

This is not to propound an ecclesiastical version of Michel's iron law of oligarchy. It is rather to recognize that the movement against religious specialization succeeded in divesting priests of real social power, and in destroying the mystical and magical forces which they manipulated, whilst at the same time it could not, in the long run, succeed in preventing the re-emergence of specialists. Professionalism is a part of the wider social process of secular society, and so even in anti-clerical movements professionals re-emerge. Their real power, when they do re-emerge, however, is in their administrative control and the fact of their full-time involvement, and not in their liturgical functions, although these will be regarded as the activity for which their authority is legitimated.

Liturgical specialization in the new development of sacramentalism becomes the basis of the new claim not only to authority, but also to status, with the added advantage of the weight of tradition behind it. Since society is more secular, and religious movements are increasingly clerical in their authority structure, laymen are now more effectively led by the 'experts' who necessarily re-emphasize the internal aspects of religious practice and religious organization, since their own wider social functions have been shorn away. The great lay figures of the Free Churches no longer appear, and so the denominations become increasingly concerned with liturgy, ecclesiology, Church property, and the professional status of the minister.

Thus the clerical class, in a secular society, cannot enjoy the social influence and privileges of priesthoods of the past: its writ does not run into the affairs of the wider society. But it has retained, like the parson's freehold in the Anglican tradition, an area for its own professional competence, and, in the case of the Free Churches, it has wrested this area back from lay control. In this case the clerical professionals have become the custodians of religious values which were themselves once laic values and, in assuming this responsibility, they have inevitably reinterpreted the character and mission of the movement to which they belong, and have returned to the more traditional preoccupations of religious specialists – the narrow concerns of the priestly role, the administration of church affairs and the assertion of distinctive competences.

These traditional competences are not now bolstered by any extensive demand for priestly mediation in the secular affairs of life. Indeed religion is generally regarded as circumscribed in its use and efficacy even by the religious. But precisely as clerics have lost the moral, social and pastoral aspects of their former role, so we can understand why there has tended to be a greater stress on their distinctive liturgical competence. The cleric who has seen his expertise in social matters, in moral matters, as a counsellor, as a therapist, as a teacher, steadily taken over by others has obviously needed the reassurance of a special area which no other profession was likely to appropriate in the light of more modern knowledge. Thus the most ancient function of all, and the one which cannot be technologized or modernized, becomes the one to which clerical professionals return. It does not even need the general ideological support of dogma – the liturgy exists, and maintains itself for itself. And this rediscovery of the indispensable priestly function by the ministers of movements which arose in a spirit almost of anti-clericalism, has led inevitably to a wider understanding among the priests of these movements and those of older established Churches. As the doctrinal issues of protest have been forgotten a new ecumenical spirit has ridden in on the tide of restored interest in the residual liturgical function of the priest.

It would of course be going too far to suggest that the ecumenical movement was solely a response to the changing role of the ministerial profession in the modern world; there are other circumstances which have encouraged ecumenical trends. One of these has been the changing extent to which religious movements are amenable to rational organization, and this factor has had its consequences very much more among the ministerial professionals than among the laity. As long as religious movements relied on immediate spontaneous voluntary support, or on the coincidence of territorial and spiritual divisions in society, so they could base their operation on existing social organization, much of it spontaneous and unplanned. But as religion has increasingly operated in a society both secular and pluralist, so the possibility has diminished that these almost 'natural' divisions would be sufficient for the organization of religion. In the modern world religion has had to compete with all sorts of other agencies seeking the time and resources of men, and particularly in America, but also in Britain and other European countries in which there is any significant degree of denominationalism, the Churches have increasingly adopted the same style of operations and similar methods of organization as the large concerns of business, education and recreation in modern society.

Despite the difference in the ultimate 'commodity' offered, this has meant that Churches have become more like their secular counterparts, and have evolved similar agencies of control and operation. In consequence the religious experts who were once, at least nominally, and sometimes actually, most concerned with the service of God have increasingly come to serve the organization. Administration has in some measure superseded spirituality, and rational business organization has replaced the distribution of grace or the reception of divine inspiration. The process has gone furthest in America, and inevitably the clerical class has been most drawn into this process.

This type of organization has made it apparent especially to these professional men of religion that where many denominations exist rational organization is often lacking. The accountancy system of business comes to be applied to religious activities and to religious property. If the Church has not yet attempted to impose 'time and motion' studies on clerics, it has none the less gone some way in this direction, by recognizing what might be called 'the wastes of competition'. When several denominations maintain large premises close together, duplicate administration, services, printing houses, missionary endeavour, fund-raising, prayer meetings – and each, often, with surplus capacity in terms of seating, and other facilities – then it becomes increasingly apparent, to men used to the rational economic thinking of the modern world, that resources are under-used. There is a new pressure for ecumenicalism from the argument for the better use of facilities. The new administrators of the Church, sometimes trained in the methods of modern business as much as in the theology of their denomination, begin increasingly to see possibilities for organizational change the only hindrances to which are the particular differences in belief and religious practice between denominations. The specific ideals for which denominations arose are then surrendered for the more rational use of resources, and for the greater convenience of administration.

There can be few human activities on which rational planning, administrative co-ordination and the regulations of bureaucratic organization have such deleterious effects as religious movements. For the demand for rationality is capable of transcending the specific religious ethic and distinctive faith of movement. We have referred to this development in the American Baptist Convention, which has steadily compromised its Baptist belief that God speaks to the individual and to the individual congregation. Having a congregational polity, divine inspiration was always regarded as necessarily local, God in the community of gathered saints. But as agencies to take care of evangelization, home missions and fund-raising at national level have evolved so it has acquired new departments at headquarters, and these departments necessarily take decisions and subscribe to activities for which there is no traditional justification in terms of 'spirit leading'. The typical denominational organization of government – the conference – has superseded the local church in the dictation of Baptist activities. A central agency of direction, itself increasingly dominated and influenced by the specialist departments of the movement, now really decides what Baptists shall do. The guidance of the individual heart and the separate community by the Spirit has been replaced by rational bureaucratic organization. Trends of this type are evident in all large religious movements, and because the clergy all increasingly share this modern rational economic spirit this in itself fosters ecumenicalism. As the Churches lose the security of acceptance and dominance in communities, and as they reorganize themselves for more centralized control of their resources, so the character of their operation changes. Economic rationalism becomes one important strand in ecumenism.

9
The Ecumenical Implications of Christian Expansion

IT would be incorrect to think of ecumenicalism as either a response simply to the changed circumstances of the ministry, or to the implications for the Churches of their use of new patterns of organization. Two of the propositions we have been examining are: that the pristine values of religious movements are steadily attenuated over time, including the tendency of minority protest movements gradually to adopt the values of the dominant organizations from which they originally separated; and that amalgamation and alliance occur when institutions are weak rather than when they are strong.

The growing weakness of the Churches has been either in their numerical support, or in the vigour and distinctiveness of their message, or both. The protest is weakened as the circumstances of the protesters (or their descendants) change: without the social basis for protestation the ideological position is insufficient to command intense allegiance. Institutions lose distinctiveness, and there is increasing conformity to the expectations of the wider society. In the mass-society conformity grows and moral rigour diminishes. Such diversity as exists, does so in a much less socially structured way, within a range of individual choices offered by persuasive agencies. Among religious movements, especially as generational transmission of religious commitment diminishes, the idea that different denominations represent diverse facets of the same truth grows.

Characteristic of the changed mood is that of the Committee of Anglicans and Presbyterians:

... we have renounced, and believe that the Churches concerned should renounce, the method of selecting and measuring such faults and errors in the past history of the Churches ... as might be judged to be responsible for our present divisions. ... mistakes have been made on both sides and ... over the generations attitudes tending to bitterness and strife have been not infrequent, but the time has come when the voice of mutual recrimination should be silent.

It is now urged that

... each separate communion, recalling the abundant blessing of God vouchsafed to its ministry in the past, should gladly bring to the common life of the united Church its own spiritual treasures.[1]

The language of condemnation and of mutual approbation must strike those used to less evaluative disciplines than theology as curious. Division, apparently, must be a matter of blame or of error, not a matter of the perception of truth, or a fact about what different parties took as the values in a given situation.

In examining some of the causes of ecumenical dispositions, it becomes evident that a number of Churches have for a time, and some are still, in the role of a Mr Facing-Bothways. The long process of discussion for reunion among the different divisions of Methodism in the last years of the nineteenth century occurred among movements which had mutually exclusive opportunities before them.

The New Connexion, as the oldest division to break away from Wesleyan Methodism, looked simultaneously to the Wesleyans and the Bible Christians in the later years of the century – although the two represented extremely

1. *Relations between Anglican and Presbyterian Churches*, London, S.P.C.K., 1957, pp. 7 and 12.

different wings of the movement which could certainly not then have been reconciled with each other. And the Wesleyans themselves, in the early inter-war years of the twentieth century were troubled lest a union with the Primitive Methodists and the United Methodists might make them into a body further removed from the Church of England, towards which, even then, some Wesleyans were inclined. Similarly, in the period following the Second World War the Church of England has made gestures to Methodists with their large element of lay preaching, and to the Presbyterians with their elective system, as well as to the Church of Rome.

Each Church must move cautiously. Always there has been anxiety lest a Church leaning towards another, might split its own following. It was after the famous Kikuyu affair in 1911 that Archbishop Davidson's judgement on this dilemma became so celebrated in words attributed to Mgr Knox. At Kikuyu there had been a missionary conference in which Anglicans, Presbyterians and Methodists had participated. After a successful occasion of co-operation the Bishop of Mombasa had celebrated Communion among those present. Opinion in England had been sharply divided. There were Anglicans who were delighted to see the spirit of ecumenicalism and Christian brotherhood given such practical demonstration. There were others who were appalled to think of the sacraments administered simultaneously to those in the Church and those outside it. The Archbishop was called upon for a judgement of Solomon, and pronounced it by declaring in effect that whilst the events at Kikuyu had been most pleasing in the sight of Almighty God, they must under no circumstances occur again.

That such ecumenicalism should have expressed itself in Africa – and in India – rather than in London, at the periphery rather than at the centre of the movement, is not surprising. There are special circumstances in the mission field which tend to make denominational differences seem less significant. Just as historical development – the changed temporal context – diminishes these differences and accelerates the attenuation of protest, so adjustment to different geographical contexts has similar consequences. Despite the initial competitiveness of missions, and the antagonisms arising from that, 'gentleman's agreements' about pagan territories and the souls of those to be saved in the territories, were a fairly early development. Once the immensity of the task of evangelization was seen in the appreciation of the size of pagan populations, and once the difficulty of Christianization was appreciated, the puny character of the resources of the missions – despite regular voluntary donations, and weekly prayer – became apparent.

The wastefulness of competition, increasingly recognized at home, became especially evident in the mission areas, where the harvest was certainly abundant and the labourers, who often fell victim of tropical climates and diseases, were certainly few. Competition, given the possibilities, became unnecessary. But more than this, since the missions faced similar problems, encountered similar resistance, similar perplexity, and had to evolve responses to local social customs – polygyny, female circumcision, puberty rites and the belief in witchcraft – which were equally alien to them all, so they had more to gain by cooperation and association than by mutual hostility. Since, too, in each mission field, missionaries no doubt welcomed discourse with fellow Europeans – even those who were religiously misguided – environmental circumstances induced a degree of association which might not have been easily possible elsewhere. In the strange new world, confessional peculiarities lost their distinctiveness: against the contrast with the pagan and the forces of evil, differences among those 'on the Lord's side' paled.

Just as the problems facing a denomination at home might involve it in the development of new agencies to meet new social circumstances, some of which were rather counter to its ecclesiological assumptions, so mission problems demanded solutions with similar consequences. Even as early as 1872, one C.M.S. missionary at the first General Missionary Conference in India, at Allahabad pointed out the trend. He saw how the missionaries of the Congregationalists were in effect bishops in the degree of local power they enjoyed, and he commented that they could not get on without a Union – both of them things contrary to pristine Congregationalist ideals about Church order. At the same time he likened the Church Councils of the (Anglican) Church Missionary Society to Presbyteries in their operation, although Presbyteries were not at all part of the Anglican tradition.[1] The Congregationalists became increasingly conscious of the limitations of Congregational polity in the mission field. In a culture entirely unused not only to the ideological aspects of Christianity, but also to many of the forms of polity which it had evolved, it is not surprising that the democratic implications of Congregationalism as it had grown up in seventeenth-century England should be an inadequate vehicle for the expression of Indian Christianity. In practice what occurred was that local missionaries gained far more informal power than they would have enjoyed normally in a Congregationalist Church, and so a practice of pragmatic rational authority evolved of a type perhaps not dissimilar from that which

1. Rev. J. Barton, *Report of the General Missionary Conference held at Allahabad, 1872–3*, pp. 300 ff., cited by Bengt Sundkler, *Church of South India*, London, Lutterworth Press, 1954, pp. 23–4.

grew up in America among the Baptists.[1] Essentially it was a response to the exigencies of a situation; to meet it the preferences of an established ecclesiological position which was in itself fundamental to Congregationalism were ignored.[2]

In the missionary situation, too, and particularly in countries like India or Africa, the assumptions of Christian exclusivism were curiously alien. Polytheistic religious systems are usually hospitable to the cults of new deities, who can be readily accommodated in the pantheon. There are diverse and incoherently distributed orders of priesthood, and a new priesthood with a new ritual and a new god is not a matter for anyone's special concern. The new cult does not detract from the old and is at most a competitor for time and resources of the lay votaries, and not to be stigmatized as a heresy. With this absence of ideological exclusivism was associated organizational pluralism, and a certain voluntaryism of religious activity. But Christianity did not accept accommodation to an existing religious situation of this kind. In the Christian tradition and despite the new ecumenism which did not yet extend to non-Christian systems, one religion eliminated adherence to another. Allegiance to one organization and participation in its affairs demanded withdrawal from others.

This disposition of Christianity must have been strange and difficult for local converts, but even more difficult must have been the appreciation that these attitudes were not only relevant in relation to, for example, Hinduism, but were equally applicable between the various different Christian groups themselves. The divisions existing between them were difficult to interpret in the new con-

1. P. M. Harrison, *Power and Authority in the Free Church Tradition*, Princeton, Princeton University Press, 1959.

2. Bengt Sundkler, op. cit., p. 39.

text, and the reasons for their separatism even more so. Indian converts could not be expected to appreciate these differences except in terms of their own social divisions, and these were certainly not applicable to the Christian denominations missioning among them. A Presbyterian missionary wrote in 1904, 'The future historian of the Christian Church in India will find many things to puzzle him – that Christians in Gujerat called themselves Irish, that others in the Central Provinces were Scottish Original Seceders, although they have never been in Scotland, were in no sense original and knew nothing about secession.'[1] What added to the perplexity of local converts was, of course, the difficulty of remaining in association with the 'right' missionary group when they moved from one area to another. In India, as in Papua (as reported by Neill)[2] and in other missionary territories, the divisions between missions became meaningless if the local population was normally mobile or increased in its mobility. Passing to other areas, the question arose, whether they could be ministered unto by the ministers of other confessions. This was yet a further pressure towards the growing ecumenicalism at the fringe.

Finally, and the missiologists themselves recognized the importance of this factor, in societies in which there were the first stirrings of nationalism the western religious movements were inevitably caught up in the development. In some ways those converted to Christianity had to establish to their compatriots that having accepted an alien religion they were none the less not to be identified with colonialists and foreigners. They had to prove themselves to be as devoted to their nation as were those who

1. J. M. Macphail, Conference, May, 1904, p. 22, cited in B. Sundkler, op. cit., p. 36.

2. Stephen Neill, *Anglicanism*, Harmondsworth, Penguin Books, 1958, p. 378.

accepted their traditional religious heritage. In India the very limited nature of Christianization imposed this upon Christians even more than in Africa, where traditional religion was not a tradition which nationalists could very easily invoke – despite some belated attempts to do so by some Pan-Africanists in the 1960s.

One manifestation of the new Christian nationalism, in all the mission territories, was the aspiration of Christians to have their own regional or national Church. The movement arose quite early in India, even before the beginning of the twentieth century. Such a national Church would necessarily have to be forged from the adherents of different missionary movements. Thus what represented an indigenous movement in the territory concerned became an exogenous pressure on Christianity to come to terms with the local situation in which national politics were more real than the old Christian divisions transplanted from Europe and America. The expansion of Christianity was thus in itself a process which, quite without regard to doctrinal truth of particular confessional positions, prompted the denominations to come together. The circumstance demanded compromise, and ecumenicalism was certainly that. As in all compromises not all of those who bargain make equal sacrifices or enjoy equal benefits. In the process some traditions must be lost, and some causes must be surrendered. The surrender arose in response to the situation, rather than from immediate conviction, even though this is what those who have canvassed ecumenism have rarely wished to acknowledge.

In some ways the development of ecumenicalism in remote geographical areas had been somewhat foreshadowed by evangelism even in home missions, in the interdenominational revivalism which had been a feature of nineteenth-century Christianity, especially in America.

The revivalists had, perhaps necessarily, emphasized certain simple and fundamental principles of their evangelical sort of Christianity. They had emphasized the issues indispensable to salvation and they had been unconcerned with the more subtle matters of denominational theology and ecclesiology. They were usually not immediately involved in any organization and could be indifferent to matters of Church order. They were generally suspicious of institutional religion, Church formality, which they saw as opposed to experimental religion. They brought Christ in regardless of the faint colourations of denominationalism.

The revivalists drew people from various backgrounds and they came in effect to reduce the significance of denominational divisions. They often sought to maximize their own semi-charismatic appeal by reducing all the distinctive status differences among their auditors. The revivalist was likely to be more successful if he could divest his hearers of their external statuses and affiliations. The technique is well known to the political leader of mass-movements, but it was used much earlier in revival movements. The revivalist hymn summarizes exactly what the mass-persuader requires to win maximum response from his audience:

> Just as I am without one plea
> But that thy blood was shed for me,

What more effectively could eliminate denominational distinctiveness?

Thus it was that in this evangelical revivalism there was a certain latent ecumenism, a latent assumption of Christian unity – not by amalgamation of organizations and hierarchies, but as a more radical individual approach to the primary religious experience. Evangelicalism was, of course, somewhat marginal – and with time increasingly so – to the settled congregations of cultural Christianity. No less than the missioning in overseas territories, it was at the fringe of the mainstream. But it did result in a new united impetus for the evangelical Churches and tended to sharpen the focus of their shared divergence from the growing force of sacramentalism.

Especially towards the end of the century men of different denominations came together in the development of a new evangelicalism with a much stronger emphasis on the affective aspects of religion in the development of the idea of Holiness, and its expression in the revivalism of Moody and Pearsall Smith, and in the Keswick Convention.

Another marginal area in which there arose the inter-denominationalism which was to pave the way for a more thoroughgoing and doctrinally justified ecumenicalism, was the new social preoccupation of Christianity. The rise of the Social Gospel in the United States in the latter part of the nineteenth century was in many ways an attempt to confront Christianity with the dire social problems which even denominationalism, with all its diversity of social class correlation, was failing to meet. In a rather different way the development of the Y.M.C.A. and subsequently the S.C.M., were both stepping stones towards the increasing association in good works at the social rather than as yet at the religious level of those who still remained doctrinally apart. The Parliament of Religions at the Chicago World Fair in 1893 had put religious organizations on some sort of common ground which was at once shocking and exhilarating, and perhaps the challenge which was then felt at the impact on modern Christian society of the Ramakrishna movement and other Eastern cults, may have moved many Christians towards a mental closing of the ranks.

The growth of local Councils of Churches, which

occurred both in Britain and the United States in the early years of the twentieth century, was a first response of the Churches to the problems they encountered in a changing society. Co-operation in a range of goodwill undertakings, and a broad recognition of some generally common dispositions among many important points of doctrinal and organizational difference, was the attitude which prevailed. Among English Nonconformists there had been longer co-operation to meet common problems, particularly in the field of education. The Protestant Dissenting Deputies were an early, if tiny, manifestation of co-operation between denominations to meet joint problems: they were the delegates of Presbyterian, Congregationalist and Baptist congregations 'in and within twelve miles of London' who were 'appointed to protect their civil rights'; and their common enemies were the state and the Established Church.[1] That eighteenth-century manifestation of denominational cooperation was a small beginning arising from a common circumstance of adversity. In the 1890s the Free Churches in England established a National Council, and later a Federal Council. The co-operation of the Free Churches was, of course, never easy, since they subscribed frequently to congregational polity, and denominational control was itself a strange and not altogether acceptable idea, even at the end of the nineteenth century, among Baptists and Congregationalists.

In the course of time these councils became more concerned with religious association rather than with association only in local good works. The amalgamations which occurred in Britain were frequently between Baptists and Congregationalists, each with strong traditions of local autonomy. The association was less dominated by clerical

1. On this see, Bernard Lord Manning, *The Protestant Dissenting Deputies*, Cambridge, Cambridge University Press, 1952.

considerations, than by the relative weakness of each movement in new areas of settlement. Theological considerations were set aside: Baptists, who traditionally believed that believers' baptism was an indispensable condition of Church life, and Congregationalists who did not, agreed to make what had been prescriptive simply permissive. Some of these unions were of particular parties within the different denominations, for the creation of distinctly evangelical Churches which were prepared to receive ministry from preachers of different denominations (usually Baptist, Congregationalist and Methodist) provided only that they stressed the emphatically evangelical aspects of religion.

In the United States the local community Churches were often more broadly based. Since the end of the First World War such Churches often became a shared response to population changes, to the abandonment of downtown areas, and to the creation of new suburbs. Their loss of denominational distinction and their concentration on organizational efficiency has not always met with the enthusiasm of all American churchmen. The tendency of some of these Churches to engage in shallow activism, community fund raising, pot-luck suppers, without realizing the significance of personal ties, has met with sharp criticism.[1] This, however, might be the cost of ecumenical endeavour.

Developments at the periphery – in the mission field and at local level – had consequences for denominational headquarters. The Churches were drawn into consultation with each other, and even movements without much central authority and with some theological resistance to its development, found themselves accrediting representa-

1. See Gibson Winter, *The Suburban Captivity of the Churches*, New York, Doubleday, 1961; Lyle E. Schaller, *Planning for Protestantism in Urban America*, New York, Abingdon Press, 1965.

tives and delegates, who, if they were to meet other denominational representatives on equal terms, had increasingly to be given more power. The attempts at revivalism in the late nineteenth century brought those of different denominations increasingly into association among the more evangelical movements that were in any case least committed to particular ecclesial arrangements, in their emphasis that acceptance of Jesus was all that really mattered. Similarly, the social enterprise of men in different denominations tended to bring them together despite theological differences. The Social Gospel in America, Christian Socialism in England, and even the social work activities of the Salvation Army, were all signs of new dispositions which were capable of ignoring denominational barriers. Even so anti-sacramentalist a movement as the Salvation Army commanded widespread recognition for its social work, and even led to conversations – albeit abortive – for the Army's association as an 'order' of the Church of England.[1] Thus the heathen overseas and the changing recognition of social problems at home were both precipitating circumstances in the promotion of the ecumenical movement.

1. On the Salvation Army see K. S. Inglis, *Churches and the Working Classes in Victorian England*, London, Routledge, 1963.

10

Ecumenicalism and the Denominations

THE first ecumenical developments in England were the reunions of the different branches of Methodism. The creation of the United Methodist Free Churches from the two schismatic movements, the Wesleyan Methodist Association and the Wesleyan Reform Movement in 1857 was the beginning. Throughout the latter half of the nineteenth century the prospect of a reunited Methodism was frequently before the minds and the conferences of the different denominations of the movement in Britain, split as it then was into half a dozen different sections. The process itself was largely a matter for the clerics in the movement rather than for the laity. The advantages of rationalization by amalgamation of local chapels, whilst often in the back of the mind of the architects of unions, could rarely be specifically promised because the strength of Methodism was essentially in the allegiance to the local chapel as much as to the specific denominational group within Methodism. Each new amalgamation was essentially a victory for the larger and more central organization over local autonomy. Whereas the process of schism in Methodism had generally brought into being movements which conferred more authority on laymen and reduced ministerial authority, amalgamation was generally towards a greater recognition of ministerial authority and away from the priesthood of all believers. It tended to be towards the norm of the dominant Wesleyanism rather than towards the more emphatic democratic practice of the United Methodists.[1] Despite the continued

1. Robert Currie, *Methodism Divided: A Study in the Sociology of Ecumenicalism*, London, Faber, 1968.

permission for authorized laymen to administer sacraments – one of the cherished rights of the Methodist schisms – the laying on of hands in ordination became a feature of the new Methodist Church after the final union in 1932. The development of elaborate liturgical forms further manifested the dominance of the Wesleyan party, with an increasing emphasis on the ministerial estate in Methodism and the diminished emphasis on lay activity.

In this development, however, Methodism has reflected a general trend within the Free Churches to return to a rather more sacramentalist and even sacerdotal position. Of the Congregationalists it has been said by one of their most respected authorities: 'In our own time we are in an age of sacramental revival (which we share with all other free churchmen) ... a movement towards higher forms of church music, more frequent Communion, and more dogmatically-based Baptism.'[1] He adds 'All this is very natural' but provides no reason why we should accept that judgement. The naturalness can be explained only in terms of the changing circumstances of Nonconformity and its increasing loss of social base in a society facing steady secularization, in which religion is becoming compartmentalized, and in which, in becoming marginal to the dominant social concerns, its internal divisions lose meaning and relevance. The situation parallels in so many ways that of the Christian missions at the fringe of Indian society. The establishment of the Church of South India was there the splendid union of a fragmented minority: the reunion of Christian Churches in Britain will not be entirely incomparable.

The whole direction of Protestant dissent in the days in which religion was a vigorous force, providing expression

1. Erik Routley, *Congregationalists and Unity*, London, Mowbray, 1962, p. 38.

for social and economic tensions, was away from the sacerdotalism and sacramentalist elements of the Established Church. Anglicanism itself was an expression of that, and the separatist Brownists, from whom the Congregationalists trace their descent, and the Presbyterians, took the process rather further. The Baptists, as a lower-class group, and the Quakers when they emerged in the seventeenth century continued the trend. Methodism cannot, certainly, be so readily seen in the same line of development, but Methodism was the reinterpretation of dissent as a revitalization of a different stratum of society at a different stage of its economic development, as it passed from a basically agrarian and trading society into an industrial society. In effect, and perhaps rather against some of Wesley's somewhat muddled aspirations for his movement, Methodism asserted its strong protest against the Established Church, and made of its meeting houses chapels. If they never completely eliminated some of the High Church ideals of Wesley, they at least overlaid them by folk practices which were a long way removed from what might be called in Redfeld's terms 'the Great Tradition' of the society.

The logical continuation of secularization begun in the historical dissenting denominations came not in Methodism, but in Unitarianism. Although largely an intellectual movement, and therefore a movement among clerics, Unitarianism became the application of the New Reason to religion. Unitarianism became the solvent of the last remnants of sacramentalism, and completed the 'demystification of the world' effectively begun by the early Lutherans and Calvinists – to trace its origins no further back. But Unitarianism took the process further. It made apparent the choice which was becoming increasingly evident, between religion and rationalism, between a mystic view of the world and belief in the intercession of God in human affairs, and the explanation of affairs in more scientific terms.

It is evident that in many respects the Nonconformist movements themselves are stages in a process of secularization of attitudes and orientations if not of actual immediate practice. They claimed less for religion, reduced religious authority, emphasized lay participation, demolished ascriptive status and mystical domination. They rejected supernatural authority except as it was individually apprehended or apprehended in the gathered community, and they rejected the institutionalization of what they saw (even if they now no longer care to affirm) as error and corruption. By making religion practical and 'everyday' they challenged the control of the Churches; they diffused an ethic throughout everyday life rather than maintaining an emotion in an institutionalized setting.

What, however, has become evident, is that in a society in which this process of secularization has gone further, the influence of the Nonconformists has been caught up and carried on if not yet to its conclusion, yet in the direction of a much more radical challenge to religious values than the challenge they enunciated. As life has been 'privatized' so the social functions of religion itself have appeared less necessary and have been less fully maintained. The demystifying tendency of the hardheaded Puritans, and the even harder-headed Unitarians, led to an attrition of the sense of the sacred in society. Once on its course this process was not held in check by the various attempts by the Churches to accommodate their message to changing social conditions. It was not checked by the disappearance of the crude social control of 'hellfire' and its replacement by a religion emphasizing joy, the love of God and personal fulfilment. As theological thinking was itself further affected by modernism and by a changed social environment, so it became apparent that society itself was becoming more secular than the Free Churches. It had received the message of these Nonconformist movements and Nonconformity had been part of the process of liberation from all religious pre-occupations.

As the cultural and social situation has changed, the Free Churches have been left occupying positions which are no longer so easily maintained as they were. The debate has passed them by, their posture has been petri-fied, and becomes decreasingly appropriate to the wider social scene. Their protest against the Church and their anti-ritualism are irrelevant. From a situation in which sacramentalism and sacerdotalism were the evil things, they have survived into an age in which secularization is the evil thing. Their balance once on the secular side against the sacerdotal now slips the other way. They now protest against the development and continuation of ten-dencies which had their beginnings in religious dissent. They are thus forced into a position of standing more with, than against, the Church from which they came out. Their mission has in some way lost its impetus, and the central ideology against which they held their distance has now itself become marginal in a radically changed society.

It is clear that on specific subjects – their acceptance of the need for reform of laws on homosexuality and abor-tion; their tolerance of divorce; their permissive attitude towards birth control – the Free Churches still retain freer access to the values of an increasingly secular society than does the Established Church itself. Their anti-sacramentalism of the past might now at least in part accord with the marginality of the sacraments in modern society, but it involves a more radical challenge to religion than the Nonconformists themselves would ever have envisaged or desired. So they are pushed into greater association with the Established Church. What was the stable measuring rod of their sense of separation has become their connecting chain. The barge-pole which kept the dissenting Churches separate from Anglicanism has become the boat-hook which will pull them together again. It is in this sense that the Nonconformists think of their sacramentalist revival as 'natural'.

The Free Churches now resist further secularization, they see in ritual a protection, a necessary and indispensable expression of religiosity. The whole process of rationalization to which their development gave expression would, were it pursued further, leave them uncertain what it was that they could be religious about. The Unitarians, who took the process furthest, have experienced precisely this, and it is no accident that it should be in this, most rationalistic of all Christian denominations, that the word Christian should have been dropped in the American title of the Unitarian movement. For the Free Churches, at least, worship is an irreducible. If one is committed to worship one has something about which to be religious and worship can be elaborated in the now re-emphasized liturgical forms. Reason is abandoned for the maintenance of practices which, whatever their justification, become the irreducible and necessary activities of religion. The strength of religion is in its dogma and in its arbitrariness, and this the Free Churches – formerly open, tolerant, amenable to reason – have now rediscovered. Thus a process of remystification of the world is almost necessary to them. Their plain old liturgies develop and are elaborated. The aesthetic appeal is added to the higher status and the centrality (within contemporary religious discourse) of more elaborate and traditional liturgical forms. So in all the Free Churches we see the growth of sacramentalism, the heightened authority and apartness of the minister, who increasingly approximates to the position of a priest of a Church of higher persuasion.

Just as the Church when faced by the development of modernism at the beginning of the century, finding that history and argument were difficult territories on which to ground the faith, returned with von Hügel and Dean Inge to a more mystical interpretation of its role and mission, so the Free Churches today have embarked on something of a similar process. In this they will, inevitably, be at some disadvantage. If ritualism is to be endorsed at all, it will always have more appeal where its historical continuity can be better demonstrated and where it sits more easily as a received – rather than a revived – tradition. But the process is seen as in some way a spontaneous thing, a new apprehension of God and the purposes of God, and – conveniently – it helps in the general development of ecumenicalism. The authenticity of Free Church sacramentalism may never be put to a test of its own, because it will not, perhaps, be a final resting place for the Free Churches. It will be, rather, a stepping stone on the way to reabsorption in the Established Church.

As it has become increasingly difficult to maintain a limited rationalism, a limited rejection of the sacramentalist and sacerdotalist aspects of traditional orthodox Christianity, so the arbitrary forms and rituals against which the dissenting Churches protested in the past have been reintroduced. If secularists could defeat religion by intellectual argument, by historical evidence, and more especially if the rational organization of the modern world could make religious communities appear anachronistic, at least the ritual practices, dogmatically supported, were a certainty.

Nonconformity in its Puritan form and even in its Methodist form (and the names 'Puritan' and 'Methodist' are themselves no accident) was the agency which helped in the re-socialization of whole generations towards the type of society in which rational responses would be appropriate and institutionalized. But as the whole society has acquired an increasingly impersonal, anonymous and intellectually controlled character, the Churches have found need to reassert the persistence of the emotional and communal functions which religion has traditionally fulfilled. Ritual has been the vehicle for this emotional satisfaction, the agency by which men are brought into contact with divine, inspirational and, often, aesthetic experience in a controlled and regulated way. Thus, it has been to the use of ritual that the Nonconformists have returned, as the point at which the quintessentials of religion can be preserved.

Just as the Anglican Church has steadily become higher in its rituals – and this is true even of the Low Church party within Anglicanism – so the Nonconformists have experienced a 'sacramental revival'. The process was already beginning at the time of the reunion of the three Methodist Churches in England in 1932. In large measure Wesleyanism swallowed the dissenting branches of Methodism, and although the right of lay administration of the sacraments was maintained, the more liturgical form of Communion practised by Wesleyans became more common, and the more liturgically controlled use of Morning Prayer was institutionalized. The status of the ministry was elevated. The expectation of many that the union would retard the drift of Wesleyanism towards Anglicanism and even towards Anglo-Catholicism was not realized; instead the union of 1932 allowed the process to continue and brought former Primitives and United Methodists into a movement much closer in mood to the Established Church than their own branches of Methodism had ever been.

Yet Methodism still necessarily maintains certain distinct differences in practice from those of Anglicans. The basis of fellowship is different, and the extent of lay involvement is still much greater than is characteristic of the normal Anglican parish. In a study of attitudes among leading lay people in Methodist and Anglican Churches in four widely separated parts of England, it has been shown just what these are that appear to be the hard core of differences between the two Churches at the present time.[1] The survey itself is clearly inspired in the recognition that so much of what goes on under the label of ecumenism arises from the convictions of clerics of different Churches talking to each other not in the language of their denominations, but in the common language of their profession. What the author suggests is 'it is lay people at the local level who will have to sort out where they stand'. And so he approached lay members of the Anglican Church Councils and the members of Methodist leader's meetings.

What this survey showed was that, as against 73 per cent of Anglicans, only 11 per cent of Methodists regarded Holy Communion as that part of Church worship which meant most to them. Some 60 per cent of the Anglicans considered that it should be taken once a week or even more frequently, whereas 75 per cent of the Methodists regarded once a month as often enough. The contrast here with the attitudes of a century ago, and the indication of the ritualistic drift, is evident when one recalls that Queen Victoria, no doubt reflecting something of Prince Albert's Lutheranism, regarded twice a year as appropriate – albeit with proper preparation for each of these occasions. Methodists revealed themselves in this survey as enthusiastic hymn-singers – a reputation they have often enjoyed with others, though not always one

1. David B. Clark, *Survey of Anglicans and Methodists in Four Towns*, London, Epworth Press, 1965.

mentioned with the fullest Christian charity: 89 per cent of them thought that this was an essential part of the Church service, whereas among the Anglicans only 54 per cent held hymns in this high regard. Whereas 89 per cent of Anglicans regarded the repetition of the creed together as essential, only 14 per cent of Methodists thought so. There were predictable differences of a similar order about how important it was to kneel for prayer, whether a choir should be gowned, and whether ministers should wear special dress. The Protestantism of Methodism was revealed in the fact that 81 per cent held that the sermon was essential to the service, against only 45 per cent of the Anglicans. (The sample had a rather less than representative number of distinctly 'Low' Anglican Churches among its total, otherwise this percentage might have been rather higher.)

On baptism, differences were no less emphatic. Some 78 per cent of Anglicans said 'Yes', and 61 per cent of Methodists said 'No', when asked whether baptism was essential to the process of becoming a real Christian. Whereas 68 per cent of the Anglicans in the survey considered that a layman should never administer the full Communion Service, only 32 per cent of Methodists thought so (a sizeable proportion in a denomination which reasserted this right of the layman in rather strong terms in 1946). On the ordination of women there were similar divergences: 71 per cent of Methodist men and an equal proportion of Methodist women were prepared to admit women to ordination, whereas only 46 per cent of the Anglican men and 37 per cent of the Anglican women wanted this innovation.

Despite these marked differences of attitude among some of the best informed lay people in the movements, such has been the propaganda for unity that most lay people regard talks by Church leaders as well worth while, even though they also recognized strong differences of attitude between themselves and their opposite numbers of the other Church. The people in the sample were asked which Church they felt had most in common with their own: 33 per cent of Anglicans chose the Methodist Church, but only 17 per cent of Methodists chose the Church of England. Of Methodists 33 per cent chose Congregationalists, and 20 per cent of Anglicans chose the Roman Catholic Church, but no Methodists chose the Roman Catholic Church. When the question of social ethics was raised, the Methodists revealed the strength of their commitment to religious guidance in daily life, which is so much more a characteristic of dissenting movements than of orthodoxy. More than three-quarters of the Methodists were prepared to express themselves as strongly disapproving of football pools, as against fewer than a quarter of the Anglicans; 57 per cent of Methodists but only 16 per cent of Anglicans disapproved of sport on Sundays; 79 per cent of Methodists but only 42 per cent of Anglicans strongly disapproved of bingo. On divorce there were again predictable differences with 44 per cent of Anglicans and 14 per cent of Methodists strongly disapproving of the marriage in church of divorced persons.

Whilst the evidence from surveys of this kind should never be regarded as more than an indicator – all attitude tests being subject to margins of error which investigators and computers rarely acknowledge – none the less the profile of response is firm enough to make evident the persistence of broad differences between the movements. Although Methodism has experienced a ritualistic revival, this has been largely a ministerial movement: the laity continues to nurture a sense of its dissent which is stronger than is acknowledged by its religious professionals. But it is the religious professionals who will hold the conversations and make the recommendations, and it is largely they who will frame and vote on the resolutions on unity, even in movements which, like Methodism, have a rather strong lay tradition. Certainly it is they who will make propaganda for union, and whose visits and interchanges will receive the endorsement of publicity by the mass-media. It is they who will prefer the sacramental revival, and who will find in ritual some objective activity which will be an exclusive (or near-exclusive) task which only the duly qualified and accredited will be permitted to perform.

The divergence between laity and clergy in their attachment to specific denominational patterns of worship, which we have noted between Anglicans and Methodists, appears to be reflected in the United States, in spite of the generally accepted superficiality of much religious commitment in American society. Lee cites a survey undertaken in preparation for a Conference on Faith and Order, which appears to have been conducted among clerics, concerning their views on the nature of the Church, the ground of salvation, the Person of Christ, and the sacrament of the Lord's Supper. Of the findings he quotes 'all the respondents could be included in the Methodist Church without increasing the diversity which is already represented by the Methodist Church. Ninety-four per cent could join the Lutheran or Presbyterian Churches without increasing the diversity in the views of the Bible which already exist in the clergy of these denominations. ... Four or five possible positions on the Lord's Supper are taken by Episcopal clergy, and these account for 96·4 per cent of the total responses.'[1]

1. Reported by Walter G. Muelder, 'Institutionalism in Relation to Unity and Disunity', in Paul S. Minear (Ed.), *The Nature of the Unity we Seek*, St Louis, Mo., Bethany Press, 1958, cited in Robert Lee, *The Social Sources of Church Unity*, New York, Abingdon Press, 1960, p. 85.

We may compare with this the findings of Glock and Stark, from a sample of lay members of churches in Northern California, which reveal marked differences between denominations. Unqualified belief in the existence of God was affirmed by 81 per cent of Catholics; 99 per cent of Southern Baptists; 81 per cent of Missouri Lutherans, 75 per cent of Presbyterians, 63 per cent of Episcopalians; 60 per cent of Methodists and 41 per cent of Congregationalists. An entirely similar pattern emerged from questions on belief in the divinity of Jesus and belief in the Virgin Birth (accepted by 81 per cent of Catholics; 99 per cent of Southern Baptists; 92 per cent of Missouri Lutherans, but only 39 per cent of Episcopalians; 34 per cent of Methodists and 21 per cent of Congregationalists). What emerged were distinctly different responses from various Churches which none the less are engaged in conversations concerning prospects of unity – Catholics and Episcopalians, and Methodists and Baptists. Glock comments, 'In the light of these findings it seems difficult to account for the hopes and activities directed towards general ecumenicalism.'[1]

Obviously there are similar spans of divergence within several movements, and considerable overlapping. None the less, what is also clear is that, if responses to questionnaires of this kind are really tapping seriously held convictions, there are also significantly different profiles of belief in different denominations, and that the divergences within are held in some specific denominational matrix of belief, practice and organization which do bear significance and meaning to lay members. A theologian like Dr Lee sees in the fact of diversity within denominations a ground to stress the similar ranges of difference in various denominations, but to see these beliefs in their wider

1. Charles Y. Glock and Rodney Stark, *Religion and Society in Tension*, Chicago, Rand McNally, 1965, Ch. 5.

ideological and social context, not merely for church professionals but for laymen who voluntarily accept them, might be to see ecumenicalism as less well supported by lay experience than by clerical aspiration.

Those concerned with ecumenism are especially preoccupied with priestly functions, ecclesiastical hierarchy and validity of ordinations. In an age when ideological and doctrinal differences are much less stressed, even by (perhaps especially by) the clergy themselves, the crucial aspects of Church unity are the questions of the degree of specialization of the priest, of differences in ritual practice, and in the organization of Church life, including the functions of the clergy the authenticity of their orders and the structure of ecclesiastical hierarchy. Thus in their conversations with the Methodists, the Anglicans necessarily insisted that they could not depart from the historical episcopate by which its clergy receive the precious gift of grace and authority which has come down through episcopal prayer and the laying-on of hands. Commenting on the Conversations some interpreted what the Report of the Conversations offered as the 'unambiguous ordination of the Methodist ministers by a bishop to the priesthood of the Church, explicit acceptance of baptismal regeneration and the Eucharistic sacrifice in terms to which no Anglicans (at any rate no Catholic-minded Anglicans) could object.'[1] Thus, whether they appreciated it or not, what High Anglicans held that Methodists would be receiving by this arrangement was *for the first time* ordination as priests in the Church of God. The former Archbishop had a different interpretation, but there can be little doubt about what Anglo-Catholics felt

1. Dr Mascall in a letter to *The Church Times* of 29 March 1963, cited in Lord Fisher of Lambeth, *The Anglican Methodist Conversations and Problems of Church Unity. Some Personal Reflections*, London, O.U.P., 1964, p. 22.

that Methodists would be surrendering in the acceptance of a Service of Reconciliation.

A noticeable confirmation of the extent to which ecumenicalism is a priestly rather than a lay movement is evidenced by the Anglican and Presbyterian conversations which occurred in the mid-1950s. The Anglican delegation of twelve consisted entirely of clerics (five of whom were bishops, one an archdeacon, and three of the remainder canons). The Church of Scotland delegation of twelve had only one lay elder among its number. The Episcopal Church of Scotland re-emphasized its title by including two bishops in its three delegates and the Presbyterian Church of England had three clerics among its four delegates. There were thus two laymen among thirty-two delegates, and this for conversations between four Churches two of which have equal representation of ministers and laity in the presbyteries and synods in their own internal Church arrangement.

The delegates were happy to discover that earlier conversations had established, in 1924 and 1949–51, the considerable doctrinal agreement between the Church of England and the Church of Scotland – this despite the gradual elimination of Calvinistic influences in the one, and their maintenance in the other over the course of centuries. Inevitably and explicitly the Churches decided not to discuss past faults and errors, so that whatever differences had existed in the past, the warranty of positions for which their predecessors had vigorously contended, were now easily and lightly abandoned, in the recognition of 'mistakes . . . made on both sides'. Earlier claims to exclusiveness were equally abandoned, and it was now conceded of Episcopalian and Presbyterian Churches that 'neither of them claim[ed] in its separateness to exhibit the whole truth and wealth of the One Church of Christ' whilst each claimed 'to possess gifts from the Head of the Church which it cannot in conscience deny or resign.'[1]

The conversations concerned themselves almost entirely with the problems of ecclesiology, so that even that section of the report entitled, 'Theological Considerations' was devoted almost exclusively to the ministry. Inevitably the conclusion was that episcopal, presbyterial and (nodding to the Congregationalists and perhaps the Baptists) the congregational systems must 'under conditions which require further study, have an appropriate place in the order of life of a reunited Church.' To this was added, 'that each separate communion, recalling the abundant blessing of God vouchsafed to its ministry in the past, should gladly bring to the common life of the united Church its own spiritual treasures.'[2] 'Each Church must allow the other a measure of freedom in interpreting the changes proposed, and seek itself to interpret them not in accordance with the *status quo ante* in its own tradition, but in accordance with the plenitude of order and practice in the enriched Church of the future.'[3] – This seems to be an invitation to establish procedures which will, as in the case of the Methodist and Anglican Service of Reconciliation referred to above, be capable of very different interpretation for each movement. It seems a strange way of negotiating, to insist that each party should be allowed to have a divergent understanding about exactly what is implied by a procedure to establish unity. Yet it is difficult to interpret the passage as other than an invitation to accept a procedure which will be open to different interpretation on the two sides.

Something of the same acceptance of diversity of interpretation is evident in the relations of the Anglican

1. *Relations between the Anglican and Presbyterian Churches*, London: S.P.C.K., 1957, p. 7.
2. ibid., p. 13.   3. ibid., p. 13.

Church with other bodies which claim, as some Anglicans do, the validity of their orders in terms of apostolic succession. In 1931 the Anglican Church entered into a relationship with the Old Catholic Church (which consisted of those Roman Catholics who rejected the doctrine of papal infallibility in 1870 and an older party of Dutch Jansenists). Each Church declared that it accepted that the other held all the essentials of the Christian faith. Since that time it has been customary for Old Catholics to be present at the consecration of bishops in the Church of England, and today it is rare that such a representative of the Old Catholic Church, or one of the other Churches in full communion with it, and with orders recognized as valid but irregular by the Roman authorities, is absent from an Anglican consecration. Of this circumstance Bishop Neill has written:

Probably about half the Anglican episcopate now has the Old Catholic as well as the Anglican succession, and before long this is likely to be true of the whole episcopate. If at any time the Roman Catholic Church wished to move nearer to the Anglican Churches [in practice almost any non-Anglican would interpret the movement as necessarily being the opposite of this – of the smaller body moving nearer to the larger] this might clear the way to happier relations. No Anglican imagines that anything is added to his consecration or ordination by Old Catholic participation; but from the Roman Catholic point of view, such orders might be held to have regained something of that regularity and validity which the Pope's Bull of 1896 denied to them.[1]

That the cost of ecumenism for the Free Churches is the

1. Stephen Neill, op. cit., pp. 373–4. The Bull referred to is the encyclical *Apostolicae curae*, 13 September 1896, in which the Roman attitude to Anglican ordinations was defined – that they were null and void. What this means for all the sacramental administrations which have gone on in the Anglican Church since the Reformation is of course a theological problem!

acceptance of episcopacy seems evident. The larger confession is always likely, in practice, to make fewer concessions than the smaller. In England the Anglican Church will undoubtedly set the tone. In 1950 the Report on *Church Relations in England* began with the basic question from the Archbishop of Canterbury, whether it would be possible for the Free Churches to take episcopacy into their own systems, thus taking one step forward towards a common ministry and common sacraments.[1] This, then, was the *sine qua non* for union. The demand is reinforced by the very diversity of the ecumenical gestures manifested by Churches in distress. The Anglicans although conducting negotiations with the Presbyterians and Methodists, have increasingly entertained ideas of some ultimate reassociation with the Church of Rome. At the very time when the 1966 Report on Anglican–Presbyterian conversations was published the Archbishop of Canterbury was in consultation with the Pope, despite the gulf which yawns between Rome and the spiritual descendants of John Knox. Since the Anglicans are looking to Rome as well as to Edinburgh and to the Methodists, they must be unwilling to make any significant compromise on the subject of the episcopate. Bishops-in-presbytery might be the way in which Presbyterians are encouraged to see the episcopate, and Bishops-in-circuit might be the emphasis for the Methodists, but for any conversations with Rome there will need to be a return to an emphasis on apostolic succession.

The ministers of the Free Churches are, as we have mentioned, generally disposed to a restoration of ritualism. We have noted, too, that the modern patterns of organization which the Church increasingly adopts create

1. From a sermon reprinted in G. K. A. Bell, (Ed.), *Documents on Christian Unity*, Fourth Series 1948–57, London, O.U.P., 1958, p. 48.

large areas of executive authority for particular departmental heads, even in congregationally organized
Churches. The Churches, in societies in which business-
take-over bids and mergers are a commonplace, are also
seeking to realize the 'economies of scale', and are coming to terms with rational bureaucratic administration and
planning. But the bureaucratic structure which is often
canvassed as the new model for the Churches may not fit
the traditional episcopal polity any more easily than it fits
the congregational polity. It must mean the gradual transfer of power from the spiritual heads of the Church to the
new class of administrators. Administration is a profession with its own values, and they differ from those of
religious organizations: administrators would require
payment on a scale rather different from that of the European Protestant ministry, and from the Catholic priesthood.[1] Administrators interpret their roles as specific,
instrumental and affectively-neutral tasks: the clerical
role is manifestly the opposite of this – it is diffuse,
effective and much of its activity (i.e. ritual) is for its own
sake, or at least for no specific empirical end.

It is possible, however, that in the short run, the significance of centralization may favour, as do all the other
circumstances, the growing dominance of the episcopal
over the non-episcopal churches. Grass-roots democracy
is not easily sustained in the religious context when other
social organizations are becoming increasingly bureaucratic, institutionalized and hierarchic. The increased
efficiency of centralized operation is too impressive in
modern society for spiritual organizations to withstand,

1. The Paul Report recommended a very extensive rational reorganization of the Church of England. See Leslie Paul, *Deployment
and Payment of the Clergy*, London, Church Information Office, 1964,
and for a comment, B. R. Wilson, 'The Paul Report Examined',
Theology, LXVIII, 536, 1965, pp. 89–103.

even though efficiency is not the appropriate criterion for them. The Methodists in Britain expected economic benefit from rationalization of their use of church premises. The union between the Congregationalist Christian Churches and the Evangelical and Reformed Churches in America in 1957, was expected to bring financial benefits in periodical publication, in the actuarial soundness of the pensions scheme (with increased numbers of clergy), and 'market opportunities and financial advantages which no businessman would deny.'[1]

What has also occurred in our society is that the clergy, in common with other professions, have become concerned about professional solidarity. Ecumenism will certainly benefit the ministerial profession, as we have seen. Already the signs grow that the clergy increasingly recognize their *professional* allegiance, and this, necessarily, at some cost to their *denominational* allegiance. Lee comments on the extent of the movement of clergy across denominational lines. He is able to show that from 1951 to 1955 the Presbyterian Church, U.S.A., received 372 ministers from other denominations, and lost 209 to other church bodies, and between 1950 and 1954 40 per cent of the ministers joining the Congregational Christians came from other denominations. Joint services, visiting preachers from other faiths, have become almost a commonplace in England in the mid-1960s. Members of Catholic religious orders are especially in demand to preach in Anglican churches.

The continuing emphasis on the divorce of material and spiritual values in the Churches (although in American religion they are seen as much less contradictory) has perhaps so far prevented the ministry of different denominations from too conspicuously comparing stipends and work conditions. The differences in status have, in the

1. A comment cited in R. Lee, op. cit., p. 120.

past, been an accepted part – sometimes a proudly accepted part by Nonconformists – of denominational commitment. Today the enhancement of status is perhaps one of the attractions of Church unity for the ministry of the smaller bodies whose polities will necessarily be abandoned when union takes place. The surrender of Congregational and Presbyterian polities will certainly mean a loss of lay influence. The Church will increasingly become the organization of its professionals, and they will be increasingly professionals emphasizing technical expertise and monopoly of sacramental functions. For the Nonconformists the merger would mean higher status, and for the Catholics (both for those within Anglicanism and for Roman Catholics if they were eventually part of such a reconciliation) there would be the reassertion of the authority of bishops and the centrality of the charisma and the sacramentalism which were challenged at the Reformation.

The Nonconformists might be induced to accept some role as an 'order' in the Church, with limited autonomy from, but ultimate submission to, the Archbishop or the Pope. The prospect has already been envisaged by an eminent Congregationalist, who has emphasized the traditional usage of the term 'Church' among Congregationalists to argue that in fact the denomination has never properly regarded itself as 'The Congregational Church' but has employed the term either for the universal Church of all believers or the local congregation itself. This argument then admits that the Church is neither exclusively congregational, nor are Congregationalists 'the Church'. They could, it is argued, therefore cheerfully regard themselves as simply an 'order' within the Church Catholic. The implication is, perhaps, that one day it might be an order within the Catholic Church.[1]

1. Erik Routley, op. cit., pp. 31–4.

This ingenious argument would need some amendment to suit the American case, where since 1957 the Congregational Churches have, as the larger body in a union with the Evangelical and Reformed Church, adopted the designation of United Church of Christ. The same argument might even appeal to Methodists. Long ago, Sidney Dimond, the psychologist of Methodist revival, tried to argue that Methodism was neither a sect nor a denomination, and clearly it was not 'the Church'; it was rather to be conceived of as an order.[1] Some modern Methodists might like it to return to that status, at least for the laity, while the ministry were absorbed as part of the professionals of the new united Church.

What must be recognized, however, interesting as the ecumenical movement may be, is that ecumenicalism, even at its most successful is not in itself a revival of religion, nor a reconversion of society. It is the turning in on itself of institutionalized religion, as its hold on the wider social order has diminished. The healing of divisions is something which restores the morale of churchmen – and in a secular society a larger proportion of churchmen are professional churchmen – in a period when the external influence of the Church is declining either in terms of numbers of Church supporters in the wider population, as in England, or in terms of Christian influence over behaviour and morality, politics, education and other institutions, as in the United States. The energy which churchmen have put into the ecumenical movement has been perhaps in rough proportion as they have lost hope of evangelization of the world. Essentially this has been a movement directed inwards into the life of the Church, not outwards into the wider society, which remains essentially unmoved by ecumenical achievement, and per-

1. S. G. Dimond, *The Psychology of Methodist Revival*, Oxford, 1926; idem, *The Psychology of Methodism*, London, 1932.

haps even rather suspicious of it. The laity who remain committed to their various denominations appear markedly less enthusiastic for actual assimilation with other bodies than do the clergy. Nor does ecumenism achieve much in the way of increasing the influence of reunited bodies. Currie has shown how reunions in Methodism, far from stemming the tide of falling membership, made no visible impact upon the rate at which loss occurred.[1] If compromise means the loss of distinctive purpose and particular commitment, it may also be that for those who remain something of their previous ardour will disappear. Ecumenism may be a policy not only induced by decline, but one encouraging decline.

The institutionalized forms of Christianity lose the commitment of the masses, and this appears true of England where Church numbers decline and America where they do not, but where Church teaching means less. That Christian belief persists in society in some residual way is not in dispute, and Christian teaching appears, from the figures assembled by Mr Argyle,[2] to be, despite diminished attendance, rather better understood in its rudiments in England than in the United States, as his citation of the following comparisons collected in different surveys, seems to suggest:

	Great Britain	United States
Church membership	21·6 per cent	57 per cent
Weekly attendance at church	14 per cent	43 per cent
Those who offered daily prayer	46 per cent	42 per cent
Those able to name four Gospels	61 per cent	35 per cent

There may of course, in the semi-compulsory teaching of religion in schools in England and its absence in America, be an easy explanation for divergences of this kind. But

1. R. Currie, op. cit.

2. Michael Argyle, *Religious Behaviour*, London, Routledge, 1958, p. 35.

whatever the specific explanation it is evident that Christianity has little specific grip on the population of the industrial nations.

In England the organized Church remains influential in different ways. It is strongly represented in the educational structure of the society. And, rather more important, the Anglican Church is still entrenched within national institutions. Its elaborate convocations still have a vestige of significance as national events, and its association with the functions of government and state ritual, give it influence out of all proportion to its active lay support. In terms of the needs of a society (which are not to be confused with the results of opinion polls, nor even of democratic elections) it is not to be lightly asserted that this is necessarily deleterious or inappropriate. It is, however, an influence of religion which does not immediately stem from the conscious choice of the public at large.

Despite the abandonment of the Churches by the people, most people in Britain, like those in America, confess a belief in God, and most of them can state this belief in more specifically Christian terms. What is apparent is that the Churches no longer cater for the emotional expression of men in society. Their answers to fundamental questions are seen by the majority to be intellectually deficient, and for most men what is intellectually discredited is not easily accepted simply because it is emotionally reassuring. The Churches themselves have, increasingly, sought to come to terms with the intellectual assumptions of contemporary society, and have themselves shown a diversified adjustment in terms of their insistence on the acceptance of particular beliefs. There has even been an increasing retreat from the moral sphere, with new 'permissive' attitudes on matters once seen as necessary subjects of social and religious imperatives.

Church unity could not but promote a further generalization of Christian commitment. The vestiges of denominational morality would necessarily be abandoned. Compromise would call for the surrender of distinctive moral and doctrinal positions. A wider tolerance of diverse moral and doctrinal opinion would be necessary. The attempt to encompass a wider and more diverse public, and to avoid unseemly schisms, would necessarily demand less specific and, as we have already seen, more ambiguous pronouncements, with latitude of interpretation. A church organization might be preserved, but much of the meaning of specific religious beliefs and their moral correlates would be abandoned to attain that end. Something of the vacuousness of American religion, as Herberg describes it, might be achieved in England – but without much likelihood that by its acceptance the majority of Englishmen would reaffiliate with the Church.

PART IV
THE SECTARIAN
AND DENOMINATIONAL ALTERNATIVE

11

The Origins and Functions of Sects

ALTHOUGH ecumenical tendencies dominate the contemporary religious scene in Britain, and are increasingly important in America, there persist a variety of movements within Christianity which manifest no immediate ecumenical disposition. These are the sects. Their response to the world is more intensely and specifically religious than that of the Churches. They have, in general, made much less compromise with the social order. They represent an alternative pattern of religious commitment in the secular society. They are themselves a feature of societies experiencing secularization, and they may be seen as a response to a situation in which religious values have lost social pre-eminence. It is in conditions in which the sacred order has been subordinated to the secular – usually the religious institution to the political institution, as in the Roman Empire or Europe from the sixteenth to the nineteenth century, or twentieth-century Japan – that sectarianism becomes most manifest and institutionalized.

They have played an important part in the development of Western society, and in this last part of the book, some attention must be paid to their description and analysis, and their relation to Churches and denominations. Sects are always somewhat exclusive bodies which impose some test of merit – of faith, knowledge of doctrine, obedience – on would-be entrants. They keep members under scrutiny and seek to regulate the pattern of their lives in particular ways. They normally have a procedure for ex-communicating the wayward and for ensuring the purity of the community.

Sects are normally lay movements, which practise their religion without an established professional ministry. They share, very often, the central functions among the senior members (in the Christian tradition, often exclusively among the senior male members) and they often condemn the employment of a special ministerial order. They are usually committed to a concept of the priest-hood of all believers, to mutual ministry of one man to the rest, or to the ministry of all men to the wider society, according to the way in which they interpret scripture. Where any sort of professional full-time ministry does exist in a movement which is generally regarded as a sect, its operation is usually closely circumscribed. It is usually not difficult to enter its ranks – whether that process is by technical instruction in the Bible and in evangelizing techniques, as in the sects which stand in the funda-mentalist scriptural tradition, or by ritual ordination, as in some of the essentially sectarian-style movements which emphasize sacramentalism and regard themselves as 'Churches'. In the former instances the status of the minister is not stressed. Indeed, the professional ministry is often seen as a mere convenience, and its activities and prerogatives are not a central subject of concern, as they clearly tend to be in Churches and denominations (as evidenced above in their central place of the questions affecting the ministry among the problematical matters in ecumenicalism).

The sect, then, tends to deny any sort of division of religious labour. Whereas the fully established Church accepts the legitimacy of differential commitment on the part of priests (and often of even more totally dedicated members of various types of religious order) and laity, the sect rejects any such distinction. All men should be equally committed, and commitment must be total. Whereas the Church accepts, and often endorses the cultural dispositions of the secular society, the sect usually condemns them, or at least withdraws from them. In the sect there are no conditions of greater and lesser sanctity, except as these are manifested in the individual's religious or moral performance. The sect rejects or regards as irrelevant the political arrangements of the wider society, whereas the established Churches come to legitimate the authority structure of the secular society, and frequently have acted as agencies of social control for political authorities. Whereas in the Church there is an objective institution which administers grace, in the sect there is a subjective fellowship and a participation in mutual love. The Church represents itself as a hierarchy, the sect as a community and a fraternity. Whereas the Church represents itself as the religious organization of the nation or the society, to which men are come at birth as members, the sect regards membership as an achievement, proved by one's capacity to live up to certain standards. The sect member both chooses and is chosen.

These distinctions between sect and Church were first made evident by the sociologists Ernst Troeltsch and Max Weber. They saw Christianity in particular as manifesting an inner dialectic between sect and Church, the struggle between spontaneity and institutionalism, between conformity and protest. Both tendencies have been manifested from the very beginnings of Christianity. In some ways it would appear that the Church itself has been assisted by the sect – prevented from becoming moribund and unduly corrupt by the recurrent protest of sectarian groups. The sects have represented the interests of particular strata which, for one reason or another, have felt themselves unaccommodated religiously and perhaps socially.

It is evident, both from the large numbers of sects which have arisen in certain periods of history, and from their diversity, that the common functions of sects for their members can be expressed in only the most general terms. But one of these functions has obviously been the heightened sense of commitment and distinctiveness which sectarianism implies. The members of the major Churches or denominations are often indistinguishable from one another in most of their secular concerns. They tend to be more characterized by their occupation, their education, or by purely personal dispositions than by their religious affiliation. But the sectarian is almost always conspicuous by virtue of his religious commitment. Whatever activity he is engaged in, the fact that a man is one of Jehovah's Witnesses, or a Christadelphian, or even a Quaker, tends to become evident sooner rather than later. This particular characteristic may often be associated with the intensity of sect life, of the drawing together of a community which is often small, and which usually demands a strong communal allegiance among its members.

The sect provides a context of social involvement which, quite apart from the specific advantages which the ideology offers to the faithful, demands responsibilities of a much more compelling kind than are found in most voluntary organizations, interest-groups, service agencies or welfare associations. The intensity of the bond may well be related to the fact that although most sectarian movements express concern for mankind at large, salvation is expected primarily for those who belong (even if theoretically other 'saints' outside the fellowship may qualify). Given the extraordinary degree of high-mindedness, public spirit within the community, and moral rectitude of many sectarians, it would be wrong to suggest that sect adherence gained its strength from enlightened self-interest understood in the very long-term view – for salvation is usually post-mortem, and sometimes not even immediately post-mortem. There is undoubtedly an appeal in terms of the prospect of salvation, but this is not in itself unmediated by a concern for rectitude, obedience, truth and the solidarity of the community itself. Even beyond these considerations, the consolation of the here and now prospect of salvation hereafter, may not be without significance in understanding the sectarian disposition.

Finally, the circumstance in which leadership roles are to be performed is of importance in many movements. The sect provides a total reference group for the individual who belongs, rather as the ghetto community provided such a group for eighteenth-century European Jews. Although the sectarian has some involvement in the wider society, and may indeed earn prestige there (especially in his economic activities, but sometimes also for his general moral behaviour) it is essentially within the sect that his status is re-evaluated and sanctified. Leadership roles are frequently important features of sect organization, at the informal level, if not at the level of formal sect structure. They may, indeed, be the more significant where no institutional leadership obtains. The sect provides a close context in which individuals can seek status, acquire power, exercise talents with the assurance that once they are socialized to the values of the movement and its expectations of them, they can receive recognition from the fraternity. So strong is this aspect of sectarian life, and perhaps of all community life in which bonds are tightly drawn and the boundaries well-defined and the demand for allegiance total, that there is little doubt that a principal cause of schism and disruption in sects is disagreement about power and status.

For groups that are religiously or socially disenfran-

chised, or whose aspirations are unconfirmed or unlegitimated in the general social order, sectarian commitment may be an appropriate substitute for all that they
believe that they forego. The sect affords a coherent
community organization, a stable pattern of order. It
provides norms and values which are indisputable. It
usually brings into being an actual fraternity in which
these values find expression and social application. It
legitimates particular aspirations, sanctions particular
modes of conduct, and usually draws into membership
those in similar social circumstances, of similar status and
with similar interpretations of the situation in which they
find themselves. The ideology of a sect welds it together,
but usually those who come forward already share a range
of social attributes which dispose them to at least some
salient features of organizational structure and ideological position of the movement they join. Those who
voluntarily associate with each other in a sectarian movement generally show considerable similarity of social
characteristics. Since men of diverse social circumstances
do not readily and voluntarily associate in any other types
of social organization (except where they are 'coercively'
drawn together, or stand in distinct and specified status
relations and authority relations) it would be surprising
to find them doing so in voluntary religious movements.

Sects display a wide range of doctrinal and organizational positions. Whilst most of the sects which persist
in contemporary Britain and America undoubtedly come
out of the fundamentalist Protestant tradition, there are
other groups of sects which emphasize very different
doctrinal positions, and some which imitate the order and
preoccupations of the major Churches. To a sociological
characterization of sectarian movements we shall shortly
turn.

Organizationally sects are hardly less diverse. Many, it

is true, attempt to establish themselves with a minimum of organization. They emphasize egalitarianism and the priesthood of all believers and, consequently, in rejecting the clerical profession, they also reject all formally instituted leadership positions. Since sects frequently reject, or disregard the status system of the wider society, they are ideologically opposed to the creation of distinctive statuses in their own organization. It can be asserted that the scriptures themselves provide very little guidance on church organization, and groups which pride themselves on the scriptural nature of their structure emphasize the early radical egalitarianism of the Church at Jerusalem, and regard the whole development of churchly offices as a manifest evidence of the corruption of the Christian Churches, and often of their ungodly nature.

In contrast are those sects which, started through the inspiration or the prophetic claims of a strong personality, have tended usually to evolve a much more elaborate, and more hierarchic authority structure. Thus the Mormon Church, which began in a distinctly sectarian way, evolved strong leadership roles from the distinctive claims of Joseph Smith to be the mouth of divine revelation to the Latter Day Saints. After his murder in 1844 the movement depended on the rigorous leadership of Brigham Young, and the whole elaborate hierarchy of lay priesthood which Smith had established. Christian Science, another movement which has many of the attributes of a sect, and which, in Europe, at least, is usually so regarded, has demonstrated since the very beginning emphatic leadership roles. Mrs Eddy was a woman who would brook neither criticism nor rivalry, and the early expulsions from her movement eliminated those who in any way challenged her authority. In her own lifetime, and especially in her declining years, Mrs Eddy established a complete bureaucratic structure for the control of the Mother Church in Boston, to which all other churches in the movement had to become affiliated as branches. The style of leadership roles in Christian Science are essentially those of business executives, rather than of religious leaders. The doctrine and social practice of Christian Science was definitively laid down by Mrs Eddy, and the Board of Directors operates essentially as a body of managers, not as prophets or as inspired leaders. At local level there is a similar absence of an ideological leadership, and the dominance of essentially business leadership in the church boards.

Movements which are called into being by a charismatic leader, almost inevitably continue to require the performance of leadership roles, and the charismatic leaders concerned tend to institute hierarchic structures even before their own disappearance from the scene. In such movements there is less emphasis on the equality of members, except perhaps in their common relationship to the original leader. There may be, and in western society there usually is, an emphasis on the opportunity for all members to achieve the positions of leadership in the movement.

Because charismatic leadership asserts itself by some special proclamation of truth, sects which begin in this way tend to be characterized by doctrines which differ considerably from the general Christian tradition. Their special teachings tend to be regarded as *necessary* for salvation (however salvation may be conceived) and as the special warrant of the movement. Thus both Mormonism and Christian Science, which were distinctly 'founded' religious systems have also distinctive teachings which deviate considerably from the Protestant orthodoxy out of which their leaders came. External circumstances somewhat eclipsed the distinctive charisma of Joseph Smith in Mormonism, and Brigham Young's part in the 'gathering of Zion' tended to alter the balance of emphasis from charismatic to pragmatic claims to leadership. None the less the original teachings remain.

Mrs Eddy also emerged in a society in which pure charisma was not easy to establish, but she succeeded in fixing her own doctrines securely on her movement and by procedures of a rather uncharismatic type – fixed by regulations and legal procedures, written into a Manual; the elimination of 'personality' from Church offices and their circumscription in the therapeutic practice of the movement – prevented any subsequent leader from ever challenging her posthumous charismatic claim. The Rev. Todd Ferrier played a simpler role in the Order of the Cross movement. Madame Blavatsky in Theosophy was, like her successor, Mrs Besant, perhaps less distinctly charismatic than magnetic. The emphasis on the realm of the arcane which might be explored, and the idea of an unfolding truth, were ideological positions which left open leadership roles, and which de-personalized knowledge in a way which restricted charisma.

The modern tendency of sectarian development, in fact, is one which leads away from charismatic leadership. It is increasingly difficult in the modern world for an individual to claim successfully to be the one messenger of the divine, to be a prophet with a special insight. Knowledge itself has to have a more objective quality, and to be capable of – or appear to be capable of – some type of rigorous scientific or semi-scientific testing. The new sect leader who stands outside the orthodox tradition increasingly accepts the model of teacher, or of *guru*. This is more the way in which man in the twentieth century expects to receive even religious truth. The more secularized society is more sceptical about personal claims to charisma, and the range of knowledge available even to simple men in modern society makes the claim to specialized knowledge, unavailable to the now institutionalized methods of investigation and inquiry, more difficult to sustain. Oracle and miracle, the stock in trade of tradition-al charismatic leaders, are less readily believed. And so it is that today the leaders of this type of new sect are con-strained to present knowledge which imitates the form and content of modern secular knowledge.

It is no accident that Mary Baker Eddy should have called her discovery Christian Science; nor that her organization and that of many movements which share the general orientation of Christian Science, should have 'teachers' and 'practitioners', have been taught in 'institutes', awarded 'degrees', be controlled by 'boards'. The cults of this type all claim to be systems of mind control, of healing, of insight which goes beyond the routinized formality of the modern world, modern know-ledge and modern organization. Yet they all tend to be organized in very much the same way as the institutions of the society in which they develop. Thus the very doc-trines which new movements proclaim often make the claim to distinctive charisma more difficult, since these teachings themselves tend to the rational or pseudo-rational. They affirm certain goals – success, health, wealth, longevity, happiness, personal freedom, mastery – and set themselves up as new means of attaining them. The goals are those which may be said to dominate the cultures of western countries, the dominant 'cultural goals' as Robert Merton calls them.[1] The movements of the type of Christian Science, Psychiana, Divine Science, Unity, Scientology, The Process, offer new non-insti-tutionalized means to gain these ends. But in doing so, they offer an objective system of truth which can be 'proved' by its results, and thus the room for the charis-

[1]. Robert K. Merton, *Social Theory and Social Structure*, Glencoe, Ill., The Free Press, revised edition, 1957.

matic claim of even the founder is somewhat diminished.

Mrs Eddy, spanning as she did the period in which old-style values and new ideals were emerging, arising in a new and still unsettled society, in which religious leadership was still part of a persisting tradition of revivalism, was able to combine the claims of the past and of the future, and to use religious terms such as 'atonement' and scientific terms like 'demonstration', in presenting her system. But the possibilities of asserting genuine charisma have diminished since her time. Even she found it hard to stand sufficiently far from her followers, especially in her earlier years, and many left her accusing her of being fond of money and of serious ebullitions of temper. Only in her later years could she attain the distance which charismatic leaders often find necessary to sustain their claims to wonder-working and oracular utterance. Her position in time allowed her to be the 'discoverer and founder' of a system which, however, in itself was held to be capable of being taught, learnt and applied rather like mathematics. Her charismatic claim, presented often in traditional terms – 'a woman clothed with the sun' – was confined to this discovery; thereafter the system itself must supersede its foundress. Since her time the charismatic leaders who have arisen in the Western world in the full sense of the term 'charisma' have been very largely confined to ethnic minorities, still shut out from the full effects of the growing rationality of modern economic systems – Father Divine and Daddy Grace among American Negroes for example.[1]

Within the tradition of more Orthodox Protestantism, no claim to charisma in the full sense of the word could possibly be admitted. The record of God's dealings with man is regarded as closed: no further prophets and no

1. For a reliable account see A. H. Fauset, *Black Gods of the Metropolis*, Philadelphia, University of Pennsylvania Press, 1944.

further revelations are expected. But in the debased sense in which sociologists often loosely employ the term 'charisma' the leaders of some dissenting movements in this tradition might be so regarded. However much they wrote or commented on scriptures, however, these leaders, in virtue of the tradition in which they stood and the appeal which they made, could hardly claim even as much as Mrs Eddy in their assertion of personal leadership.

Mrs Ellen White, nineteenth-century leader of the Seventh Day Adventists, had visions, and professed to know why the advent so keenly expected in America in 1843 by the followers of William Miller, had not occurred. But the revelations she received were all in terms of a reassertion of various scriptural prescriptions, concerning in particular the keeping of Saturday as the sabbath, and particular diatetic laws. But Mrs White was regarded only as 'a special guide'.

Dr John Thomas, founder of the Christadelphians, saw his own copious writings as merely a commentary elucidating scripture in terms of adventual problems. He refused to arbitrate on disagreements among his followers and his successor claimed for him no more than that his work was 'the application of a singularly constituted brain to the study of the holy oracles'.[1] Pastor Russell, whose writings established the Watchtower Truth Society, the International Bible Students, or Jehovah's Witnesses as they came to be generally known, was not particularly revered in his own lifetime, and has been virtually forgotten as the movement has passed under other leadership. His immediate successor Judge Rutherford, who was certainly given to dramatic pronouncements, hardly attained semi-charismatic stature, and after his death the

1. For an account of the Christadelphians, see B. R. Wilson, *Sects and Society*, London, Heinemann, 1961.

direction of the movement passed very much to a committee, of whom the Chairman, Nathan Knorr, has only gradually emerged even as a strongly identified personality. Much the same would necessarily be said of most other leaders of new sects – Alexander Campbell, who brought the Disciples (and the Churches of Christ) into being; or John Nelson Darby, the powerful leader of the Exclusive Brethren. It is true that General William Booth, the founder of the Salvation Army, told his leaders to obey God, and 'the General next to God', but his message was essentially in the scriptural tradition. He too, was no more than a leader, however powerful and energetic, who stood firmly on the scriptures.

Even those movements which emphasized the operation of charisma in the life of the Church, necessarily institutionalized it and consequently circumscribed the extent to which any individual could claim a unique commission to act as the mouthpiece of God. Edward Irving, the founder of the Catholic Apostolic Church, which sought to restore the offices of the Church which it derived from the gifts of the Spirit described in the Epistles, found that claims to power were widely distributed throughout his Church once the various offices of apostles, angels and evangelists had been distributed, and often he was himself subject to the charismatic utterances of others.

The later Pentecostalists of the early twentieth century from their disorderly beginnings in Topeka, Kansas, Chicago, and in the Asuza Street Mission in Los Angeles, found it more difficult to establish Church organization on essentially Pentecostal criteria. There was never any effective claim to leadership at anything more than local level on the basis of the charismatic gifts of the Holy Spirit within that movement. After their first enthusiasm, Pentecostalists quickly came to recognize that their particular teaching and practice was no more than an added blessing to the evangelical fundamentalist tradition in which it arose. It was not a necessary doctrine for salvation, but merely a fulfilling confirmation to those who were saved. Pentecostalists did, of course, promulgate their teaching widely, and sought to bring men to salvation by the promise of this extra blessing, but neither Aimee Semple MacPherson in Los Angeles, nor the leaders of the Assemblies of God, attempted to suggest that speaking in tongues was an imperative performance for those who would be saved.[1]

Pentecostalism was frequently closely associated with the revivalistic tradition in fundamentalist Protestantism, and its leaders such as George Jeffreys in Britain, or Oral Roberts or A. C. Valdez in America, stood in the old tradition of revivalism of R. A. Torrey, D. L. Moody and Charles Finney. None of these, however, can be described as more than a figure enjoying 'derived charisma'. They were messengers and not prophets, and their power was recognized as a mixture of the claims of the salvation which they preached (but which only Christ could give) and their personal gifts in preaching. Undoubtedly sects which adopted revivalistic techniques were affected by the employment of these means to achieve their ends, but the fact that they were prepared to use mass revivalism indicates a tendency for the movements concerned to evaluate the preaching of the gospel, and the bringing of men to salvation rather more highly than the accretion of numbers into their own movements.[2]

1. For a largely theological account of Pentecostalism, see N. Bloch-Hoell, *The Pentecostal Movement*, London, Allen & Unwin, 1964. See also B. R. Wilson, op. cit.

2. On this subject see, B. R. Wilson, 'The Pentecostal Minister: Role Conflicts and Status Contradictions', *American Journal of Sociology*, LXIV, 1959, pp. 494–504.

Although some sects begin with a new charismatic message, and others, such as the early Plymouth Brethren, begin with a number of 'seekers' coming together to explore the scriptures and seek out God's purposes and commands, and some arise around a new practice, such as the Pentecostal fellowships which arose spontaneously in a number of places in Britain, America, Scandinavia and elsewhere in the first two decades of the present century, there are others which begin in a process of schism. Schismatic groups are not usually dominated by charismatic leaders: they come out of existing fellowships on a variety of grounds, some more ostensible than actual. The demand for organizational change, especially by excluded groups or those who consider themselves to have too little access to control, is a common circumstance. The schisms of Methodism which occurred in late eighteenth-century England and in the first half of the nineteenth century were divisions on grounds such as these, and were essentially concerned with the greater representation of the laity in church affairs.

Sometimes the point on which schism occurs is ostensibly doctrinal, but, in general, divisions on matters of doctrine appear to be rationalizations for other deeper causes. This is especially evident when, after a fellowship has divided on a doctrinal issue, one party unites with some previously separated group with which it had – until reconciliation – doctrinal differences. Power, struggles of personality, occasionally the development of new practices, of a social, ethical or – perhaps less commonly – liturgical kind, are the usual causes for the emergence of schismatic groups. Some movements seem almost to thrive by divisions; Christian Science, where central control was strong, undoubtedly increased its branches when difficulties caused local churches to split – as long as each sought to remain in association with the

Mother Church. As long as no issue of teaching was involved local splits could have more the character of binary fission than of real schism.

Other movements, where schism goes deeper, may none the less find the pattern of feuding fellowships a certain revitalization of basic teachings. Division can provide a new charging of the emotions, and a new commitment to the cause. The history of the Plymouth Brethren and of the Christadelphians, are examples of this process.[1] The rival groups are often directed essentially to each other, and this appears to be especially so in movements in which there is a strong emphasis on equality and democratic participation (though the word 'democracy' is not one usually favoured), and in which the members of the sect are virtually a self-selected community of the elect who live as much of their lives together as they can.

It is frequently the case that sects which begin with a charismatic impetus, and some of those which are called into being by a revivalist, begin with a firm commitment to the reunification of Christendom. That a particular leader thinks that he can induce the Christians of the world to leave the institutionalized Churches once these have been shown to be corrupt, may seem strange, and yet this is a common aspiration in the early stages of the development of a sect. The leader or revivalist sees his mission as being to all mankind, and even while a new sect is forming around him, he often condemns vigorously the sects and denominations into which the Church of Christ has been divided.

Even those with highly distinctive teachings hold out

1. The salutary influence of internal conflict was long ago recognized by sociologists; see, Georg Simmel, *Conflict*, Glencoe, Ill., The Free Press, 1955 (translation by Kurt Wolff of 'Der Streit', Chapter 4 of Simmel's *Soziologie*, 1908).

this hope. Mrs Eddy thought that the Churches would accept her discovery of Christian Science at least in the early periods after her discovery in 1866. Alexander Campbell thought he was drawing Christians together on the basis of a restored commitment to the Scriptures. The early Plymouth Brethren had much the same vision, and so did some of the leaders of Pentecostal movements. There is often an almost recognizable pre-sectarian phase in the emergence of a movement that becomes a sect – a phase in which the hostility of the world is not anticipated and in which the institutionalism of the movement's own arrangements has not occurred, and has thus not yet established a very conscious human organization to sustain and disseminate the movement's teachings, and to organize its liturgical activities. Everything still appears to be at the direct behest of the Holy Spirit. Of course, quite apart from this early, and often soon abandoned, assumption about converting all Christendom, many movements continue to regard themselves as the only faithful expression of the true fellowship of Christ, even though those which stand in the central fundamentalist tradition cannot elevate fellowship in their group into the criterion of ultimate salvation, which, necessarily in evangelical teaching, rests on faith.

Sects which begin in schism rarely make universal claims of this kind. They are often more animated by the issues of the immediate division on which they have come into separate existence, and frequently are preoccupied with the wickedness of those whose fellowship they have recently left. Their emphasis understandably cannot be on the bringing together of all the faithful, and tends almost of necessity to be on the importance of separating from evil, of purging the dross. What begins as a dispute about doctrine (even if, as we have noted, that may often be a rationalization for a conflict of personalities or a dispute about power or status) often becomes a dispute about the proper conduct of meetings; to the charges of heresy are added charges of improper devotional attitudes, inadequate dissociation from worldly men, and, eventually, charges of immoral behaviour. Schism has to be justified, and is justified in terms of the impossibility of associating with those whose lives so little conform to Christian norms and whose beliefs are a distortion, if not a perversion, of the truth. Again, the manner in which a movement comes into being affects the range of ideological response which it can manifest.

Sectarian movements are not all of a kind, and one way of distinguishing them is in terms of their broad response to the wider society. These responses embrace their theology, organization and social ethics and practice, and they are always rejections of, withdrawals from, or amendments of, the dominant pattern of social conformity. In western society four principle responses can be recognized, which we might conveniently label as *conversionist*; *revolutionist*; *introversionist*; and *manipulationist*.[1] Briefly characterized, *conversionist* sects are fundamentalist evangelical sects, emphasizing literal interpretations of the Bible, and being primarily concerned with converting sinners, often by revivalist techniques. They are sects that often rely rather heavily on strong leadership. Methodism began with this broad orientation, although it did not begin specifically as a sect, and in both Britain and America soon ceased to be a sect. Salvationism and Pentecostalism provide other examples of sects of this type.

The *revolutionist* sects are the adventists who respond to

1. For a more extended treatment see B. R. Wilson, 'An Analysis of Sect Development', *American Sociological Review*, 24, (1) 1959, pp. 3–15. See also Elmer T. Clark, *The Small Sects in America*, New York, Abingdon Press, revised edn, 1949.

the world by predicting its overthrow and the establishment of a new dispensation when Christ returns. This type of sect is more emphatically hostile to the wider society, and although often seeking recruits, less specifically concerned with this end than with prophetical exegesis. Many contemporary adventist sects had their origin in the preaching of William Miller in America in the 1830s and 40s. The Seventh Day Adventists, the Christadelphians, and less directly, Jehovah's Witnesses owe their beginnings to that outcrop of adventist preaching.

The *introversionist* sects are those which have withdrawn from the world and which cultivate their own inner holiness. Some begin with inspirationalist tendencies, and others evolve steadily from an early – often revolutionist response. They are not usually interested in conversion except very nominally. Some Pietist movements, particularly those beginning in eighteenth-century Germany, are representative of this type of sect, and some nineteenth-century Holiness movements evolved this type of response to the world. So has that branch of the Plymouth Brethren known as Exclusive Brethren: for some time, too, Quakers occupied this position.

Those sects labelled *manipulationist* are rather further removed from the central Christian tradition. They do not reject the world, nor withdraw from it, but rather offer their votaries a new *gnosis* with which to conduct themselves in the world, and, often, with which to gain the goals which are approved of in the wider society – health, wealth, longevity, psychological security, intelligence, resilience, happiness and success. Very often these movements claim to have a monopoly of the means by which these ends can be gained. They are orientated essentially to the present world and have no developed eschatological position. They offer a system to be learned, and sometimes liken the deity to a principle or even a formula with which the secrets of living can be learned. The group life of this type of sect is often minimal, in contrast to introversionist, revolutionist and conversionist sects. Many of these owe their beginnings to the healing activities of Phineas P. Quimby in Massachusetts. The New Thought movements (Unity, Divine Science) began then, and Christian Science was certainly immensely influenced by Quimby.[1]

There are other sectarian responses – *thaumaturgical* (mainly spiritualist groups in the Western world), *reformist* (exemplified in the present-day Quakers), *Utopian* and *ritualist*,[2] but none of these has the generative importance of the other types of sect for contemporary western society.

Sects are not, of course, static. They evolve over time, and there is, as we have indicated in the case of revolutionist sects which become introversionist (and in the case of the Quakers, passing through this phase to become a reformist sect), a tendency for their response to the wider society to change over time. But sects are the most intense collective manifestations of the religious disposition to be discovered in secular society. They represent a continuing and deeply religious alternative to the religious compromise which is often, if not always, involved in ecumenism.

1. On the New Thought movements generally, see Charles S. Braden, *Spirits in Rebellion*, Dallas, Texas, Southern Methodist University Press, 1963.

2. An account of the leaders of ritualist sects, though with little information about their following, is given in Peter F. Anson, *Bishops at Large*, London, Faber, 1964.

12

Emerging Denominations and Persisting Sects

THE term 'sects' is often employed as a term of abuse, both by the man-in-the-street and by the leaders of major religious movements. It would, however, be easy to underestimate the social importance of sectarianism in the development of western society. Sociologists have been much more aware of its significance than have theologians. Montesquieu noticed the frequency with which piety, tolerance and commerce were associated. The piety was itself at least partially a sectarian phenomenon, and the tolerance was a condition which only the emergence of strategically influential, but socially deviant, religious interest-groups – namely sects – made necessary. Both Max Weber in his thesis on the particular significance of Puritan dispositions and theology for the development of capitalist society, and Ernst Troeltsch, paid special attention to sectarianism, and the tendencies which it promoted in society. Subsequently H. Richard Niebuhr, in seeking to explain sociologically the origins of denominationalism, proposed a theory about sect development which must be briefly restated.[1]

What, however, is evident, once we have recognized that there are distinct differences between groups of sects, is that not all of these writers were thinking of the same thing when they wrote of sects. Both Troeltsch and

1. Max Weber, *The Protestant Ethic and the Spirit of Capitalism*, London: Allen & Unwin, 1930; Ernst Troeltsch, *Social Teachings of the Christian Churches*, New York, Macmillan, 1931; H. Richard Niebuhr, *The Social Sources of Denominationalism*, New York, Holt, 1929.

Niebuhr mistook the part for the whole, and each a different part, and in very different social contexts, at that. For Troeltsch sectarianism was either of a mystical or an adventist kind, or, in terms employed more recently, his sects were essentially revolutionist or introversionist movements. Niebuhr, however, was very much more concerned with groups which showed a conversionist disposition. Niebuhr's thesis about denominations is capable of being seriously misleading, if it is assumed that the sects of nineteenth- and twentieth-century America, which became denominations are a continuation of, or are of the same type as, much earlier essentially revolutionist and introversionist movements.

Niebuhr recognized that the denominations in the United States in the 1920s, when he was writing, corresponded broadly to the social divisions which prevailed among men. In extending his thesis he suggested that there was a dynamic relationship between sects and established denominations – broadly that every sect which did not wither away, might be expected to develop into a denomination. He went further, in suggesting a basic circumstance which promoted this development: as each narrow and exclusive sect, emphasizing voluntary adherence, recruited its own second generation – the children of its founders – so, it became a denomination. Once there were inborn members the sect, he held, had ceased to be a sect. It moved from the early exclusiveness to a less rigorous acceptance of members, to a position of reduced tension with the world, and eventually to the acceptance of the legitimacy of other religious movements. The analysis made evident some of the salient characteristics of the denomination. Niebuhr wrote:

. . . by its very nature the sect is valid only for one generation. The children born to the voluntary members of the first generation begin to make the sect a church long before they have arrived at years of discretion. For with their coming the sect must take on the character of an educational and disciplinary institution with the purpose of bringing the new generation into conformity with ideals and customs which have become traditional.[1]

Our concern is less with the correlation of social class divisions and denominations, than with the further thesis that religious movements begin as sects, with all the characteristics of voluntary adherence, separation from the world, exclusiveness, hostility to the dominant culture, and the total commitment of members, and then pass within the course of one generation into denominations: to this issue we shall shortly turn. In passing we might acknowledge the extent to which Niebuhr's insight into the social basis of denominationalism was warranted. New religious movements are frequently vehicles for sections of society which are otherwise unaccommodated socially and religiously. When the productive relations of a society are changing, new groups of men find some need for a reinterpretation of their position.

New classes, then, seek their own transcendental justification, and do so all the more vigorously for being excluded from the existing distribution of social honour and religious sanctity. Their demand for status, for gratification is likely to respond to the transcendental promise of status *in the next world* if the immediate prospect of status in this one is withheld. And yet, what the history of Protestant denominationalism makes evident is that there is no agency so effective in providing men with improved status and respectability *in this world* as that which promises them these things in the next. Becoming religious, accepting the promise for deferred rewards is itself an agency not only of discipline, but also of enhancing status in this world. The sect which persuades

1. H. Richard Niebuhr, op. cit., p. 19.

men that they are the poor, 'the least the lost the lowest and the last', promises them ultimate salvation in the after-life, also offers a foretaste of heaven in the assembly, establishes its own inner status structure, induces members to behave in respectable ways to each other, and to conduct themselves as veritable saints *manqués* in the wider society. It is part of the return to fundamentals manifested by groups that emerge in this way.

Although the sect is religiously an outsider group, in terms of the behaviour of its members it frequently brings them to a level of meticulous conformity with – sometimes slightly old-fashioned – values and practices. Often it appears to fossilize the moral standards of an earlier period, or to bring to the urban context the values of a more orderly agrarian background. Often, too, its adherents appear to be those who have come from this background, who have experienced the chaos of social life under new conditions, and who have forged a new pattern of order which is an adaptive response to their new circumstances. Nor is it surprising that religion is the agency of this moral renewal of communities. Religion canalizes the emotions, and provides legitimate expression for emotional upsurge, whilst at the same time regulating and disciplining the emotional life of communities.

Thus the Puritans, the Quakers, and the Methodists were all examples of groups who found some sort of legitimation for their life activities, and some new form of expression for the emotional, economic and social disruption with which they were faced. The Methodists provide the obvious example of a dislocated new working class, drawn from those settling in the newly industrialized areas. It offered a democratic theology, in which all men by an act of will might claim salvation, and might soon thereafter become *assured* that they were destined for the heavenly life hereafter. It was the first mass working-class movement, with stable organization and nation-wide association. Its polity was autocratic in spite of its democratic theology, and only gradually did the lay Methodist acquire parity of esteem with the ministerial class, and only through a number of schisms from the parent Wesleyan body through the course of the earlier half of the nineteenth century. But Methodism with its band meetings, its circuits and its lay ministry was a significant testimony to the effect of rational principles of organization on which it rested. It offered new emotional outlets – lusty hymns for pub ditties, order and a clear status structure for the chaos and uncertainty of life in the newly settled industrial areas, opportunities for expression and leadership, status and respectability, and eventually the regard of the wider society.

From this example it becomes evident that newly emergent social groups, are, at least in the context of a society in which the religious view of the world dominates, likely to need and to evolve new patterns of religious belief to accommodate themselves in their new situation. Niebuhr suggested that the reason for this development was that established Christianity was, in such circumstances, too closely identified with the dominant strata, making it inappropriate to accommodate new classes. New strata, with new perceptions of the world arising from their particular life experiences, and the acute sense of deprivation they suffered could not be fitted into the existing pattern of religious life – hence the sectarian impulse.[1]

The dominant religious expression is normally closely

1. The theory of relative deprivation as the source of sectarianism has recently been given much more systematic expression in Charles Y. Glock, 'The Role of Deprivation in the Origin and Evolution of Religious Groups', in Robert Lee and Martin E. Marty, *Religion and Social Conflict*, New York, O.U.P., 1964.

associated with the ruling strata of traditional society. Its leadership is normally another expression of the power, and another confirmation of the status of established ruling *élites*. If religion has any significance at all, it must, if the society is to maintain its way of life, and if the pattern of social order is to persist, be integrated with that way of life. No ruling class could afford – in a society in which religion is taken seriously – to encourage religious movements to evolve with leadership drawn from sections of society other than its own. In conditions of stability there is perhaps little need for such developments. Only when the social order has been disrupted are the displaced elements likely to seek religious expression of their social experience. This was as evident in the Tai-ping rebellion in China, in the Hau-Hau movement among the Maoris of New Zealand, among the Kimbangoists of the Congo, or the Mau Mau movement in Kenya. It is not, then, simply a matter of social class expression, it is the expression of dislocated groups.

In western society, with the development of stronger political institutions, with the process of rationalization, religious expression ceased to be of such transcendent importance to the way of life of society itself, and conditions developed which allowed rulers to indulge sectarian groups and to tolerate them (particularly where they had evolved socially and economically important functions). The new sects participated in and reinterpreted the central religious traditions of the society, adjusted to the needs of their own circumstances, or with emphasis on such teachings as were of greatest appeal to their clientele.

Just as established religion is institutionalized, so it is likely that new sectarian movements will experience this same process over the course of time. Niebuhr's thesis that only for the first-generation adherents is sect life a valid experience mistook the sequence common among certain types of sect in America for an inevitable process. Just as new religious movements do not necessarily represent a particular social class, but may represent any dislocated group, so the sect may not so quickly become a denomination. There may be factors which prevent this development, and these may be ideological, organizational, social structural, or, perhaps, in some circumstances, purely adventitious. What is most evident is that certain types of sect, with distinctive responses to the world are more disposed to undergo this denominationalizing process than are others.

Niebuhr's thesis assumes in the first place that all sect members are recruited at the same time, that there is a first generation and that all those who come into the sect subsequently are 'second generation' – the children of the founders. This in itself is a simplification. Some sects are more disposed to accept outsiders than are others, and this circumstance in itself may affect the extent to which a sect is denominationalized. Much depends on the terms in which recruitment occurs, how lightly and with what consequences for the movement itself.

A movement which is distinctly adventist tends to recruit those who have strong antipathies to the wider society, who exult in the prospect of its overturn. These people are not likely to be those who would welcome the sect's becoming more adjusted to the wider society. Thus as long as a revolutionist sect retains its central ideology, and without regard to the changing emphasis occurring among inborn members, there is likely to be a strong ideological check to the process of becoming a denomination. Since such movements are often careful about admission – and demand some doctrinal competence – they provide their own means of retarding any tendency to become a denomination. Nor, in such a movement, is it quite enough to suppose that those who are the children of existing members are automatically sect members themselves. They, too, must prove their worth before admission, and although in many instances the choice of whether to join the community or not may be very extensively influenced by home background, associations and friendships, none the less in many sects there is still an examination of suitability and adequate understanding of sect teachings, for instance among Quakers as well as among Exclusive Brethren and Christadelphians. Thus, although there is some force in the Niebuhr argument in some cases, there is no *necessary* development of sect into denomination in one generation.

Obviously, however, in other cases the disposition of a sect to develop in this way is more evident. The conversionist sect is distinctly disposed to take in large numbers of outsiders, if it can win them over. What is crucial to sect development here is not a generational process, but rather a recruitment policy. Recruitment policies may be even more propitious for denominationalism than the internal recruitment of the second generation. The conversionist sects which adopted revivalist techniques often won a large number of converts but the cost of doing so was that of bringing in a great many unsocialized persons who had little knowledge of, and in some cases no special interest in, the distinctive teachings of the sect itself. They were drawn in by the main promise of salvation, and the way in which it was presented. The emphasis on success by revivalism has often meant that there is a relatively lightly committed clientele, of a rather volatile disposition. These are not the stuff out of which persisting sects are made. In consequence the conversionist sect, even before it comes to recruit the second generation, is inclined to move towards a denominational position.

Conversionist sects have some difficulty in retaining their second generation, which is often not in need of the (usually) rather emotional orientation of the sect, and the ecstatic exercises in which it engages. The lower mental and emotional stability of many of those it recruits tends to reduce the likelihood of stable family commitment in these movements, and consequently even in conversionist sects, where Niebuhr's argument is most plausible, the second generation is less likely to be crucial than Niebuhr supposed. Although this point has certainly some validity for some American nineteenth- and early twentieth-century movements, the forces moving the Pentecostal and Holiness sects towards the denominational position which many of them are near to attaining, appear to have been very much more the forces of revivalistic recruitment policies in association with other organizational elements rather than the automatic acceptance of the second generation.

Whilst generational change is undoubtedly one factor in the evolution of sects, it is not, then, necessarily, the crucial determinant which Niebuhr sought to make it. Nor does it necessarily lead to denominationalism. We might more adequately say that the attenuation of protest may be in part a failure of the second and subsequent generations to maintain the perspective of their predecessors. There is certainly a difference between those who are converted to a revolutionist sect, and those who accept adventist teachings at their mother's knee. One can expect a marked change of personality type in revolutionist movements especially between those who come in as converts, and those who grow up with these teachings as family and community orthodoxy. They have not so emphatically chosen to be separated from the world (although they must usually make a definite subscription to sect teachings) so much as decided not to join the world. But these generational shifts of temperament whilst of great importance for the life and continuance of a sect are not, as Niebuhr supposed, particularly in the direction of a readier acceptance of the dominant culture and of other religious movements. It is not the fact of protest and separation which changes, but rather that the *terms* of the protest and the *terms* of separation change.

After the early period of their emergence, all sects which persist experience a process of institutionalization in which customs are hardened, procedures are routinized, practices are stabilized and an even tenor of life is established. Even in sects which emphasize ecstatic experience the same process can be observed: the occasions for ecstasy become delimited and regulated, the operation of charisma becomes circumscribed, the extent to which inspiration may legitimately influence people is gradually defined. This development, then, means some change in the life practices of the sect and perhaps in its response to the wider society. It may also mean that over time there is less direct desire on the part of the members to fulfil all their own offices, and there may be that development of a division of religious labour which characterizes denominations and Churches. Thus a group which either assumes or has conferred upon it the responsibilities for ministry, or for organizing meetings, or for publishing a magazine, tends sometimes to emerge. This process is obviously one in the direction of the denomination.

It can arise, however, from other circumstances than simply that of generational change. If a movement grows the problems which face it in relation to the activities which it undertakes, especially the work of evangelism if that is a sustained activity, but also missionary work abroad, fund raising, the printing and circulation of publications, may all dispose it towards change in a particular direction. This may occur even in spite of a doctrinal position which opposes such developments, a process we have already noticed in the case of the American Baptist Convention in spite of the frequent protest of those (usually rural and remote) churches which embrace the movement's traditional theology most vigorously. The denomination has evolved an elaborate centralized executive control – so much so that some of its members even refer to the powerful departmental heads who are all nominally only Baptist ministers like any other as 'bishops in business suits'.

The emergence of a paid ministry, and then of a central council, which effectively bring lay control to an end, and which eliminate local control, are the threats which all persisting sects have to face. Where there is intense initial hostility to anything but lay and local control – and this is often a position of sects – the process may be retarded or even completely prevented. In a more rationally organized society the process is harder to resist. Even where central control is kept in lay hands, or partially in lay hands, there often emerges a certain type of layman who comes to exert influence. Often it is the reasonably well-to-do layman who comes to accumulate power – the man who has leisure, perhaps because he is retired or because he has the type of job or the private means which allow him to devote himself to things which interest him. Even in groups as radically opposed to a ministry as the Exclusive Brethren, the Christadelphians and the Quakers, this tendency has been evident. Occasionally movements react against the process, as when the Quakers ceased to 'record' the names of 'ministers' in the 1920s in England. (These ministers were laymen, but laymen whose 'ministry' was regarded as appropriate and acceptable in the movement.)

Thus it is evident that although sects do not necessarily

follow a predetermined path of development, they are none the less not static communities entirely unaffected by their own existence over time or by influences of the wider society. Sometimes that wider society can precipitate particular sectarian responses, sometimes in the direction of obliging a sect to abandon a particular sectarian position, and sometimes inducing the sect to return to a more vigorous emphasis on its separateness from the world. The two processes can even occur simultaneously, and from rather similar circumstances. An example from the history of the Christadelphians will suffice to illustrate the point.

During the First World War, the Ministry of War in Britain declared itself prepared to consider exemption from military services on conscientious grounds of individuals who belonged to particular religious groups, if they were vouched for by the leaders of the movement to which they belonged. The Christadelphians who were conscientious objectors had always rejected the idea that they had leaders, and they were equally ill-disposed on Biblical grounds to appoint committees or to evolve any centralized agencies of sect government. Yet to ensure the best treatment for their own young men who, when conscription began in England in 1917, were likely to be called to the colours, they were obliged to entrust negotiations with the Ministry to someone whom the Ministry officials, at least, could regard as a leader of Christadelphians. A committee evolved under the leadership of a man with time and means to support himself in this role, and thus external pressure induced the sect to depart from one of its entrenched positions. To treat with the wider society at all – even to claim its right to exemption from it – the sect had to evolve agencies which the wider society could recognize. At the same time the very fact that the nation was involved in war was a circumstance which made all Christadelphian boys aware of their separated condition, and the very fact of military service meant that they had to decide fairly early whether they wished to become members of the movement or not (since the Christadelphians were not prepared to vouch for anyone who had not been a member for some time before he was eligible for service). All this then meant that Christadelphians gained an enhanced sense of their differences from other men. Their group adhesion had to be reaffirmed in the face of external constraints and their sectarian tendencies were reinforced.

That sects undergo a process of change is clear. But they are likely in most cases to remain as sects, particularly where they are not orthodox fundamentalist conversionist groups, and particularly where they exist in a much more stable environment than that of the United States at the end of the nineteenth and beginning of the twentieth century. At that time, in a society growing by extensive waves of immigration and with the optimism which a rapid rate of economic growth and of the exploitation of new land, new labour and new capital permit, social mobility was already an accepted expectation and a buoyant myth in America – not only for individuals but even for religious movements. Every sect could expect to grow into a large denomination. As we have already seen the absence of an established church made this prospect all the more attractive – there was nothing from which to preserve social distance.

Even those movements which were not distinctly conversionist showed tendencies towards the loss of sectarian characteristics over time, given the extraordinary circumstances of American society. Thus the Seventh Day Adventists and Jehovah's Witnesses, although in many ways still sects, have undoubtedly been affected by the conversionist and expansionist ideal which prevailed in American society. The Witnesses have a fixed teaching that those who will reign with God can number only the 144,000 fixed in the Book of Revelation, but they accommodate a great many others (the 'millions now living' who 'will never die' in the words of the late Judge Rutherford, former leader of the Witnesses) by predicting that their future will be in the new kingdom to be established on earth. Thus even the restrictive doctrines of adventism are interpreted in such a way that optimism and evangelism are warranted. Although the Witnesses remain a revolutionist sect, they have adopted expansive recruitment policies more usually associated with conversionist sects.

But in other cases sects have changed in response in a way rather less influenced by the immediate environment, and rather more in accordance with essentially internal pressures. Thus some revolutionist sects have tended over time, as adventual hopes have been disappointed, to become more preoccupied with the means of their own insulation from the wider society. They have tended to become more concerned with the condition of their own society, with their own inner holiness. Sometimes, because the struggle with the world has slackened, or the prospect of Armageddon somewhat receded, they have developed the proclivity for schism within, often over matters which to the outsider seem trivial in the extreme. Generational change may have given an impetus to a changing response from that of rebellion to that of acceptance of the internal sect order, from revolutionism to introversion. Thus the Quakers and the Christadelphians have shown marked tendencies in this direction, the Quakers in the eighteenth and early nineteenth centuries and the Christadelphians most conspicuously in the period between the wars.

Introversion is often a secondary position for sects, and

may in turn give way to another response. The Quakers evolved from their intensive inner community concern to a much more evangelical persuasion in the mid-nineteenth century. Theologically less orthodox than the bulk of evangelical denominations (and perhaps rather less concerned with doctrinal matters than are most sects) their position changed into one of justification of their own prosperity in the world by a growing disposition to philanthropy. Their educational interests were reinvigorated. As their community became rather more open to the wider society once they abandoned their peculiarities of speech and dress in the 1850s, and as evangelicalism had brought them into wider social contact, so they evolved a growing social philanthropy. As they ceased to be a group whose leadership was characterized by the successful owner-manager and became more markedly a group led by professional people, so the style of philanthropy shifted from the disbursal of moneys to the increased concern with good works. They became a reformist sect.

There are some indications that, after a period in which a devotional attitude has been more pronounced among Christadelphians, some among them now begin to show much more concern for 'good causes' in the wider society, from which not so long ago they would have held aloof. This change, too, has been accompanied with the change of social status of Christadelphians and appears to be associated with some of the well-established and well-educated professional people who (principally by intergenerational social mobility) are today to be found among Christadelphians. Thus it can be seen that sectarian change may be from one sectarian response to another rather than from the sectarian position to denominationalism. Even a reformist sect remains still somewhat apart and separated, and indeed perhaps the effectiveness of their reform programme virtually demands this disinterested detachment to make their goodwill effective and acceptable.

The terms Church and denomination are often loosely employed; some sociologists, following Troeltsch, tend to think of the two polar cases and to assume a steady movement from sect to Church. But in fact the Church is a religious organization which sees itself as coterminous in the society in which it exists, assuming the identity of the political and the religious community. Obviously in the case of the Roman Church, the Church continued to assume its writ to run throughout a society which had ceased to be politically integrated. It was always prepared, however, as its attitudes to voyages of discovery illustrates, to extend its area of religious authority as the political sovereigns with whom it had influence extended their own domains. Theoretically everyone in the society is born into the Church, and when the political authority is prepared to exert its monopoly of physical coercion in the interests of religion, it can go a long way to make theory into fact. Yet the sect may claim to precede the Church.

In Christianity it is clear that there was a Christian sect, both in the Holy Land and in the Empire before there was a Church, and only theological and ecclesiological casuistry could possibly suggest otherwise. The sect, then, exists as the protest group which calls a challenge to the wider society and its religious institutions. In the Christian case it became in time a Church, but not without the recrudescent manifestation of sectarianism. Troeltsch takes this back to the sectarian emphasis of the gospels themselves, seeing in Jesus the original emphasis on sectarianism and in Paul the disposition to institutionalize religion and so to establish some sort of Church.

There may be something to the argument that it is pre-

cisely the inner dialectic in Christendom between institutionalized Church and protesting sect which has prevented Christianity from becoming itself as moribund a
religious system as Buddhism had become before the
modern era. The sect has continually pressed the Church
to recognize the need for vigour, and has continually
challenged the corruption and the institutional and ritual
deadness towards which at times it was disposed to give
way. In England and America, Methodism can be seen as
the most vigorous reassertion of principles in the face of
a largely docile established religion. The way in which
some churchmen have responded to faith-healing and
Christian Science, and to Pentecostalism, suggests that
these sects, too, have in some contexts been responsible
for stirring religious professionals to re-examine their
practices and their assumptions about pastoral care, worship and liturgy.

The denomination is, however, a very much later
phenomenon. The sect as a protest arises readily in circumstances of social disturbance. The Church we see as
emergent in societies in which there is at least some claim
to present or past political cohesion on the basis of which
it claims its own sphere of operation. The denomination,
however, depends on very much more circumscribed
social and political conditions than either sect or Church.[1]
It is voluntary but not exclusive. It admits new members
without exacting tests of merit – almost on a formal
statement of belief and willingness to join. It does not
claim an exclusive monopoly of religious truth, and is
prepared to take its place among other religious organizations and often to co-operate with them in affairs of
common interest. It is prepared to accept a measure of

1. See David A. Martin, 'The Denomination', *British Journal of
Sociology*, XIII, 1962, pp. 1–14; idem, *Pacifism*, London, Routledge,
1965.

religious specialization – a professional ministry and full-time executive agencies. It may carry a certain emphasis on lay participation from its sectarian past, but it will also have evolved a considerable bureaucracy, even in those instances where it is ecclesiologically committed to the automony of local congregations.

It no longer emphasizes hostility to the world, but accepts in large measure the values of the wider society with only marginal issues of difference, and only perfunctory demands for different and higher standards from its own members. Thus contemporary Methodism asserts the importance of teetotalism and is opposed to gambling but in practice many even quite committed Methodists do drink, albeit in moderation, and one of the great bene-factors of the Methodist Church in Britain has himself been responsible for the promotion of one of the largest mass-gambling recreations in the country. The moral tone of the denomination is relaxed, and part of the process of movement from sect to denomination, where this occurs, is in the changing attitude to matters of morals. Two examples from the Disciples of Christ (known in Britain as the Churches of Christ, which, confusingly, is the name of a more radical schism from the Disciples in the United States) illustrate this point.

Fifty years ago those within this denomination would certainly have frowned at the idea of members going to the theatre, and might have gone further than this to register disapprobation. Today in a congregation of this move-ment there may well be a young people's theatre club. But the changed attitude to the wider society became evi-dent even in the very early years of this movement, for this was one of the archetypical denominationalizing sects of Niebuhr's theory. As the Disciples, or Campbellites, as, from the name of their leader, they were often known to others, rose in social status, so their attitude changed even to education – often a subject of concern to sectarians. In 1831, Alexander Campbell declared in a way very typical for the sectarian leader:[1]

The Saints have derived their qualifications to perform their Master's service, not from poring, for years over the profane remains of heathen historians, divines, priests and moralists ... not from the unintelligible wranglings of contentious and contending doctors of human Divinity ... not from theological seminaries those prolific, filthy hotbeds of sophistry, error, prejudice, nonsense and factions ... but from the unadulterated oracles of the truth of God.

But within only ten years, so rapidly had the need of ministering to the converted arisen that Campbell could say –

To hear an uneducated preacher or teacher of religion ... whose every sentence is a sin against the laws of language; who, with inquisitorial tortures, murders the King's English at every turn – to hear such a one reproach a man of celebrity with theological errors – is an ebullition of human folly more disgusting than any other I can imagine.

And again: 'Schools for prophets, as well as schools for languages and sciences are yet required and all men feel the want of them.'

The influence of an education-conscious society made itself felt on the rapidly expanding sects, and the need for a literate ministry became, as with other movements, one of the early requirements which prompted the denominationalizing process. Much the same story could be told for other conversionist sects at a much later date in England. The various Pentecostal movements began with local lay evangelists, but in providing them with educa-

1. This and the following quotation are from Oliver R. Whitley, *The Trumpet Call of Reformation*, St Louis, Mo., Bethany Press, 1959, pp. 88 and 89.

tion for revivalist work brought into being seminaries and steadily – though less swiftly than the Campbellites – came to distrust education less and less.

The denomination then emerges usually – though some would contend not always – as a result of evolution from a sect, even though by no means all sects follow this evolutionary path and, when they do, not for the reasons or in the time-span which Neibuhr suggested. Whether any denominations exist which were not for a time – however brief – sects or of strong sectarian disposition is perhaps a matter for disputation: what is clear is that the denomination does come on to the scene only at a certain stage in history. Certain social pre-conditions are necessary for it. There must be tolerance, and there must be an acceptance of a certain pluralism. The divergent needs and arrangements of different social strata, different ethnic groups, or different town or country populations, have implicit acknowledgement in the fact of denominationalism. Thus the denomination cannot realistically be seen simply as midway in a linear scale between sect and Church: it is essentially the creation of specific historical circumstances, and becomes a significant form of religious organization in those conditions in which tolerance is extended to sects. Tolerance, indeed, is one circumstance which permits the sect to become a denomination. Tolerance, we may suppose, however, becomes established only when religious thinking and the religious view of the world have already ceased to be central features of the way of life of a people.

If tolerance is one condition for the emergence of denominations the possibilities of social mobility are another. Whereas the sect rejects the secular society, its values or its means of attaining them, the denomination, as we have seen, largely accepts these goals and the institutional means. It is in this circumstance, in the case of denominations which have evolved from sects (and there can be no doubt this is most of the major denominations in contemporary Europe and America) that sectarian ideals are sometimes surrendered. Thus as the Methodists in both England and America became more respectable, so the sectarian elements evident in their early history, and especially in the early nineteenth century, disappeared. The strict rules of the early Wesleyan conferences concerning the appropriate numbers of petticoats which women might wear, the appropriate length of hair, the height from the ground of women's garments, and the prohibition of frivolous talk, were all of them relaxed.

In America, as the meetings of Methodists became more centred on the chapel and less on the home meeting of the Methodist class so there was a shift from simplicity and lay control to increased concern with churchly equipment. The search for personal holiness was steadily abandoned, and concern with financial support for the increasingly large and often Gothic-style churches, became of more moment for the ministry. As Methodists rose in the social scale, so there was a demand that their places of worship should show a certain congruence of status with that of the participants. Discipline became more lax, and an increase in Church ceremonial was associated with a fuller acceptance of the wider society. Education tended to replace devotion as a central concern of the denomination, and the Church sought social acceptability by involvement in a wide range of good works: Christians now proved themselves less by the exemplary conduct of their own lives and more by their helpful participation in the wider society. Sometimes the helpfulness could be reduced to strictly monetary terms in conformity with the rationalization of activities, and the impersonality of the role structure of modern society.

Denominationalism is a distinctive pattern of religious adherence appropriate to modern industrial society. The denomination is not the form to which all or even most sects evolve, nor is it a part way position towards the emergence of a Church. It is a mutation which in some respects owes something to the way in which the Churches have themselves evolved in the modern world. In the pluralist society it is clearly impossible for a Church to continue on the assumptions which it could make in a society in which religious and political institutions were necessarily mutually supportative. Even though Roman Catholics are organized territorially in the usual parochial system even in dominantly Protestant societies, the organization has no significance except internally for the Church. The Church, despite its traditional claims, operates in fact as one religious movement among many, and although, by virtue of ancient claims to authority and superiority, it sometimes manages to gain concessions not always accorded to smaller sects, it is often in much the same position in relation to the law. It is perhaps harder for Mormons to gain tax exemptions for their temples (which are not open for public worship) than for Catholics to gain it for the chapels of enclosed orders, but the anomaly has to do with the prejudice which prevails against 'newer' religions, and the vague but persistent idea that the older the form of religious organization the more legitimacy it has.

Despite its claim to specific titles, its size and its appeal within Christendom by virtue of ancient status, the Roman Church in Britain, and the Roman and Episcopalian Churches in America, are from a sociological point of view only denominations. In America, and in Wales, too, for that matter, there is no 'Church' in the strict sense: the American, it has been said, used to denominationalism, has no conception of what is meant by the

Universal Church.[1] Thus the denomination becomes, in effect, the pattern even for old Churches in the pluralist society, and even more fully in the increasingly secularized society. Sect, Church and denomination stand in dialectical relation, in a time-related sequence. The sect existed first; the Church came to gain near monopoly; the denomination emerged as the typical religious pattern in the unreligious and irreligious society.

Sects sometimes become denominationalized, though sects also persist. The Churches, too, in effect, have been denominationalized in secular society. Ecumenism is perhaps a way in which they seek to find their way back to circumstances in which they can again make claim to churchly status.

1. Willard L. Sperry, *Religion in America*, Cambridge, C.U.P., 1945, p. 10.

Conclusion

THE concept of the Church, as it has been understood in the social sense, is one which acquired its full meaning and realization in European feudal society. It claimed, within a given territory, the monopoly of spiritual power, just as the state claimed the monopoly of political and military power. In European history one Church presided over several nascent states, and this but reflected its claim to transcendence and universality. For, although in the age of more emphatic nationalism the Church tended to become closely identified with the state, and this was especially true in Protestant Christendom – indeed to the point of accepting the dominant authority of the state – the earlier conception was of a Church unconfined by national ethnic boundaries. But the Church relied, for the effective recognition of its claim to a monopoly of spiritual power, on the coercive power of the political authority.

As the institutions of society grew apart, and as religious institutions and functionaries lost, first their control of, and later much of their access to, various social activities – diplomacy, education, the regulation of trade, etc., so the civil authority gained in power, and, having less need for the good offices of the Church, was less disposed to protect its ancient privileges. The emergence of new classes with new skills and resources, who were unaccommodated in the Church, but whose social importance sometimes won for them the protection of princes, created a pluralism which became the first properly instituted invasion (there had been many unlegitimated invasions before) of the Church's claim to spiritual monopoly as far as the temporal sovereign's writ could run.

The ecclesiological theory of the Church remained. But once tolerance was extended to organized dissenters the Church, sociologically viewed, was reduced to the status of a denomination, albeit for a very long time a dominant and privileged denomination. In America, despite the 'establishment' of particular confessions in various states, denominationalism was, from the very creation of the federation, the norm. Religious pluralism has its official foundation-stone in the American constitution, although its modern beginnings go back to sixteenth- and early seventeenth-century Europe. The growth of religious diversity in the United States made evident the untenability of the social concept of 'the Church' in that society, although those religious organizations which inherited the ecclesiology and the associated liturgical practices, continued to behave as if they were in fact Churches. In political and social affairs, of course, they could not do so.

In Europe, where established Churches did persist in most countries, loss of effective authority affected the Churches even in societies where there was near unanimity of religious belief. In Germany, Scandinavia, Holland, Switzerland and Britain, Protestantism created the conditions for an earlier manifestation of religious tolerance than occurred in Catholic countries, but as religion lost political influence, dissent, even in Catholic countries, became increasingly tolerated. More important, anticlericalism became a significant manifestation of political radicalism.

What was begun by the tolerance necessary in increasingly diversified societies, was continued by the process of secularization itself. When large numbers effectively ceased to be religious, all religious movements were reduced to the status of denominations and sects. The process, was, inevitably, the more painful in those societies in which the fiction of the concept of the Church had persisted. In America, as we have seen, secularization drained the religious content, without too radically affecting the form, of religious institutions. So persistent indeed were the forms, that in that pluralistic society, sects could expect, especially in the nineteenth century when expansion and optimism were so manifest, to graduate into denominations, and even to acquire for themselves the liturgical, architectural and (sometimes) the ecclesiastical styles which had previously been exclusively associated with those more ancient religious institutions which had in the past been – and which still laid claim to being – Churches. Thus some commentators have, mistaking the form for the social reality, been prepared, rather inappropriately, to discuss the process not as one of denominationalism, but as one 'from sect to Church'. Church was, however, merely the high status towards which some sects were aspiring, without, however, any realistic prospect of attaining it.

In the secular society there are, strictly speaking, no Churches. There are denominations, some of which have special historic privileges, and some of which suffer some historic liabilities (for example the preclusion of Roman Catholics from certain offices of state in England). But whereas denominational claims are, given the high level of manifest public support, sustainable in America, even these become difficult to sustain in Europe, where the secularization process has not merely (or not so markedly) drained away the content of religious beliefs, but has also caused public support to ebb. In some European countries those religious institutions which once boasted the name and the reality of Churches are, with secularization, faced with being reduced to the status of sects; that is to say, of being reduced to relatively small, heterodox groups who believe and practise things which are alien to the majority.

They differ from sects, however, in lacking the intensity of commitment.

It is in response to this circumstance of secularization that the Churches of the past have sought to shore up their claims to status. Their dominant response has been ecumenicalism. Since what secularization has eroded has been the intensity of specific belief, the sense of superiority and apartness, this solution has been all the easier to accept. Clearly, in this process, those Churches which have remained largest and which have managed to maintain their more traditional practices have some advantage. The ritual dance of ecumenism emphasizes steps known as 'drawing together' and 'growing together'. A close observer of the dance might notice that the gyrations and revolutions of some of the dancers are far more numerous in a short space of time than those of others. The attempt to discover a more firmly legitimated basis of faith and order – beginning with the Tractarian movement of the nineteenth century in England – has led to an attempt to restore the security of the past, however much of it may be done in the name of action appropriate to the present. The sentiments of returning to the first century of Christianity come readily to the lips of modern churchmen, even when they are emphasizing the need for change to keep up with the twentieth century, and restoring liturgical practices from the twelfth or thirteenth centuries.[1]

Yet if it is the Roman Church which, liturgically, ecclesiastically, and theologically stands to gain, it can do

1. See for example Leslie Paul, *Deployment and Payment of the Clergy*, London, Church Information Office, 1964, and the discussion which followed – Bryan Wilson, 'The Paul Report Examined', *Theology*, LXVIII, No. 536, 1965, pp. 89–103, and the contributions of Leslie Paul and Bryan Wilson, *Theology*, LXVIII, Nos. 538 and 539, 1965, pp. 202–6 and 245–6.

so in these departments only by surrendering control in others. What affects liturgy and ecclesiology and theology as an academic discipline, affects only the Church. It has little consequence for society at large. Where ethics are concerned, however, matters are rather different. The secular society, with its acceptance of more technical and scientific procedures, will not brook interference of the traditional kind, in, for example, matters relating to marriage and birth. It may, indeed, eventually, also re-assert the control it was steadily acquiring until the past decade perhaps, over education, as the financial demands of modern education steadily outstrip the resources of private agencies – even of religious organizations. Other religious movements have in the main abandoned the attempt to influence society in these matters except by pious injunction. Eventually the Roman Church must do the same.

Ecumenicalism, then, is a response which might save the Churches from becoming sects, since 'from Church to sect' would appear to be the order of the day for religious organizations in secular society. Sects have always been anathema to churchmen, indeed to most Christians, even including those who, in the eyes of other Christians and of the secular world, are themselves sec-tarians. And this, even though there can be no doubt that the intensity of religious commitment, the most individ-ually influential and pervasive religious view of the world undoubtedly exists in sectarian movements. En-thusiasm has never had much appeal to churchmen, and lay intensity has often been a matter for concern and re-proach among those who have become professionals of religious organizations. The ecumenical alternative to sectarianism – although Christianity was certainly sec-tarian in the now so popular first century – is associated with the liturgical revival and the reassertion of the

episcopacy even in denominations which began by dis-
avowing both.

Both, as we have seen, have a special appeal to the professionals of the Churches. They improve the claim to
social status on the part of the ministry; they emphasize
the antiquity of the religious role, and hence reassure its
performers of the legitimacy, permanence and usefulness
of their chosen calling. Liturgicalism reasserts the monopoly of the professional, by providing him with the
equivalent of skills and techniques which he alone is
licensed to practise. Episcopacy enhances the promotion
prospects of the cleric, and perpetuates the claim to high
dignity, association with ruling *élites* and the maintenance
of the religious institution in some nominal position of
high social importance.

Given an organization with all the capacity for persistence displayed by the Churches – their claims on latent
sentiment, their operation at crucial times of personal
and familial crisis, their association with the kinship
structure, and especially with the childhood of many
people – one sees the clerical profession as a self-per-
petuating incumbency. The forces of ecumenism are
clerical forces, and the forces of the new ritualist movement are clerical forces. We witness the struggles of a profession for survival in the Protestant countries of Europe.
The choice is principally between the loss of organizations,
positions and social influence, as in the case of sects, or
the maintenance of organizations, the multiplication of
positions, the reassertion of professional expertise, and
the close identification with the cultural goals and styles
of secular society, as in the case of religious institutions
in America. There is a third position and it appeals to a
minority of the clergy in Europe. As the ministry becomes
an entrenched but increasingly functionless intelligentsia,
so this minority interprets its role increasingly as involve-

ment with social and political affairs. From the secure base of religious livings, they sally forth on what are largely political crusades. This is the tradition of dissent, of course (even though it is often Anglican and Catholic clergy who are involved), but it is not religious dissent. It is the use of a religious base for political action. In general, the choice of the clergy has been ecumenicalism, liturgicalism and the attempt to identify with the goals of secular society and to show where religious organization (even if not religious ideas and values) fits in.

The social basis which facilitates the development of ecumenicalism is the diminishing diversity of society. The disappearance of ethnic, regional and pronounced stratificational differences reduces the significance of the religious divisions which reflected them. That significance has, of course, been affected, too, by the process of secularization itself. Were secularization not involved it might be possible to predict a return to the Durkheimian case of a unitary religion expressing the social solidarity, cohesion and shared values of an undiversified society. Those functions of religion were manifested in a simple society, but we can seriously doubt whether, even with a less diversified society of the future, and with ecumenism, we shall in any sense return to the position in which religion would operate as the integrative agency of modern society.

The whole significance of the secularization process is that society does not, in the modern world, derive its values from certain religious preconceptions which are then the basis for social organization and social action. It is rather that ecumenical religion will, as Herberg suggests it does in America, merely reflect the values which stem from social organization itself. Even with its votaries in contemporary society, religion does not begin to compare in its influence with the total religious world view which prevailed in simple society, and the subsumption of all activities and all institutions in the religious orientation to the world. The diversification of society destroyed the dominance of religion, and redistributed its functions. The diminution of diversity (and it is a diminution in only certain areas, in fact) does not restore religion to its former pre-eminence, nor return to it the functions which it once performed.

Social cohesion, and some measure of social consensus – at least concerning innumerable patterns of action in everyday life – must prevail in all continuing societies which are not experiencing anarchy. But even if this cohesion were attributed to the primacy of shared patterns of values, norms, conventions and orientations to the world laid deep in the socialization process, still one need not suppose these values to be specifically religious or to be today actively supported by religious commitment and religious organization. It is clear, of course, that they owe, in origin and development, much to religious conceptions of society in the past.

We may rather turn to the complex dovetailing of our institutional arrangements; to the mixture of inducement and coercion which prevails within the work order of our society; to the largely autonomous body of duly instituted law; to the elaborate interaction of supply, demand, knowledge of the market, and knowledge of consumers, which structure much of the provision of a modern economy, to see what it is that maintains the cohesion of contemporary society. That certain values, norms, and conventions enter into this highly intricate picture is self-evident. That they have a primacy or a determinacy seems very much more disputable. That they are ultimately religious ideas, and rest on religious practice and institutions for their validity and legitimacy, seems highly questionable.

Social cohesion is but one of the functions which have been generally ascribed to religion. In this essay no attempt has been made to examine the fulfilment of these functions in modern society, but what has perhaps become broadly apparent is that the secular society does not appear to depend in any direct way on the maintenance of religious thinking, practices or institutions. In a society with diminished diversity in public affairs, and the relegation of various moral matters to the private domain, religion, too, may have become a largely private concern. Indeed religionists have increasingly tended to describe religion as an individual matter, and a personal matter. Such has been the drift especially of the more evangelical branches of Christianity. Does religion, then, become merely a matter for private predilection? Or a matter of individual demand for emotional support in circumstances of extremity? Do we then see a return, for the mass of men, to the occasional conformity of the past? Those occasions being primarily the occasions of trauma in the life-cycle of the individual or of the nuclear family.

There is, however, one function which appears to have been vitally performed particularly by the Protestant manifestations of Christianity, and which assumed great importance in the development of modern society. The voluntary act of religious association implicit in Protestantism – in its various denominations and in many of its sects – entailed a distinctive commitment of goodwill to a group which was neither specifically kinsfolk nor neighbours. Without the primary affectivity of kinship relations this goodwill had none the less to be manifested. Clearly, the implications for such a response are deeply laid in earlier Christianity: they are found in the parable of the Samaritan, and in the oft repeated dictum 'We love him because he first loved us' which has applications for relations within the fraternity as well as for the relations of man to his God.

In Protestantism, however, was reacquired the voluntary character of earliest Christianity, and this has been of importance for the development of modern society. But Protestantism added something more to the detached goodwill which was implied in the formation of voluntary religious societies, and this it did by transcendental reinterpretation of the social roles of the new trading strata which were becoming important in the late fifteenth- and early sixteenth-century Europe. The work ethic which was emphasized in Calvinism, in Puritanism generally, and subsequently in Methodism and the various Holiness sects, was an ethic which rested on an essentially extraneous motivation to be committed to work. The disinterested devotion to the calling relied on the detachment of work and material reward, and the assertion that work was a spiritual activity and a moral obligation. The strong informal assumption was that, whatever material ends were gained, the real end of fulfilling one's calling in this world was a heavenly reward. It was the uncertainty of that reward in Calvinism, and the strong informal assumption that, although God's will could not be known, achievement in this world was an intimation of the real blessings which God would bestow in the next, which induced the disposition to work.[1]

Thus, with work regarded as a religious and moral duty, material reward is, at least ideologically, displaced. A disinterested commitment is established. But, as Max Weber stressed, once these work dispositions had been

1. On this see Max Weber, *The Protestant Ethic and the Spirit of Capitalism*, London, Allen & Unwin, 1930; J. Milton Yinger, *Religion in the Struggle for Power*, Durham, N.C., Duke University Press, 1946; Talcott Parsons, *The Structure of Social Action*, Glencoe, Ill., The Free Press, 2nd edn, 1949, Ch. XIV.

established, and society had been re-socialized for a new work order, the religious agent of this change was no longer necessary for its continuance.[1] Role-performance, in the post-Protestant society, comes to rely on a secularized value-structure in which work is no longer a sacred calling. Today a man works without the higher sense of purpose which the Protestant ethic communicated. Protestantism replaced the immediate material inducement to work by a more remote spiritual one, and this was perhaps a necessary ideological justification for that age; but in so doing it created a more involved nexus between what a man did and his reward for it. His remote prospective spiritual interest became effectively a type of disinterested commitment in the everyday activity of his life. The disappearance of a religious interpretation of economic activity, may mean that role-performance is now evinced without specific commitment and without devotion. The nakedness of the interest relation is borne home. Work, which ceased to be part of life itself with the passing of agrarian society (that is for farmers), became a *calling*, and was recognized as a distinctive activity of life, sanctified in religious terms, and is gradually transformed into being a *job*, supported strictly by the institutional order and an unmediated interest relationship.

It might be maintained that this development, which is clearly part of the secularization process, is itself part of the process of man's increasing rationality, his recognition of 'real' facts. One might, however, also ask, whether work is made more bearable for the worker, and its performance more valuable for society, if disinterested devotion is lacking. Unreligious societies have attempted

1. Max Weber, op. cit., p. 70. At the end of *General Economic History*, New York, Collier, 1961, Weber remarks, 'The religious root of modern economic humanity is dead, today the concept of the calling is a *caput mortuum* in the world.' p. 270.

to find other ways of motivating men, of winning their disinterested goodwill: it is not clear that any appeals have been more effective than was that of the Protestant ethic.[1]

Disinterested devotion, or disinterested goodwill, has, however, significance for other things besides work relations. Although Victorian industrialism would not have been possible without a widely diffused work-ethic, there may be a time when, in an age of automation, society's work order will function without these ingrained habits of work of the past. Even then, however, disinterested devotion might still be necessary to society's functioning, at least as the radical alternative to institutional coercion. Anyone who has compared the pattern of civic and political life in underdeveloped countries with those of advanced society, must be impressed by the differing degrees of disinterested commitment and detached goodwill which prevails in advanced society, and the extent to which advanced societies rely on these dispositions for their normal functioning. The maintenance of public order and social control depend, in large measure, on the diffusion of disinterested goodwill, and on a certain level of public and individual honesty (as distinct from the purely communal honesty which prevails in simple, often even in peasant, societies). The extension of kin-group and neighbourhood affectivity into generalized and impersonal goodwill, has been an achievement which has kept the corruption, crime, nepotism of modern society within bounds. It has facilitated a pattern of very general socialization – all class, regional and ecological differences

1. In this connexion see Reinhard Bendix, *Work and Authority in Industry*, New York, Wiley, 1956; and for an examination of some of these issues in a very different cultural context, Robert N. Bellah, 'Reflections on the Protestant Ethic Analogy in Asia', *Journal of Social Issues*, XIX (1), Jan., 1963, pp. 52–60.

notwithstanding – in which a strongly internalized sense of impersonal individual honesty has been very widely created. And in all of this the teachings of Christianity, and originally the implications of the teachings of Protestantism in particular, and the voluntarism of denominational allegiance, have played perhaps the most important parts. Less advanced people rely very much more on the social control of the group, on public surveillance of individual behaviour; when those societies are urbanized and industrialized, bribery and corruption become widespread patterns of public behaviour.

As modern societies advance, however, and with the decline of religious values in the process of socialization and of the impact of religious institutions in public life, we see also new patterns of crime and delinquency in the industrialized nations. The disinterested devotion which was vital to the creation of the capitalist work order and to the public life of industrial nations, and which rested on a religious idea-system, appears as a type of moral capital debt which is no longer being serviced. In an achievement-orientated society, in which monetary success is neither circumscribed (as it was in Catholic Europe) or mediated by religious values (as it was in Puritanism and Methodism), but in which it is legitimated in essentially hedonistic terms, the increase of crime and of public disorder must be expected.

Secular society has little direct regard for religion. It would be too early to say that it functions without it, or that it could ever do so. The secular society of the present, in which religious thinking, practices and institutions have but a small part, is none the less the inheritor of values, dispositions and orientations from the religious past. The completely secularized society has not yet existed. Whether indeed our own type of society will effectively maintain public order, without institutional coercion, once the still persisting influence of past religion wanes even further, remains to be seen. It may be, that in response to the growing institutionalism, impersonality, and bureaucracy of modern society, religion will find new functions to perform – but that, perhaps, would be not the religion which accepts the values of the new institutionalism, the religion of ecumenism, but the religion of the sects.

Appendix

THE CONDITION OF NONCONFORMITY

THE purpose of this essay has not been to document the statistics of secularization, and in the text the readily available figures for the Church of England have been used as an index of the changing circumstances of religious commitment in England. To augment these data some general information on the principal Nonconformist denominations in England is presented here. The figures for the Methodists are for Great Britain, but since Methodism has never had a very extensive following in Scotland or Northern Ireland, this divergence is not particularly important. The three movements have a sufficiently similar theory of what constitutes membership to make comparison possible, at least in a broad sense. No statistics are provided for Roman Catholics here, since the available figures rest on assumptions so radically different that comparison becomes meaningless. That there has been a marked increase in priests, communicants and churches in Roman Catholicism, is apparent; Roman Catholics now constitute a very significant proportion of the religiously committed and religious-active population in England.

The Methodists since 1935. (All figures are for Great Britain)

	1935	1945	1955	1965
Ministers	4,674	3,475	3,414	3,408
Members	847,675	752,659	744,659	701,306
Sunday Scholars	1,187,056	706,237	802,654	495,696
Teachers	191,286	110,743	128,239	93,326

Source: *The Minutes of the Annual Conference of the Methodist Church*, London: Methodist Publishing House.

The Congregationalists since 1935. (All figures are for England and Wales)

	1935	1946*	1955	1965
Ministers	2,714	2,042	1,948	1,776
Members	439,448	385,545	342,137	198,488
Sunday Scholars	451,764	280,075	287,013	150,423
Teachers	58,923	37,044	37,862	23,480
Churches	4,406	4,447	4,057	2,799

* 1946 has been taken because no summary of statistics was published in *The Congregational Year Book* for 1945.

Source: *The Congregational Year Book*, London: The Congregational Union of England and Wales.

The Baptists since 1935. (All figures are for England and Wales)

	1935	1945	1955	1965
Ministers	1,908	1,762	1,849	1,964
Members	375,383	344,784	301,162	269,527
Sunday Scholars	430,199	275,589	307,257	235,312
Teachers	55,677	36,326	40,878	—
Churches	2,979	2,976	3,042	3,048

Source: *The Baptist Handbook*, London: The Baptist Union of Great Britain and Ireland.

Selected Bibliography

THIS bibliography is in six parts, and includes all but the incidental works cited in the text, and some others. In the first part are included general works in the sociology of religion, strictly defined; that is to say, books about religion written by sociologists or employing a sociological perspective. Then follow three sections: Secularization; Ecumenicalism; and Denominationalism and Sectarianism. All of them include both sociological and other works on these subjects. In the case of ecumenicalism there is scarcely any strictly sociological literature, although there is a rapidly growing theological literature of which only a fraction is cited here. The fifth section is devoted to other works which have been cited in the text, many of them being sociological studies. Finally, a few books of importance for those interested in some of the issues raised in this book, have been included in the final section. In the case of translations, and of older works, the original title, place and date of publication have been given.

General Works in the Sociology of Religion

ARGYLE, MICHAEL, *Religious Behaviour*, London, Routledge, 1958.

BERGER, PETER L., *The Noise of Solemn Assemblies*, New York, Doubleday, 1961.

BERGER, PETER L. and LUCKMANN, THOMAS, 'Sociology of Knowledge and Sociology of Religion', *Sociology and Social Research*, 47 (4), July, 1963, pp. 417–27.

DURKHEIM, EMILE, *The Elementary Forms of the Religious Life*, Glencoe, Ill., The Free Press, 1954 (translation by J. W. Swain of *Les formes élémentaires de la vie religieuse*, Paris, Alcan, 1912).

EISTER, ALLAN W., 'Religious Institutions in Complex Societies', *American Sociological Review*, 22 (4), 1957, pp. 387–91.

GLOCK, CHARLES Y. and STARK, RODNEY, *Religion and Society in Tension*, Chicago, Rand McNally, 1965.

GREELEY, ANDREW, *Religion and Career*, New York, Sheed & Ward, 1963.

HARRISON, PAUL M., *Authority and Power in the Free Church Tradition*, Princeton, Princeton U.P., 1959.

LENSKI, GERHARD, *The Religious Factor*, New York, Doubleday, 1961.

MOBERG, DAVID, *Religion as a Social Institution*, Englewood Cliffs, N.J., Prentice-Hall, 1962.

O'DEA, THOMAS, 'Five Dilemmas in the Institutionalization of Religion', *Social Compass*, 7, 1960, pp. 61–7.

O'DEA, THOMAS, *The Sociology of Religion*, Englewood Cliffs, N.J., Prentice-Hall, 1966.

TROELTSCH, ERNST, *Social Teachings of the Christian Churches*, New York, Macmillan, 1931 (translation by O. Wyon of *Die Soziallehren der christlichen Kirchen und Gruppen*, Tübingen, Mohr, 1912).

WEBER, MAX, *The Protestant Ethic and the Spirit of Capitalism*, London, Allen & Unwin, 1930 (translated by Talcott Parsons from *Gesammelte Aufsätze zur Religionssoziologie*, Tübingen, Mohr, 1920, Vol. 1, but originally published in 1904–5).

WEBER, MAX, *The Sociology of Religion*, London, Methuen, 1965 (translated by Ephraim Fischoff from *Wirtschaft und Gesellschaft*, Tübingen, Mohr, 1925).

WEBER, MAX, *Essays* (edited by Hans Gerth and C. W. Mills, London, Routledge, 1948, Part III (translated by the editors from *Gesammelte Aufsätze zur Religionssoziologie*, Tübingen, Mohr, 1920–21.

YINGER, J. MILTON, *Religion in the Struggle for Power*, Durham, N.C., Duke U.P., 1946.

YINGER, J. MILTON, *Religion, Society and the Individual*, New York, Macmillan, 1957.

Secularization

ACQUAVIVA, SABINO S., 'The Psychology of De-christianization in the Dynamics of Industrial Society', *Social Compass*, 7, 1960, pp. 209–25.

ACQUAVIVA, SABINO S., *Der Untergang des Heiligen in der industriellen Gesellschaft*, Essen, Ludgerus Verlag, 1964 (translated from the Italian by Eberhardt Kenngott).

BLACKHAM, H. J., *Religion in a Modern Society*, London, Constable, 1966.

HERBERG, WILL, *Protestant, Catholic, Jew*, New York, Doubleday, rev. ed., 1960.

LIPSET, S. M., 'Religion in America: What Religious Revival?', *Columbia University Forum*, II, 2, 1959.

LUCKMANN, THOMAS, *Das Problem der Religion in der modernen Gesellschaft*, Freiburg, Verlag Rombach, 1963.

MARTIN, DAVID, A., 'Towards Eliminating the Concept of Secularization' in Julius Gould (Ed.), *Penguin Survey of the Social Sciences*, Harmondsworth, Penguin Books, 1965, pp. 169–82.

MATTHES, JOACHIM, 'Bemerkungen zur Säkularisierungsthese in der neueren Religionssoziologie', *Kölner Zeitschrift für Soziologie und Sozialpsychologie*, Sonderheft 6, 1962, pp. 65–77.

Ecumenicalism

BELL, G. K. A. (Ed.), *Documents on Christian Unity*, Fourth Series, 1948–57, London, O.U.P., 1958.

BEVAN, R. J. W. (Ed.), *The Churches and Christian Unity*, London, O.U.P., 1963.

CLARK, DAVID B., *Survey of Anglicans and Methodists in Four Towns*, London, Epworth Press, 1965.

CURRIE, ROBERT, *Methodism Divided: A Study in the Study of Ecumenicalism,* London, Faber, 1968.

EHRENSTROM, NILS and MUELDER, WALTER G., (Eds.), *Institutionalism and Church Unity*, London, S.C.M. Press, 1963.

FISHER OF LAMBETH, LORD, *The Anglican–Methodist Conversations and Problems of Church Unity*, London, O.U.P., 1964.

KENT, JOHN, *The Age of Disunity*, London, Epworth Press, 1966.

LEE, ROBERT, *The Social Sources of Church Unity*, New York, Abingdon Press, 1960.

NEILL, STEPHEN and ROUSE, RUTH, *A History of the Ecumenical Movement*, Philadelphia, The Westminster Press, 1954.

ROUTLEY, ERIK, *Congregationalists and Unity*, London, Mowbray, 1962.

S.P.C.K., *Relations between Anglican and Presbyterian Churches*, London, S.P.C.K., 1957.

S.P.C.K., *The Anglican–Presbyterian Conversations*, Edinburgh, St Andrew Press, and London, S.P.C.K., 1966.

SUNDKLER, BENGT, *Church of South India: The Movement Towards Union, 1900–1947*, London, Lutterworth Press, 1954.

TAVARD, GEORGE H., *Two Centuries of Ecumenism*, Notre Dame, Ind., Fides, 1960.

Denominationalism and Sectarianism

BLOCH-HOELL, NILS, *The Pentecostal Movement*, London, Allen & Unwin, 1964.

BRADEN, CHARLES S., *Spirits in Rebellion: The Rise and Development of New Thought*, Dallas, Texas, Southern Methodist University Press, 1963.

BREWER, E. D. C., 'Church and Sect in Methodism', *Social Forces*, 30, 1952, pp. 400–408.

CALLEY, MALCOLM J. C., *God's People: West Indian Pentecostal Sects in England*, London, O.U.P., 1965.

CLARK, ELMER T., *The Small Sects in America*, New York, Abingdon Press, rev. ed., 1949.

COHN, NORMAN, *The Pursuit of the Millennium*, London, Secker & Warburg, 1957.

DAVIES, RUPERT, *Methodism*, Harmondsworth, Penguin Books, 1963.

DIMOND, S. G., *The Psychology of Methodist Revival*, London, O.U.P., 1926.

DIMOND, S. G., *The Psychology of Methodism*, London, 1932.

ERVINE, ST JOHN, *God's Soldier: General William Booth*, London, Heinemann, 1934, 2 vols.

FAUSET, ARTHUR H., *Black Gods of the Metropolis*, Philadelphia, University of Pennsylvania Press, 1944.

FRAZIER, E. FRANKLIN, *The Negro Church in America*, Liverpool, Liverpool U.P., 1964.

GLOCK, CHARLES Y., 'The Role of Deprivation in the Origin and Evolution of Religious Groups', in Robert Lee and Martin E. Marty, (Eds.), *Religion and Social Conflict*, York, O.U.P., 1964.

GOLDSCHMIDT, W. R., 'Class Denominationalism in Rural California Churches', *American Journal of Sociology*, 49, 1944, pp. 348–55.

ISICHEI, E. ALLO, 'From Sect to Denomination among English Quakers', *British Journal of Sociology*, 15 (3), 1964.

LIPSET, S. M., 'Religion and Politics in the American Past and Present', in Robert Lee and Martin E. Marty, (Eds.), *Religion and Social Conflict*, New York, O.U.P., 1964.

MARTIN, DAVID A., 'The Denomination', *British Journal of Sociology*, XIII, 1962, pp. 1–14.

MARTIN, DAVID A., *Pacifism*, London, Routledge, 1965.

MULDER, WILLIAM, *Homeward to Zion*, Minneapolis, Minnesota U.P., 1957.

NIEBUHR, H. RICHARD, *The Social Sources of Denominationalism*, New York, Holt, 1929.

O'DEA, THOMAS, *The Mormons*, Chicago U.P., 1957.

PIKE, E. ROYSTON, *Jehovah's Witnesses*, London, Watts, 1954.

POPE, LISTON, *Millhands and Preachers*, New Haven, Conn., Yale U.P., 1942.

POPE, LISTON, 'Religion and Class Structure', *Annals of the American Academy of Political and Social Science*, 256, 1948, pp. 84–91.

SMITH, TIMOTHY L., *Called Unto Holiness: The Story of the Nazarenes. The Formative Years*, Kansas City, Mo., Nazarene Publishing House, 1962.

STROUP, H. H., *Jehovah's Witnesses*, New York, Columbia U.P., 1945.

TAVUCHIS, NICHOLAS, *Pastors and Immigrants: The Role of a Religious Elite in the Absorption of Norwegian Immigrants*, The Hague, Nijhoff, 1963.

TAYLOR, P. A. M., *Expectations Westward*, Edinburgh, Oliver & Boyd, 1965.

WARNER, LLOYD, *Democracy in Jonesville*, New York, Harper, 1949, pp. 153 ff.

WEARMOUTH, R. F., *Methodism and the Working Class Movements of England, 1800–1850*, London, Epworth Press, 1937.

WHITLEY, OLIVER R., *The Trumpet Call of Reformation*, St Louis, Missouri, The Bethany Press, 1959.

WILSON, B. R., 'An Analysis of Sect Development', *American Sociological Review*, 24 (1), 1959, pp. 3–15.

WILSON, B. R., 'The Pentecostal Minister: Role Conflicts and Status Contradictions', *American Journal of Sociology*, LXIV (5), 1959, pp. 494–504.

WILSON, B. R., *Sects and Society*, London, Heinemann, 1961.

WILSON, B. R., (Ed.), *Patterns of Sectarianism*, London, Heinemann, 1967.

Other Works Cited

ALFORD, ROBERT R., *Party and Society*, Chicago, Rand McNally, 1963.

ALLEN, PHILIP J., 'Childhood Backgrounds to Success in a Profession', *American Sociological Review*, XX, 2, 1955.

ANSON, PETER F., *Bishops At Large*, London, Faber, 1964.

BATTIS, EMERY, *Saints and Sectaries*, Chapel Hill, N.C., University of North Carolina Press, 1962.

BELLAH, ROBERT N., 'Reflections on the Protestant Ethic Analogy in Asia', *Journal of Social Issues*, XIX (1), Jan., 1963, pp. 52–60.

BENDIX, REINHARD, *Work and Authority in Industry*, New York, Wiley, 1956.

BOULARD, F., *An Introduction to Religious Sociology*, London, Darton, Longmans, Todd, 1960 (translated by Michael Jackson).

BRIDSTON, KEITH R. and CULVER, DWIGHT W. (Eds.),

The Making of Ministers, Minneapolis, Augsburg Publishing House, 1964.

CAMPBELL, ERNEST Q. and PETTIGREW, THOMAS F., *Christians in Crisis*, Washington D.C., Public Affairs Press, 1959.

CARLTON, E. J., *The Probationer Minister: A Study Among English Baptists*, unpublished M.A. Thesis, University of London, 1964.

COMTE, AUGUSTE, *Cours de philosophie positive* (1830–1842) translated by Harriet Martineau as *The Positive Philosophy of Auguste Comte*, London, Chapman, 1853.

COMTE, AUGUSTE, *Fundamental Principles of the Positive Philosophy*, London, Watts, 1905 (the first two chapters of *Cours de philosophie positive*, translated by P. Decours and H. Gordon Jones).

COX, HARVEY, *The Secular City*, New York, Macmillan, 1965.

COXON, A. P. M. *A Sociological Study of the Social Recruitment, Selection and Professional Socialization of Anglican Ordinands*, unpublished Ph.D. Thesis, University of Leeds, 1965.

DURKHEIM, EMILE, *Suicide*, London, Routledge, 1952 (translation by George Simpson of *Le Suicide*, 1st edition, 1897).

FICHTER, J. H., *Social Relations in an Urban Parish*, Chicago, University of Chicago Press, 1954.

FICHTER, J. H., *Religion as an Occupation*, Notre Dame, Ind., University of Notre Dame, 1961.

GILLESPIE, C. C., *Genesis and Geology*, New York, Harper Torchbooks, 1959.

GLOCK, CHARLES Y., RINGER, BENJAMIN B., and BABBIE, EARL, *To Comfort and to Challenge*, Berkeley and Los Angeles, University of California Press, 1967.

GORER, GEOFFREY, *Death, Grief and Mourning*, London, Cresset Press, 1965.

HALÉVY, ELIE, *Histoire du Peuple Anglais au XIXe Siècle*, Paris, Hachette, 1923–46, 4 vols. (translated by E. I. Watkins and D. A. Barker, London, Benn, 1949–60, 6 vols. – in 7).

HALMOS, PAUL, *The Faith of the Counsellors*, London, Constable, 1965.

HAMMOND, PHILLIP E. and MITCHELL, ROBERT E., 'Segmentation of Radicalism – The Case of the Protestant Campus Minister', *American Journal of Sociology*, LXXI (2), Sept., 1965, pp. 133–43.

HOBSBAWM, ERIC J., *Labouring Men*, London, Weidenfeld & Nicolson, 1964.

HUGHES, STUART, *Consciousness and Society*, New York, Vintage Books, 1961.

INGLIS, K. S., *Churches and the Working Classes in Victorian England*, London, Routledge, 1963.

LANDIS, BENSON Y., *Yearbook of American Churches*, New York, National Council of Churches of Christ in U.S.A., 1964.

LASLETT, PETER, *The World We Have Lost*, London, Methuen, 1965.

LIPSET, S. M. and BENDIX, R., *Social Mobility in Industrial Society*, Berkeley, University of California Press, 1959.

LITTELL, F. H., *From State Church to Pluralism: A Protestant Interpretation of Religion in American History*, New York, Anchor Books, 1962.

MANNING, BERNARD LORD, *The Protestant Dissenting Deputies*, Cambridge, C.U.P., 1952.

MARSHALL, T. H., *Citizenship and Social Class*, Cambridge, C.U.P., 1950 (reprinted in idem, *Sociology at the Cross Roads*, London, Heinemann, 1963).

MITFORD, JESSICA, *The American Way of Death*, London, Hutchinson, 1963.

MERTON, ROBERT K., *Social Theory and Social Structure*, Glencoe, Ill., The Free Press, rev. ed., 1957.

NEILL, STEPHEN, *Anglicanism*, Harmondsworth, Penguin Books, 1958.

PARETO, VILFREDO, *The Mind and Society*, London, Cape, 1935 (translation by A. Livingston and A. Bongiorno of *Trattato di Sociologia Generale*, Florence, 1916) 4 vols.

PARSONS, TALCOTT, *The Structure of Social Action*, Glencoe, Ill., The Free Press, 1949.

PAUL, LESLIE, *The Deployment and Payment of the Clergy*, London, Church Information Office, 1964.

PEEL, JOHN, 'Birth Control and Catholic Doctrine', *London Quarterly and Holborn Review*, October, 1965, pp. 315–27.

REISS, ALBERT J., *Occupations and Social Status*, Glencoe, Ill., The Free Press, 1961.

SCHALLER, LYLE, E., *Planning for Protestantism in Urban America*, New York, Abingdon Press, 1965.

SIMMEL, GEORGE, *Conflict*, Glencoe, Ill., The Free Press, 1955 (translation by Kurt Wolff of Ch. IV, 'Der Streit', of *Soziologie*, Leipzig, 1908).

SPERRY, WILLARD L., *Religion in America*, Cambridge, C.U.P., 1945.

STYCOS, J. MAYONE, *Family and Fertility in Puerto Rico*, New York, Columbia U.P., 1955.

STYCOS, J. MAYONE, BLACK, KURT and HILL, REUBEN, 'Contraception and Catholicism in Puerto Rico', *Millbank Memorial Fund Quarterly*, 34, 1956, pp. 150–9.

TÖNNIES, FERDINAND, *Community and Association*, London, Routledge, 1955 (translation by Charles P. Loomis from *Gemeinschaft und Gesellschaft*, Leipzig, 1887).

VEBLEN, THORSTEIN, *The Theory of the Leisure Class*, New York, Macmillan, 1899.

VEBLEN, THORSTEIN, *The Place of Science in Modern Civilization*, New York, The Viking Press, 1919.

WARD, CONOR, *Priests and People*, Liverpool, Liverpool U.P., 1961.

WEBER, MAX, *General Economic History*, New York, Collier, 1961 (translation by Frank H. Knight of *Wirtschaftsgeschichte*, edited by S. Hellman and M. Palyi, München, Duncker und Humblot, 1924).

WHITE, ANDREW D., *A History of the Warfare of Science and Theology*, New York, Dover Publications, 1960, 2 vols. (reissue, 1st edn, 1896).

WILLIAMS, ROBIN, M., Jr., *American Society: A Sociological Interpretation*, New York, Alfred Knopf, 1961.

WILSON, B. R., 'The Paul Report Examined', *Theology* LXVIII, 536, pp. 89–103.

WINTER, GIBSON, *The Suburban Captivity of the Churches*, New York, Doubleday, 1961.

Facts and Figures about the Church of England, London, Church Information Office, 1962, and (No. 3) 1965.

Mainstream Religion: A Study of the Content of Religious Broadcasting, Rugby, U.K., William Temple College, 1963.

Men for the Ministry, London, Church Information Office, 1965.

Television Audience and Religion, London, Social Surveys (Gallup Poll), 1965.

The Family in Contemporary Society, Report of a Group convened at the request of the Archbishop of Canterbury, London, S.P.C.K., 1958.

Additional Works

ABELL, A. I., *The Urban Impact of American Protestantism 1865–1900*, Cambridge, Mass., Harvard U.P., 1943.

ABRECHT, PAUL, *The Churches and Rapid Social Change*, London, S.C.M. Press, 1961.

DEMANT, V. A., *Religion and the Decline of Capitalism*, London, Faber, 1952.

HOPKINS, C. H., *The Rise of the Social Gospel in American Protestantism 1865–1915*, New Haven, Conn., Yale U.P., 1940.

MAY, H. F., *Protestant Churches and Industrial America*, New York, Harper, 1949.

MAYFIELD, GUY, *The Church of England: Its Members and Its Business*, London, O.U.P., 1958.

MACLEAR, J. F., 'The Making of the Lay Tradition', *Journal of Religion*, XXXIII, (2), 1953, pp. 113–136.

NIEBUHR, H. RICHARD and WILLIAMS, DANIEL D. (Eds.), *The Ministry in Historical Perspective*, New York, Harper, 1956.

PAGE, CHARLES H., 'Bureaucracy and the Liberal Church', *Review of Religion*, XVI, 1952, pp. 137–50.

SPINKS, G. STEPHENS, (Ed.), *Religion in Britain since 1900*, London, Dakers, 1952.

VAN VLECK, JOSEPH, Jr, *Our Changing Churches*, New York, Association Press, 1937.

WICKHAM, E. R., *Church and People in an Industrial City*, London, The Lutterworth Press, 1957.

The Annals of the American Academy of Political and Social Science, 'Religion in American Society', 332, November, 1960.

Index

279